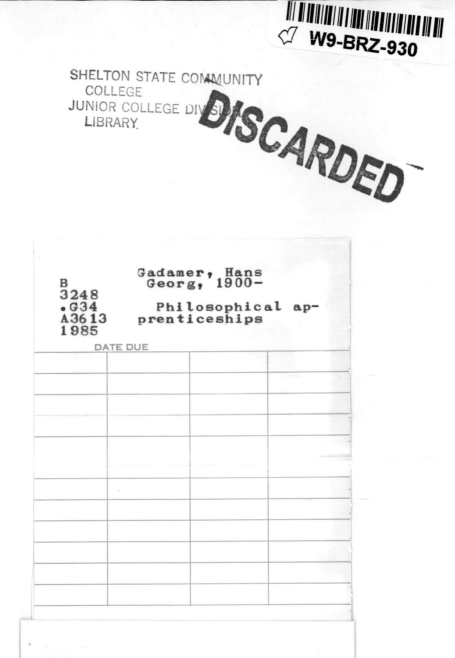

Philosophical Apprenticeships

Philosophical Apprenticeships

Hans-Georg Gadamer
translated by Robert R. Sullivan

de nobis ipsis silemus

The MIT Press, Cambridge, Massachusetts, and London, England

English translation © 1985 by the Massachusetts Institute of Technology. This work origi-
nally appeared in German under the title *Philosophische Lehrjahre* , © 1977 by Vittorio Klos-
termann, Frankfurt am Main, West Germany. The essay "On the Origins of Philosophical
Hermeneutics" was originally published in German in volume 3 of the series *Philosophie in
Selbstdarstellungen*, edited by Ludwig J. Pongratz, © 1977 by Felix Meiner Verlag, Hamburg,
West Germany.

This book was set in Baskerville by The MIT Press Computergraphics Department
and was printed and bound by The Murray Printing Co. in the United States of America.

Library of Congress Cataloging in Publication Data

Gadamer, Hans Georg, 1900–
    Philosophical apprenticeships.

    (Studies in contemporary German social thought)
    Translation of: Philosophische Lehrjahre.
    Bibliography: p.
    Includes index.
    1. Gadamer, Hans Georg, 1900–   . 2. Philosophers—
Germany—Biography.   3. Philosophy, German—20th
century.   I. Title.   II. Series.
B3248.G34A3613   1985   193 [B]   85-81
ISBN 0-262-07092-8

Contents

Contents

Translator's Introduction

De nobis ipsis silemus, Gadamer's implied promise to keep silent about the self, is a direct refusal to think and write as Descartes thought and wrote in the *Meditations.* Descartes's rejection of historical and traditional prejudices as the starting points of knowledge forced him to fall back upon the isolated self in his quest for a certain foothold for knowledge. He held unprejudiced "self" knowledge to be certain because of its autonomous location outside the flux of contemporary opinion and the handed-down literary tradition upon which opinion is based. Descartes, as Gadamer noted in *Truth and Method,* was the first modern to give the term "prejudice" the bad reputation it has in the modern world.[1] Gadamer, in turn, has taken as his self-appointed task the restoration of historical and traditional prejudices to their pivotal position as the conditions of possibility of whatever understanding we can have.

Gadamer's epigraph is thus a straightforward attack on the Cartesian prejudice against prejudices. Gadamer instead begins with the prejudices of his teachers and credits them with having truth value. But never does he take these prejudices as final positions. They are rather the conditions of an apprenticeship, which is nothing other than a productive discourse. Therefore—because he did not take the prejudices of his teachers to be the final outcomes of discursive learning—Gadamer was able to move on from a first apprenticeship with Paul Natorp to second and third apprenticeships with Martin Heidegger and Rudolf

1. Hans-Georg Gadamer, *Truth and Method* (New York: Crossroad Publishing Co., 1982), pp. 239–240.

Bultmann. *Philosophical Apprenticeships* is thus a kind of institutionalization of the Gadamerian concept of prejudices. Apprenticeships are conditions of learning in which tradition can be passed down from hand to hand, just as prejudices are conditions of understanding that must be accepted as starting points for human discourse.

Gadamer's early apprenticeships with Natorp, Heidegger, and Bultmann were not his only ones. There were also productive intellectual relationships with Nicolai Hartmann and Paul Friedländer that are not given separate treatment in this book. But as compensation there are fascinating glimpses of other contemporaries to whom Gadamer did not so formally apprentice himself. It is delightful to read about Gadamer's lifelong relationship with Karl Löwith and his brief meeting with Max Scheler on a Marburg streetcar, and one only regrets that Gadamer did not know Hannah Arendt well enough or Leo Strauss long enough to write detailed portraits of them. He only knew Arendt in passing in Marburg; and though he ran into Strauss often in the institute library in Marburg, he did not begin an intense intellectual relationship with him until a 1933 trip to Paris, when Strauss had already been forced to emigrate from Nazi Germany.

Interspersed with these memoirs are autobiographical chapters that recount the progress of a distinctly academic life. We are given a firm picture of what it was like to be a boy in Wilhelminian Germany, a scholar in the Marburg of the Weimar period, a struggling graduate assistant in the intellectual disintegration of the Nazi period, and finally a full professor in Heidelberg after the Second World War. These chapters provide us with a glimpse of a composite historical experience most of us have been spared. This is the experience of living a single life in a historical sequence of four German states, with the corresponding social and psychological challenges this posed to the unity of that life. We experience through Gadamer the sinking of the *Titanic* and the final years of what for us was the Victorian era, the carnage of the First World War, the normative disorientation of the Weimar period, and the threatening atmosphere of the early Nazi years. We roll up in a "bomb carpet" with Gadamer during a Second World War air raid, share with him a nocturnal interrogation by Soviet officers, feel what it was like to sleep on a park bench in postwar Heidelberg, and sense the pain of the 1960s student upheavals through the suicide of a colleague. The entire German twentieth century is here channeled to us through the life of one man.

What makes Gadamer's biography even more interesting and downright improbable is that it has still another chapter, not yet complete and thus not to be found in this book. This is the story of his American career. For more than ten years now, Gadamer has taught every fall at Boston College, from which place he has sortied out to other American campuses to give public lectures, his impact and popularity steadily growing in the process. Gadamer was not part of the sea change that brought such a wealth of German intellectual talent to the United States in the 1930s, but he is the doyen and prime example of a new generation of international professors who, with the help of the airplane, have brought about a second sea change in the German–American intellectual relationship. Along with such figures as Jürgen Habermas and Paul Ricoeur, Gadamer has paved the way for the reception in the United States of a revived German intellectual life.[2] Clearly one part of this intellectual revival has been the renewal of the critical theory once so closely associated with the early members of the Frankfurt School. The other part has been the rise of philosophical hermeneutics as a direction in thinking with a sufficiently distinct identity to enable it to become something of a "school" in the United States. The balance of this introduction will explore what philosophical hermeneutics is, how it arose, what its significance is, and what its problems look like.

Gadamer has been described as a follower of Heidegger, and in a certain obvious sense this is true. His mind was deeply marked by Heidegger's Marburg lectures in the early 1920s, and he is still Heidegger's ardent admirer. But as Gadamer noted in a recent letter to Richard Bernstein, he was already well prepared for his confrontation with Heidegger's 1923 lectures by his earlier acquaintance with the writings of Kierkegaard, the poetry of Stefan George, and the provocative figure of the "Platonic Socrates."[3] There is good reason to push this claim for what it is worth.

So long as Gadamer's philosophical hermeneutics is viewed as an offspring of Heidegger's thinking and as a *philosophy*, it tends to be seen in a very one-sided manner. A slight twist of the camera's lens brings everything into a much sharper focus: Philosophical hermeneutics

2. Ricoeur is French, but his thinking bears the strong imprint of its German origins.
3. Richard Bernstein, *Beyond Objectivism and Relativism* (Philadelphia: University of Pennsylvania Press, 1983), p. 265.

traces its origins as much to philology as it does to philosophy. It is as much the love of argumentative language as the love of knowledge that provides its cutting edge. This is not to deny the great impact of the young Heidegger or the Western philosophical tradition on the even younger Gadamer. It is rather to argue that the study of the dialogue-poetry of Plato, which began with Gadamer's 1922 doctoral dissertation under Paul Natorp, continued with a philological apprenticeship under Paul Friedländer, and culminated in Gadamer's habilitation thesis on Plato's dialectical ethics, written for Heidegger in 1927 and 1928, is at least as decisive a thread in the development of his hermeneutics as is the tradition of systematic philosophy.

Heidegger's contribution to Gadamer's thinking was mainly negative: It helped push the young Gadamer away from the dominant Western philosophical tradition. Although Heidegger's goal of *Destruktion* was aimed at the entire Western metaphysical tradition, it helps in locating Gadamer's thinking to set Heidegger in the context of the German nineteenth century. The mainstream of nineteenth-century German philosophizing was represented not so much by Hegel as by his followers, the Hegelians. Their achievement, if one can call it that, was to fabricate enormous systems of thought that clearly did more to smother than to encourage independent thinking. The basic premise of this epigonal work was the existence of an objective truth in terms of which the world could be seen as an "expression" by the systematic philosopher. This tendency can rightly be called "scientism." The implied premise of opponents—such as the critical young Marx (not the scientistic mature Marx), Kierkegaard, and Nietzsche—was that there is no truth that is "objective" in the sense that it can be described and calculated and restated in a rigorous formula. Truth is frail and human, more a matter of "truth-for-us" than "truth-as-such." With this as their standard, the three aforementioned thinkers set forth to do battle with the philosophical establishment. It was this underground tradition that the young Heidegger reopened and developed after the First World War.

All of this is well and good and immediately attractive, but it also raises the spectre of relativism. If there is no "objective" truth, then by what standard can one judge the "human" truths arrived at through the activity of philosophizing? The question is trivialized if one insists on maintaining an absolute position on either side. An absolute objectivism leads to an insistence on rigorously theoretical and empirical science, and an absolute relativism leads to an insistence that anything goes, that if God is dead, everything is permitted or everything is forbidden. Insofar as philosophy seeks to encourage thinking rather than kill it, it tends to avoid these sublime extremes. Yet in the Weimar Germany of Gadamer's youth, relativisms of all sorts seemed to gain the upper hand, if only momentarily, over the old objectivisms that had characterized the thinking of the nineteenth century.

One popular intellectual event did more to encourage the dichotomy between objectivism and relativism than any other single factor, and it deserves at least passing notice in our attempt to shed light on the origins of Gadamer's hermeneutics. Oswald Spengler's *The Decline of the West*, whose first volume was published in 1918, was a curious and highly popular anticipation of the Heideggerian thesis in respect to the Western metaphysical tradition. Spengler argued against the privileged position of the West among world civilizations, and in so doing he effectively "relativized" the West's claims to cultural superiority. No one in Weimar Germany took Spengler more seriously than did the classical philologist Werner Jaeger. He even set up a quasi-political movement designed to combat Spenglerian relativism. It was called the "New Humanism" or the "Third Humanism," and it involved Jaeger in academic politics all across Germany throughout the Weimar period.[4] But more significantly for our story, Jaeger clothed his objectivistic ideology in the most respectable of academic garb in his 1923 book entitled *Aristotle*. Here Jaeger argued that Aristotle's biography as an ethical thinker was a consistent move away from the subjectivistic, mythical, and clumsily doctrinaire thinking of Plato toward the clear objectivism of an empirical ethical science. Most critics of Jaeger in the 1920s attacked his appropriation of Aristotle, but the young Gadamer was one of the first to criticize Jaeger's developmental scheme and the role it assigned to Plato.[5]

The discovery that the Platonic Socrates had no systematic and objectivistic philosophy—that his profession of ignorance was not irony but rather the plain truth, and that as a consequence he was compelled to fall back on discourse—was liberating for the young Gadamer as it had been for Schleiermacher before him. Yet Gadamer made his

4. See the excellent piece on the "Third Humanism" by Horst Rüdiger in his *Wesen und Wandlung des Humanismus* (Hamburg: Hoffmann & Campe, 1937), pp. 279-297.
5. Hans-Georg Gadamer, "Review of Jaeger's *Aristotele*," *Logos* XVII (1928): 132-140. See also Gadamer's review article, "Die neue Plato Forschung," *Logos* XXXII (1933): 63-79.

discovery not through Schleiermacher, nor through Nietzsche, who apparently completely misunderstood Socrates,[6] nor even through Heidegger, who—if one is to judge by his booklet called *Plato's Doctrine of Truth*—learned nothing from Gadamer's 1928 habilitation thesis.[7] Gadamer's vision of the "Platonic Socrates" as a man who had no dogmatic answers to difficult questions about human moral virtues can be traced back to the thinking of Paul Natorp who, with his thesis of "hypothetical" rather than "objective" Platonic ideas, did more to clear away the dogmatism of Plato interpretation than any other philologist of his generation.[8] The overall result was a revolution in German philology. If Plato had no doctrine at all in his moral philosophy, then one was thrown back fully on the immediate phenomenon of his dialectical language. What thinkers like Paul Friedländer, Julius Stenzel, Karl Reinhardt, and Kurt Singer discovered was that Plato's literary work was not a makeshift for expressing a hidden doctrine but rather the heart and soul of his thinking. Truth in Plato was not a truth-as-such but a truth-for-us. It was not an objectivistic otherworldly doctrine but a this-worldly experience of dialectical language. The emphasis thus shifted away from systematic philosophy in the direction of a pure philology of the Platonic dialogues.

Once again we do well to recall that the problem of relativism cannot be treated absolutely. On the one side, there is a sublime absurdity to the claim that everything goes, but on the other there is an equally sublime absurdity to the expectation that the solution to the problem of relativism is going to be airtight. The former position denies even the possibility of philosophizing; the latter replaces philosophy with scientism. The turn to dialectical language is equivalent to a turn away from both extremes toward a dynamic center. Platonic language presents a symbolically structured world, a fused network of truths-for-us that are constantly being resubmitted to the testing ground of question and answer. In this crucible of language, the irre-

6. See Werner J. Dannhauser, *Nietzsche's View of Socrates* (Ithaca: Cornell University Press, 1974).
7. Martin Heidegger, "Plato's Doctrine of Truth," in William Barrett and Henry D. Aiken, editors, *Philosophy in the Twentieth Century* (New York: Random House, 1962), vol. 3, pp. 251–270.
8. Paul Natorp, *Platos Ideenlehre* (Darmstadt: Wissenschaftliche Buchgesellschaft, 1961). Natorp's extraordinary 1921 revision of his book did not change the key insight into the hypothetical quality of Plato's ideas. What Natrop did was to abandon the application of this key idea. In 1903 he had argued that Plato was a premature version of a modern Cartesian natural scientist. In 1921 Natorp moved away from his interest in science to emphasize Plato as a metaphysical and mystical philosopher. But hypothetical ideas remained very much in place as tentative opening moves needed to get a dialogue started.

ducible relativity of the universe is not negated by an absolute mind
capable of responding to relativity with an absolute mathematical
reformulation of it. The relativity is, instead, brought into symbolic
structures that are manageable but, with the passage of time, can do
nothing other than become "prejudices" if the *understandings* reached
in creative dialogue are treated as absolutes. What was once fused
must now be defused. The everyday language of Platonic philosophizing
is in no way a closed system of propositions, an absolute making of
a claim to objectivity. It is an open dialogue that refuses to accept the
despair of relativism but does not respond to this abyss by creating
a sublime antiworld of speech. This was not a perfect response to
relativism (or absolutism), but it was the course Gadamer chose to
follow in the 1920s.

I mentioned earlier that Gadamer undertook an important apprenticeship with Paul Friedländer that is not included among the separate
memoir chapters of this book. This relationship with Friedländer needs
to be sketched to fill in an important gap in Gadamer's early story.[9]
Along with Werner Jaeger and Karl Reinhardt, Friedländer was one
of the prize pupils of the great German classical philologist Ulrich von
Wilamowitz-Moellendorf, and as such he was expected to continue
the Wilamowitz tradition of classical philology. This tradition laid emphasis on constructing philology as a science that did not make value
judgments on Greek thinkers, assuming instead that they and their
thought had been fully systematized by the methods of modern historicism and critical analysis. This attitude made classical philology
into the handmaiden of academic philosophical research. Such a sub-
ordination was especially disastrous in the case of Plato's thinking,
where philosophers assumed a "hidden" system—the doctrine of
ideas—and then proceeded to treat Plato's language as a "makeshift"
that had to be analytically dissected to get at the underlying doctrine.
This was a startlingly modern prejudice, and Friedländer was one of
the first of Wilamowitz's pupils to rebel against the master's prejudice
in the period after the First World War, telling Wilamowitz in affec-
tionate but no uncertain terms that he had bolted to the Stefan George

9. Heidegger also worked closely with Friedländer in the early Marburg years. See Martin
Heidegger, *Basic Writings* (New York: Harper & Row, 1977), p. 14.

school of thinking in respect to classical philology.[10] The George Circle, represented in this field by Kurt Hildebrandt and Heinrich Friedemann, had even before the First World War argued that there was no "system," no hidden doctrine of thought in Plato, and that the Platonic center of gravity was to be found in his words and his myths.[11] Plato's language was not a "tool" to express a different and hidden set of entities called his "ideas," but rather a complete universe from which thinking could not be separated out. Everything that could be understood about Plato was *unverborgen*, or unhidden. Plato's thought was up front in his philosophical comedy and in his language, and thus no hermeneutics of suspicion that pushed beyond the circle of language to find "hidden" biographical or historical or ethical meaning was acceptable to the George Circle. This was a radically antisystematic insight, and it served to spark a whole generation of young Germans into rereading Plato. It was this view that Friedländer transmitted to his young apprentice.

The vast majority of Gadamer's published writings in the 1920s and 1930s are an attempt to articulate this philological and poetical approach to philosophy. Of the one book and nearly twenty review articles, essays, and book reviews published in this period, not one can be characterized as an exercise in conventional philosophizing. Every significant piece Gadamer did in this formative period adopted a philological approach to philosophical questions. At first the result was unproductive. There was no one, not even Heidegger, who recognized that Gadamer was engaged in giving basic form to what would only much later become known as philosophical hermeneutics. From being an *Assistent* in the Marburg philosophy seminar of the middle 1920s, Gadamer advanced to become a *Dozent*, a category that corresponds roughly to the American assistant professor but does not have tenure and does not pay as well. The attainment of the coveted position of *Ordinarius*, the tenured full professorship with the curricular power of an American department chairman but without the administrative responsibilities, did not come to Gadamer until 1938, and by

10. See William M. Calder, "The Credo of a New Generation: Paul Friedländer to Ulrich von Wilamowitz-Moellendorff," *Antike und Abendland* 26 (1980).
11. See Hildebrandt's attack on Wilamowitz in "Hellas und Wilamowitz," *Jahrbuck für die geistige Bewegung* I (1910). Friedemann was the first Georgian to argue that Nietzsche had been mistaken in his interpretations of Plato and Socrates, doing this in a doctoral dissertation written under Natorp and published as *Plato seine Gestalt* (Berlin: Blatter fur die Kunst, 1914) by Stefan George's personal press.

this point the main lines of his "philological" approach to philosophical hermeneutics had been fully worked out. But this in no way means that they had been recognized. Recognition would come only twenty years later when Gadamer conceptualized what he had long been doing in his Plato studies and set out this conceptual framework in his *magnum opus*.

What then was Gadamer's philosophical hermeneutics in this period, thirty years before the appearance of *Truth and Method*? It was the claim, made in piecemeal fashion, that moral philosophy does not have definitive answers but is rather a matter of raising definitive questions that clear a space for an unprejudiced talking through of human values. What we take to be answers, even those that come from Socrates, are only "prejudices," to use one of Gadamer's later terms. They are the initial conditions of the possibility of reaching agreement and understanding, but they are not final positions. Plato's ethics are not doctrinal but are thoroughly dialectical in the classical sense of the term. Ethics is not a matter of imposing otherworldly doctrine upon life but rather a matter of submitting privileged doctrine to the testing ground of lively discourse. The Platonic Socrates is always willing to do this. He privileges none of his "cloudy" ideas and thereby reveals that they are hypothetical rather than doctrinal. What then begins is a *play* of hypothetical ideas, and it is in the play or relatedness of ideas that the ethical life is lived. The participating dialecticians strive to reach an *understanding*, which is no more than an agreement arrived at. And since they know that their agreement is no more than a judgment that with the passage of time is bound to become a prejudgment or *prejudice*, they also know that the ethical life is an endless conversation. They are always thrown back upon the language that is the medium of the dialectician's life. Being that can be understood is language.

But however much the title of Gadamer's first book suggests that he was on his way to becoming a moral philosopher, his emphasis on dialectics reminds us of his awareness that moral philosophy could be constructed at the individual level only at the risk of privatizing it.[12] The individual part is to be interpreted in the context of the public whole, which in Gadamer's first book was nothing more than a language

12. Hans-Georg Gadamer, *Platos dialektische Ethik* (Hamburg: Felix Meiner, 1981), first published in 1931.

community made up of the conscious participants in the ongoing ethical dialogue. Hence it was probable, even predictable, that Gadamer would turn his attention to a consideration of Plato's political writings. He early grasped Plato's *polis* as a "city coming into being in speech" and hence focused on Plato's relation with those other makers of language, the poets, as well as on the theme of Plato's educational state. What was painstakingly but clearly worked out was the political institutionalization of the microcosmic dialectical language community. Gadamer's writings from 1934 to 1942 can well be characterized as a kind of "political hermeneutics" because of his emphasis on the moral context that sustains the ethical individual.

Gadamer's early writings, with their emphasis on philology, thus contain a political dimension that is not to be found in *Truth and Method*. The high points of the thinking of these years stand out as way stations for a new and startlingly radical way of conceiving politics. The chief point is that the modern dichotomy between ethics and politics finds no counterpart in the classical world. Politics is there a continuation of ethics by collective means, and the ethical life of the individual is a microcosmic restatement of the agreed-upon results of the discourse community. The modern privatization of ethics leaves politics in the lurch. The public realm deprived of its ethical dimension is necessarily a war of all against all, a realm in which the reasonable person must learn how to do evil for the sake of survival. In this context "political science" arises as a study of power and power relationships, and its tendency to fall back on *method* is a consequence of its loss of classical *truth*. That truth was nowhere more dramatically restored for Gadamer's generation than in Plato's *Seventh Letter*, a document that emerged as a cornerstone for the new Plato interpretation. The *Seventh Letter* revealed that Plato chose philosophizing as the preferred way of doing politics because of the profound ethical crisis in which Athens found itself. Hence the impulses that went into Gadamer's early thinking were essentially the same as those that motivated Plato. Philosophical hermeneutics was first of all a different way of doing politics.

All of these considerations suggest that philosophical hermeneutics emerged as a variation on the theme of *deconstruction* so popular in contemporary philosophy. This is indeed the case, and it is this intent upon liquidating the doctrinaire aspect of philosophical thinking that links Gadamer not just to the hypothetical ideas of Natorp's Plato interpretation, but also to the *demythologization* of Rudolf Bultmann's biblical exegesis, the *destruction* of the Western ontological tradition intended by the early Heidegger, and the kind of work that would later be done by such contemporaries of Gadamer as Hannah Arendt, Karl Löwith, and Leo Strauss. More significantly, the deconstruction of the tradition of interpreting Plato as a doctrinaire thinker is precisely the aspect of Gadamer's thinking that, abstracted into a philosophical argument, provides *Truth and Method* with its thread of continuity. Each of the forms of consciousness that Gadamer deconstructs in *Truth and Method* is conspicuous by being privileged to stand outside the ongoing conversation that constitutes dialectical ethics. The alternative that Gadamer presents to privileged *aesthetic consciousness* is the to-and-fro of living consciousness at play, and the alternative to the privileged *historical consciousness* of the nineteenth century is Gadamer's concept of "effective" historical consciousness, which is more being than being conscious. But only in the third part of Gadamer's major work does it become clear that the deconstruction of all privileged positions is a bold and unconditioned move to language. Language is not a "tool" that the privileged consciousness may use to "express" its positions. It is rather a phenomenon that speaks us before we speak it, and this means that we can never step outside of it and stand over against it. All privileges are temporary achievements, bound to be seen by a new generation as prejudices, and thus doctrine—the thinker's peculiar privilege—is always being dissolved back into the dialectical process.

Like critical theory, to which it admittedly bears many similarities, the philosophical hermeneutics that began in the Marburg of the 1920s is not so much a philosophy as an antidote to philosophical dogmatism. It is a kind of "negative dialectics" that aims above all at the liquidation of fixed and fast-frozen positions. In contrast, the critical theory of early and contemporary Frankfurt School thinkers has never rid itself fully of the taint of Marxist dogmatism. Partly this is because contemporary critical theory has not been willing to discuss its privileged "humanitarian" prejudices; and this taint has allowed philosophical hermeneutics to make something of an end run on critical theory in the United States. This is not to suggest that the humanitarian prejudices of contemporary critical thinkers are not worthy positions, but that the failure to submit them to discourse condemns critical theory to remain a modern *Weltanschauungs* philosophy rather than becoming what the young Karl Marx and the members of the early Frankfurt School presumably hoped it would become. It is this cutting edge, this unconditioned willingness to submit everything to discourse, that finally distinguishes philosophical hermeneutics from critical theory.

With the permission of Professor Gadamer, I have added to this book the chapter "On the Origins of Philosophical Hermeneutics," which gives as succinct and comprehensive a description of his thinking as I have found. I would like to thank Thomas McCarthy for giving me the opportunity to do this volume, Professor Gadamer for untold hours of conversation, Frau Jacqueline Chevalier-Finch for numerous translation suggestions, the MIT Press for excellent editorial assistance, the CUNY-PSC Research Foundation for a helpful grant, and my wife Karin for the steady support that makes projects like this one possible.

Philosophical Apprenticeships

Nicolai Hartmann

Paul Natorp

Max Scheler

Gadamer and Heidegger, August 1923

Martin Heidegger

Gerhard Krüger

Hans Lipps

Karl Reinhardt

Karl Jaspers

Karl Löwith

Breslau

A child of the turn of the century who returns to his memories in the last quarter of that century, the son of a professor and himself a professor, what should he discuss? How it was then? But what aspect of those times? Certainly not simply the things that flare up in memory from earliest childhood: the red roundness of an Edam cheese, a spinning fan in the window on Aftoller Street in Marburg, the fire engine pulled by heavy stallions thundering along the Shoe Bridge in Breslau. Such early remembrances are ridiculously intimate and irrelevant because of their very communicativeness. People today are more interested in early memories in which the progress of technical civilization reveals itself: the transition from gas lighting to electric lighting, the first automobiles. What earthquaking jolts those automobiles gave! Later, during the First World War, I was allowed to ride with an uncle in his army truck for a stretch of about a hundred kilometers. Breathtaking! The first cinema, the first telephone in my parents' home with its turning crank (number 7756—why does one remember such a thing?), my first bicycle—one could still see three-wheelers for adults—the first Zeppelin over Breslau, the news of the sinking of the *Titanic*, which, based on what I snatched from my parents' tabletalk, absorbed me much more deeply than the Balkan Wars: "If peoples out in the backlands of Turkey want to slug it out. . . ." Finally the outbreak of the war, my boyish zeal and what struck me as the highly unusual earnestness of my father. One scene at the dinner table made an especially deep impression on me. As my father argued that the loss of life in the sinking of the *Titanic* was "like a whole village going down," I rejected the comparison contemptuously with: "Oh, well, just a bunch of farmers. . . ." I had to apologize to our maid who was from the country and was just then serving us—a lesson I never forgot.

A breath of Prussian military tradition also blew over me as a child. During summer vacations in Misdroy, I was active every year as an eager soldier and strategist in a "beach company" that received its marching orders from officers of the general staff. At that time, following 1912, I was above all interested in "strategy," due to a childlike inclination to the art of the Napoleonic field marshal and to the military studies of the German Wars of Liberation that were then filling the newspapers. People said I had an officer's career in front of me—until I was pulled away from this by dreams of the inner man, poetry, and theater.

Also very childlike was my participation in the centennial exhibition arranged in Breslau to commemorate the Wars of Liberation. For a thirteen-year-old this was above all a confirmation of patriotic pride. A special satisfaction for me was that a piece from our old garden, a sandstone urn in the classical style, was shown on the exhibition grounds. Also not forgotten is how I became acquainted in the neighboring Rummel Square with the first cake baked from coconut fat— a piece of German colonial propaganda. Given the Silesia of that time, swimming in butter and eggs, the coconut fat was unusual, no, crazy!

Another slowly entangling network of relationships that formed me was that of the school. It was made up of schoolmasters of the old stamp, who no longer actually gave thrashings but who did throw chalk at the heads of inattentive children and loved to raise lumps on their heads. School was about wonderful games for the learning of foreign languages. It was about teachers, often so unusual with their tics, their ways of speaking, and especially their vulnerabilities.

I was deeply moved by the first funeral for a teacher who had died in the war. On this occasion the headmaster, that fearful man, was overwhelmed by emotion. Other puzzling phenomena were encountered for the first time, and they call up their own reflections—for example, a disagreement between two teachers over whether religion originated in fear. The pluck of the hard-boiled Enlightenment thinker who represented this thesis impressed me more than his somewhat bigoted opponent, who in any case corrupted almost everything with his pretentious Greek classes. Then the war closed in on our age group too. The highest classes dwindled in response to increased draft calls. Fatality reports continuously came in from the front. These were the hunger years, a time of revolution, graduation, and the beginning of university studies. All this passed by as in a daydream.

When I began my university studies in the spring of 1918, I was eighteen years old and anything but mature—a bashful, clumsy, inwardly turned kid. Nothing pointed to *philosophy*. I loved Shakespeare and the ancient Greeks just as much as the classical German writers, and I was especially fond of lyric poetry. But during my school years I had read neither Schopenhauer nor Nietzsche. Breslau in the war years was a quiet place, a province in a nearly patriarchal sense, more Prussian than Prussia, and far from the fronts.

My father was a pharmaceutical chemist, a significant researcher, a self-conscious, accomplished, energetic, and capable personality— a man who drastically embodied authoritarian pedagogy in the worst way but with the best of intentions. With body and soul he was a natural scientist, yet his interests were broad. I remember that once during the war I had to go to his institute to get a wire frame—Bohr's 1913 atomic model—for a presentation he was to hold at home for a circle of people. Another time I had to read for him a paper by a French chemist on the theory of benzene rings, as I recall. He knew no French. But on another account, quotations from Horace, he was superior to me. (So far had the schools declined even in my youth!) My inclinations to literature and theater and on the whole to the least profitable arts he disapproved of from the bottom of his heart. I was in no way clear in my own mind about what I wanted to study. Only that it would be the "human sciences." That was beyond question.

If one began, as a bashful eighteen-year-old, very much on one's own, to muddle around in the work of academics, one quickly found oneself downright lost, dissipating one's energies hopelessly. German literature with Theodor Siebs, Romance languages with A. Hilka, history with Holtzmann and Ziekursch, art history with Patzak, music history with Max Schneider, Sanscrit with O. Schrader, Islamic with Practorius—on all these I nibbled. Unfortunately, though, not on classical philology. The influence of my school in this area was minimal. There, too, was Wilhelm Kroll, a brilliant and witty storyteller whom I admired greatly, a friend of my parents. He took an interest in me and defended my scholarly interests to my father, just as years later the physicist

Clemens Schaefer, himself something of a philologist, was to defend me.

Psychology had only the briefest hold on me. This came about as follows: Full of zeal and curiosity, I systematically put together my class schedule according to the catalogue offerings. "Systematically" meant "take as many courses as possible." And so once upon an early (7:00 A.M.) April morning in 1918—an undernourished city kid who was still not needed as a soldier—I found myself in the psychology department. This, I thought to myself, is going to be interesting. I was thinking deep thoughts about Shakespeare's and Dostoevski's profound knowledge of human nature. Then there entered a professor in black habit, clearly a Catholic priest, into an auditorium where whole rows of benches were decorated with similar black habits. He held forth with great eloquence in a language nearly incomprehensible to me—it was Swabian. It took me a long time to guess that the *kemir* I kept hearing about was in fact a chemist. Then, after what seemed like a few hours, the professor made a few observations taken from the child psychology of William Stern. What he said struck me as strange. I screwed up my courage after the period and asked him whether he had not gotten things backwards. He was taken aback but referred to his notes once again and said, "Oh, yes, you are correct!" That was too much for me, that an eighteen-year-old should be instructing a professor, so I stole away. The professor was Matthias Baumgartner, a brilliant student of medieval philosophy who, for reasons related to the concordat with the Catholic Church, was compelled to give lectures in psychology even though he understood nothing of the subject.

My liberation from my parents was due to a book by a middling literary figure: Theodor Lessing's *Europa und Asien*, a spirited and sarcastic work of cultural criticism that bowled me over.[1] At last I had found something else in the world besides Prussian efficiency, performance, and discipline. Later, at a higher level, this initial orientation would be strengthened when I encountered similar cultural criticism in the circle of the poet Stefan George. Of course the dissolution of my frame of values that was the result of my early education also manifested itself in a new political orientation. This much was required

1. References cited by Gadamer will be retained in the original German if they have not been translated into English. If they have been translated, then the English title will be given and the German omitted. [*tr.*]

by the appetite we had in those years for finding contradictions. Meeting representatives of the Social-Democratic, Democratic, and Conservative parties—their names are forgotten today but were then noteworthy— meant above all a confrontation with the art of political speech and with democratic-republican ideas that had been foreign to my school and my parents' house. The extent to which the early influence of my parents remained operative was questionable. Noteworthy was that one day—I was still a freshman—Thomas Mann's *Reflections of a Nonpolitical Man* came into my hands and I found it wonderful. A little later the second part of Kierkegaard's *Either/Or* in a similar manner awoke in me sympathy for the judge Wilhelm and, unsuspectingly, for historical continuity. Today I would say that Hegel held the upper hand over Kierkegaard.

The first book of philosophy I picked up was Kant's *Critique of Pure Reason*, in a paperback edition published by Kehrbach. It was in my father's library. In his time when one took the Ph.D. one still had to pass a small examination called the *philosophicum rigorosum*, even if one was a natural scientist. For this he had crammed Kant, the natural thing to do in Marburg (and he was coached by the young Albert Görland). Thus was I initiated to philosophy during my first academic vacation. I really brooded over the book, but not the slightest under-standable thought slipped out of it.

I was also on bad terms with the university library. One day, bashful first-semester student as I was, I screwed up my courage and put in a request at the university for a recommended book, Cassirer's *Freiheit und Form*. When I went back to inquire the next day, without a word the sullen, one-armed lending librarian threw my call slip at me, embellished with a mysterious cipher. That sufficed nearly to frighten me to death.

But still I stuck with the philosophers. I did not, however, remain for long with the solemn lay preacher Eugen Kühnemann, who with a splendidly intonated voice and a fulminating rhetoric introduced me to the secrets of the "logical squares." His style was to me what the rhetorical pomp of Protagorus was to Socrates. It sounded too beautiful. I was dazed but not taught by it. In contrast were the polished pre-sentations of Richard Hönigswald and the tortuous chains of argument of Julius Guttmann. All three were neo-Kantians. Although I was still a third-semester student, an exception was made and I was admitted to Hönigswald's extraordinarily well-conducted seminar. I still recall what the seminar was about and how I "distinguished" myself: I could not grasp why the relation between meaning and word should be different from the relation between meaning and sign. But anyway, with the first intrusion into philosophy all of the signals were put into place. They pointed toward Marburg.

Marburg

When sometime around the year 1930 the professor of Romance philology Leo Spitzer was about to leave Marburg for a position in Cologne, he delivered a speech at a farewell banquet on the question, "What is Marburg?" I recall quite well how he named a list of institutions and persons and about them said, "All of this is not Marburg." (Some were of course insulted.) The first name of which he said "This is Marburg!" was that of Rudolf Bultmann. In fact, looking back at the 1920s, if I were to say today what Marburg then was, the name Bultmann would not be absent, but there would be other names next to his, some of them older. At that time, when a young man with philosophical interests "went to" Marburg, this meant that he went to study with the Marburg School. Hermann Cohen had left Marburg after he became emeritus, and he had died in 1918; but Paul Natorp was still teaching, along with younger men such as Nicolai Hartmann and Heinz Heimsoeth. Yet 1919 and the following years were not the time for a calm continuation of scholastic traditions. The collapse of the empire, the founding of the new republic, and the weakness of Weimar provided the backdrop for the distinctly frantic search for orientation that confronted the young people of the time. Even in remembrance it is difficult to find an orientation for that period. Germany then was about as much up to democracy as the world today is up to dealing with its own technological perfection.

I had come from Silesia, one of the military crown lands of the German Empire. I shared the common opposition among young people to throne and altar, accompanied by the unusual burden that my interests and opinions deviated not only from the National-Liberal tradition of my family but also and above all from my father's deeply rooted conviction that the natural sciences were the only honest sciences. He had tried to win me over to his point of view but soon enough saw me as one of the "prattling professors." In fact, that was the case.

The boldest and freest ideas were being discussed in the circle around Richard Hamann, the art historian. Hamann was beginning at that time to work on the large collection of photographs of French cathedrals that he had put together before the war. Many photos in the now-famous Marburg picture archive thus bear the clumsy inscription of my own hand. Hamann was a genius when it came to exploiting human labor power. His excursions were feared because he demanded as much of the participants as he did of himself. In Hamann's circle I found my first friend, Oskar Schürer, then a follower of the generation of expressionist poets connected with Kurt Wolff's publishing house. A steady stream of visitors was always coming to see Hamann. I recall running into the heavyset figure of Theodor Däubler there. Of course there were Marxist intellectuals in his circle, insofar as there were any such persons in the petit-bourgeois Marburg of those times. Hamann loved everything that could irritate and shock the complacent bourgeoisie. He beamed on the day Georg Kaiser's *Gas* was performed in the civic center. It was put on by one of those traveling troupes that, in the absence of full-year contracts, guaranteed work for actors during the summer period. He took pleasure when his own art exhibits provoked the embittered resistance of the bourgeoisie. In his way he was a character, and I recall one time when I asked a philologist for advice on my studies and with no inhibition he replied that I should do this and that and "not immediately run to Hamann." Above all he advised me to practice the source-material research methods of Edmund Stengel, which I did with profit. But I still ran to Hamann. Certainly he was a highly unbourgeois spirit. Of high intelligence and a sovereign nature, he was a convinced advocate of the coming culture of substance against the earlier egotistical culture, and he had his strongest influence in his Rembrandt Institute. The impressionism in life and art that the young Hamann had described in 1907—an analysis in the spirit of Georg Simmel—lay behind him. But still the "total tour of Western culture" (his "kilometer lecture course," in which he commented at race-car speed on photo after photo) was the achievement of a born sociologist who preferred teaching students to see new contexts to dwelling on individual works.

Soon still another group appeared, one whose vehement cultural critique stood up to the spirit of the time. Its center of gravity was Friedrich Wolters, a close friend of Stefan George. He was an economic historian, and on Wednesday afternoons from four to five o'clock he poured forth well-rounded descriptions of the cultural barbarism of the nineteenth century. I was later a participant in his seminars, too, and they were better characterized by their charming dignity than by the sharpness of the inquiry. I met there a large group of his older and younger friends: Walter Elze, later a military historian; Carl Petersen, with whom Wolters carried out a number of literary undertakings; the von den Steinen brothers; Walter Tritsch; Rudolf Fahrner; Ewald Volhard; Hans Anton; and finally Max Kommerell, who would later teach in Marburg for a few precious years. It was a circle of young people that took shape in the way a church does: *extra ecclesiam nulla salus.* I myself stood outside the circle, having been branded an "intellectual" and a novice, as I later learned. But this did not prevent Hans Anton from visiting or receiving me—of course under cover of darkness—nor did it prevent Anton, years later, from sending his friend Max Kommerell to my house and thereby sponsoring a new and productive friendship.

Wolters wore wonderful velvet jackets and a magnificent watch chain reminiscent of a medieval banker, and he maintained very friendly relations with me. When I contracted polio in 1922 and was placed in strict isolation, he was among the first who broke the rules to visit me. I recall a conversation with him in which I, still suspect on account of my philosophical interests and most likely because of an incomprehensible mode of speaking, said something on the category of individuation, no doubt under the influence of a lecture by Natorp. Wolters raised his finger in warning: "Individuality—you should protect yourself from it." To this I responded, "No, no, *individuation.*" To this Wolters responded, "Ach, so, that's something else." To me it was clear that there was no distinction but that he did not know this. Anyway, whatever he said was a standing challenge for me. The values of the George Circle embodied a corporate consciousness at a high spiritual level at a time when society was atomizing. This was provoking, but one could not help but admire the Circle for its compactness and self-certainty. In this way the poet Stefan George became an increasingly powerful presence in me, especially after I was led deeper into the world of poetry by Oskar Schürer (something that my literary studies had not done) and after Ernst Robert Curtius had opened my ears to the unique melodies of this verse. The poet himself I ran into only once at the Barfüsser Gate, but I could not look him straight in the eye, blinded as I was by the immortality of this profile.

Of course, there was not much left to save with me. I was a young *philosophe* and was quickly at home in the philosophy department. That was then still located up on the hill, and I was very much a child of the flatlands due to my Breslau youth. Early in the morning, greeted by the rising sun and still half asleep, I hurried from my parents' house on Marbach Street over the Dammelsberg to Paul Natorp's seminar. There I was greeted by the large, wide-awake eyes of the ice-gray little man, who with a soft and thin voice led a discussion that was in fact no discussion at all. Much stronger than the impression made by Natorp was that made by the "senior" in the seminar, a really corpulent young man most certainly thirty years of age who patronized all newcomers. As administrator of the seminar he made his importance felt by not entering the room through the same door we used. Instead, with a loud clattering of keys, he used a second door on the front side of the horseshoe table, the one also used by the professor. Later we moved into what had hitherto been the theology department in the old university building. It offered a view onto the chicken coop of the great fort, and it was above all in these quarters that I was introduced to philosophy by Natorp, Nicolai Hartmann, and later Martin Heidegger.

I should mention that Natorp occasionally made a deep impression on me due to the artistic tempo of his presentations. I recall one talk on Dostoevski and another on Beethoven during which the lights in lecture hall number ten suddenly went out but Natorp continued to read his written text with the help of a candle. Such things were not at all unusual at that time. These power failures were somehow connected with the transformations that were then integrating the Eder Valley Dam into the overall electric system. But for Natorp's essense and its effect, these doings were symbolic: with the failure of the all-unifying light system, the mystical candle shed light on his solitary meditations. I even did my doctorate under Natorp, a man of wonderfully few words. When one had nothing to say in his presence, then nothing occurred to one, and so for the most part both of us kept quiet. But sometimes on Sundays he invited a circle of people to his house for poetry readings, above all dramas from Rabindranath Tagore, whose deep mystical sense often inspired me. Some years later Tagore came to visit Natorp, and I recall the university ceremony that took place. In places of honor, alongside the excellent university trustee von Hülsen and the rector, Tagore and Natorp sat next to each other. What a contrast! What similarities! Two inwardly turned faces, two honorable old graybeards, standing out from all around them, both men of deep inwardness and convincing presence. Yet the erudite and sharp methodologist Natorp looked thin and slight next to Tagore, whose large, craggy face and appearance gave him the form of a man from another world.

My connection with and patient cultivation of the "senior" of the seminar, described above, led to my becoming his successor. This occurred after the promotion of this gentleman (who had meanwhile, I believe, become a good thirty years old) and manifestly at his urging. *Canis a non canendo*: I had just turned twenty. I now came into possession of the large ring of keys and, more significantly, was given unhindered access to the most recent publications, which in consequence of my sluggish administration of the library remained for a long period on my desk or in my files. This led to a downright disagreeable incident. It was 1924, and suddenly books began to disappear in wholesale lots; when finally a newly procured edition of Thomas Aquinas (the symbol of the entry of Heidegger into Protestant Marburg) took flight from my own filing cabinet, there was a great stir. In league with the police I made a dozen searches in the houses of harmless and innocent students, who blushingly produced one or another book for which they did not have the lending slip. Finally one of the house searches led in the direction of an unknown student from the Ruhr Valley who suffered slight delusions of grandeur. Today I can still appreciate how difficult it must have been for the person in question to bring back to Marburg the 200 volumes he had taken to his hometown, supposedly to help him complete a dissertation on "The Idea." This was the time of the Ruhr War, and it was only by means of a student with an Austrian passport who came to my aid—it was Fritz Schalk, later a professor of Romance philology—that the materials concerning "The Idea," including the Aquinas edition, found their way back to our library. The whole episode was not exactly a page of glory in the history of my administration of the seminar.

Nicolai Hartmann also had a strong influence on all of us at this time. His approach and his schemes, though, did not endear themselves to me. He sketched all kinds of things on the blackboard—spheres of subjectivity, spheres of objectivity, spheres of categories—but I had already gotten used to a slick dialectical style with Richard Hönigswald, and so this kind of didactic crudeness did not sit well with me. Nonetheless I was soon fascinated by the cool dignity and meditative penetration of the new teacher. And when Nicolai Hartmann, as he became more friendly, went with me after a lecture to the Café Vetter or the Café Markees, I felt myself quite elevated as he developed far wilder schemes on the venerable marble tabletops. In these schemes the ontological determining forces of values, in continuation of even more strongly determining categories, found their representation. These were things he only confided to washable surfaces, but above all I was elevated when he applauded my childlike, sharp-witted objections. It was still somewhat unusual that a young professor would let himself become so friendly with a young student, that he called me by my first name, unusual that I could go at any time to his house, to be received by him or his charming wife, almost like a son. Hartmann had been a student at Petersburg in Russia and still held to the daily rhythm of his Petersburg period. He rose at noon and was not fully awake until after midnight. Alone and doggedly he would write his books, often right up to dawn. Everything would be handwritten with a straight pen and completely reworked three times. Only the third draft ever seemed to him ready for printing and was allowed to emerge from his smoke-filled study to see the light of day. These were still hard times, and coal was scarce. Hartmann sat in winter in his unheated room in a quilted robe, a hot-water bottle in his foot-muff, holding his writing hand flexibly, ready from time to time to wrap it around the thick head of his stubby pipe. He was a man of great patience and endurance. He loved Handel's largos, and his own style had something of an andante con variazione. He exerted a civilizing influence in an artful manner, like a patient and possessed goldsmith, cold and unredeemed. The snide Max Scheler, who from the outset was very positive about Hartmann's *Metaphysik der Erkenntnis* (1921), is supposed to have said to Hartmann: "Your industry coupled with

my genius—*that* makes a philosopher."[1] This did not exactly do justice
to Hartmann, but it caught quite well the iron discipline that characterized the man. Our evening discussions, in which Hartmann brought
together a circle of students, began at about seven o'clock but revealed
themselves in their full brilliance only after midnight. When Heidegger
came to Marburg and scheduled his lectures for seven o'clock in the
morning, conflict became unavoidable, and we ceased to be worth
much after midnight in Hartmann's circle.

Nicolai Hartmann possessed a wonderful gift for associating with
young people in a comradely manner. In the hours between the afternoon lecture and the seminar, he often went with me to the bulwark
at the Weidenhäuser Bridge, and there we skipped flat stones on the
water. Hartmann had practiced this art on the Neva River in Russia
and brought it to a high level of mastery. But this is not all that I
learned from him. To his rites belonged not just the weekly discussion
orgies but also each semester a cave party. This took place at the
White Stone near Cölbe, which we reached on foot and where we
built a fire in the cave and squatted through the night, playing and
talking until the early morning hours. Especially interesting was our
teakettle game, a well known game of riddles in which simple yes/
no questions often plunged us half-educated logicians into despair. As
Aristotelians we finally found a way out by answering "in a certain
sense" instead of "yes" or "no." A good deal of wit was lavished on
the development and execution of this riddle party, and no doubt
something of the ambiguity of the kettle game is contained in every
expression of philosophy. *Distinguendum*, certainly, but more than this:
One must see things together, so to speak. In other words, the dialectician is a synoptic.

Nicolai Hartmann had a special passion for stargazing. He had
purchased a huge Zeiss telescope, so big that he could not carry it
alone into the open. Whenever I visited him on a beautiful evening,
I always feared the inevitable: "Ach, Hans-Georg, shouldn't we gaze
a little at the stars?" He was quite happy when he was able to locate
a double star or other interesting stellar phenomenon. My enthusiasm
was not so great.

1. There are two versions of this famed quote from Scheler, and Gadamer uses both in
Philosophical Apprenticeships. One version uses the term *Fleis* (industry), the other the term *Fleisch*
(flesh). I have retained Gadamer's inconsistency in the translations. [*tr.*]

He went around with me as he would with someone his own age. When, hardly twenty-two years old, I handed in my dissertation, with no embarrassment he informed me that Natorp had written a very nice report, that he himself had come to opposed conclusions on all points, and that on this basis they had agreed on a *summa cum laude*. Today, I venture to say that they were both wrong. When once during my Heidelberg years I perceived a certain dissatisfaction among my students because I was always giving them back their dissertations to be reworked, I asked myself whether I was perhaps demanding too much. I therefore asked my wife to read my dissertation, which fortunately was only in typescript. The result was: "You would not have accepted this as a dissertation."

It was true. I still knew nothing but what I had learned in general courses on how to argue sharply and in a few careful Plato readings. Thus my first meeting with Martin Heidegger came as a complete shock to my immature self-confidence. Rumors about Heidegger had been whispered about in student circles for a long time. Marburg students who had been to Freiburg reported on the unusual mode of expression and suggestive power of Husserl's young assistant. When Heidegger sent a manuscript to Natorp, one that would serve as the basis of his call to Marburg, I became acquainted with it and was immediately spellbound. The way in which the hermeneutic situation of an interpretation of Aristotle was worked out, with Luther and Gabriel Biel, Augustine and the Old Testament brought into play and with Greek thinking in all its peculiarities and freshness appearing in outline—I still do not know how much of this I really understood. Despite my title of doctor, I was still a twenty-two-year-old boy who thought rather murkily, who reacted portentously to murky thinking, and who still did not really know what was going on.

Husserl's phenomenology had already become known to us in Marburg, and this was not simply due to Natorp's famous 1917 review of Husserl's *Ideas* in the journal *Logos* or to Nicolai Hartmann's predilection for phenomenological description in the sense of a philosophical propaedeutic. In those days there were true apostles of phenomenology who expected from it the salvation of the world. I still recall how I heard the term for the first time in 1919. It was in Richard Hamann's introductory art-history seminar, where a kind of revolutionary discussion club came together for an exchange of views. Helmut von den Steinen led this memorable conversation in which

the number of proposals for the renewal of the world was exactly
equal to the number of participants. There was even a Marxist, if
memory serves me correctly, and of course he was from Hamann's
circle. One person expected from Stefan George the renewal of Germany, another expected as much from Rabindranath Tagore, a third
conjured up the giant figure of Max Weber, and a fourth recommended
Otto von Gierke's theory of communal law as the foundation of a
new political attitude. Finally someone declared with decisive conviction
that the only thing that could reconstitute us was *phenomenology*. I
accepted this devoutly and completely and without even a shred of
knowledge to back it up. And I did not learn anything more about
phenomenology when I turned to the older students. There was a
doctoral student of Natorp who with the latter's permission instituted
a very informal colloquium on Husserl's *Ideas* (such a thing was then
possible without a full reform of the university), but this and my own
reading of Husserl's work did not take me much further.

My real introduction to phenomenology came through a meeting
with Max Scheler. In 1920 Scheler gave two presentations in Marburg,
one on "The Essence of Remorse" and the other on "The Essence of
Philosophy." Both became chapters in his book *On the Eternal in Man*.
But Scheler's presentations were quite different from these spirited
but poorly written chapters. There was something demoniacal, not to
say satanic, in his philosophical passion. It was through Ernst Robert
Curtius, with whom I had an honorable and personally rewarding
relationship, that I was brought together with Scheler. I found his
questions highly surprising. He did not ask me about Natorp or Hartmann. Instead he questioned me initially about Rudolf Otto, "Saint
Otto," a dignified English presence who then held forth with unap-
proachable coolness on theological ethics. I had gone to a lecture class
of his, but only once. After about ten minutes in which he had spoken
about something or other, he said with the full understatement of an
English gentleman: "We come now epsilon to love." And now Scheler
questioned me about Otto, without doubt a significant and famous
man, because he found him "phenomenological." And Scheler also
questioned me about Erich Jaensch. I wondered about this too. What
kind of philosophical interest could experimental psychology possibly
have? We did have a fellow student who had prepared a dissertation
with Jaensch on the learning capacity of chickens, and we certainly
questioned this student, whenever we ran into him, as to how his

chickens were doing. Sometimes he even assured us of their willingness to learn. About Jaensch himself I obviously knew nothing—he seemed to me to be not at all philosophically interesting. And so the personal meeting of the immature young student with the famous guest was not without disappointment for me. But certainly, when I listened to those lectures of Scheler, I sensed that there was also a serious side to phenomenology.

Among my more pleasant prerogatives at this time was an afternoon walk with Ernst Robert Curtius. He suffered immeasurably from the small-mindedness of the Marburg life-style. When he wanted to have a good time, he would buy a railroad ticket and travel to Giessen, there to eat a good meal at the station restaurant, something he claimed could not be done in Marburg. Whenever I came, he would rise from his *liseuse* and begin immediately to tell me about his midday nap's reading. This would be Homer or Virgil or some other classical writer—he read these effortlessly without a dictionary and also without a shred of humanistic fuss. Once he said: "What a skeptical people the Greeks were. When Telemachus is questioned as to who his father and mother might be, he answers: 'My mother is called Penelope but who my father is, such a thing one can never know exactly, but it is said to be Odysseus.'" And what more he managed to discover: "Here, take a look at this. This name you are going to hear more of." It was one of the first volumes of Marcel Proust's great novel, which Curtius was, so to speak, introducing to Germany at that time.

But what I want to tell concerns Natorp. I climbed the stairs to Curtius's apartment. He lived at 15a Rotenberg Street as a subtenant of Max Deutschbein, a professor of English studies (I myself later lived there for a while). To my amazement, Paul Natorp was standing before the door, looking like a little urchin with his long cape and his dwarf's beard. Naturally I was more than a little astounded, but imagine the amazement of Ernst Robert Curtius when instead of the lone young student, he also finds at the door Privy Councillor Natorp. It is un-forgettable to me how everything in Curtius transformed itself. He showed all the good manners for which a young man is always indebted to an honorable older gentleman. Hardly had an amused, questioning look grazed me when the derisiveness, sarcasm, and superiority with which he usually sought to project himself disappeared and he showed a truly moving humility. From a scoffer such as Curtius, this deeply impressed me.

Marburg was not a place of great salons. But there was one house where anyone newly arrived in the academic world would be introduced ceremonially. I was often at these introductory dinners, which were modest in keeping with the times and which in winter sometimes took place in insufficiently heated rooms. My friend Oskar Schürer lived there. It was the house of the wife of Privy Councillor Hitzig, at 1a Rotenberg Street. It was rumored that this woman was a blood relation to ninety-one living German professors—and in fact she was a great-grandchild of Leopold von Ranke.

This was admittedly more a meeting place for the initiated or for those just admitted to the circle of the initiated. We, in contrast, were young people who were slowly trying to find ourselves. In one way or another, we were all in the same boat. Today I can still see before me the long seminar table in the *Haus am Plan* and recall my astounded attention when a young student with a very tender, soft, almost girlish voice brought up a few clever things about Nietzsche in Nicolai Hartmann's seminar. That was Jacob Klein, with whom I subsequently became friends and who later made an international reputation for himself in the field of Greek philosophy and mathematics. And I can also recall how Gerhard Krüger first drew attention to himself in a colloquium of Natorp's. This might have been one semester later in the new seminar room in the old university. Long years of working together would make us good friends.

I can also remember, as if it were yesterday, how I came to be friends with Oskar Schürer: We had gone to a recitation evening given by an academician and fell in next to each other. In the way these things go, everyone stayed in his place and suffered silently the unbearable pathos of the person giving the paper. Suddenly our glances met, we let loose with an earthshaking explosion of laughter, and Oskar and I found ourselves on the way to the door. Schürer was seven years older than me and was the commanding personality of my first Marburg years. I could tell a good deal about him. His gift for getting near people was unique, and my friendly relations with the many professors who have been described in these lines I owed to the attentiveness people gave me as a young friend of his. The only persons he did not have contact with were the philosophers. As a man with an astute eye and a way with words that would awaken one's intuition, he was just the right corrective to my altogether premature tendency toward abstraction. Schürer was educating himself at this time in science, and he eventually became an art historian. Later he became known through his book on Prague. He died prematurely in 1949 as a professor at Darmstadt. As in 1944 I would deliver the eulogy for Max Kommerell, so in 1949 I would do the same for Oskar Schürer, the older of the two and my first friend.

Another house in which a circle often met was that of the publisher of the upper Hessian newspaper, Dr. Carl Hitzeroth, a passionate art collector. I was easily the Benjamin of this circle, to which Ernst Robert Curtius, Oskar Schürer, Siegfried Kaehler, and Albert Hensel belonged. I recall as if it were today how Hitzeroth showed graphic reproductions of Hans von Marée's drawings and how Curtius reacted to my enthusiasm: "What a scene you'll make when you see Marée's large paintings in the new state museum in Munich!" It was characteristic of this circle that someone would ask the clumsy question of who we each thought was the world's greatest painter. Everyone answered "Rembrandt" with the exception of Kaehler, who preferred Michelangelo. This most certainly was because of the vital energy of Michelangelo's figures, loved as a consolation by this tender and suffering man. By the way, the convergence on Rembrandt showed how a period of inwardness united everyone (and it also reflected the nearness of the city of Kassel).

I no longer recall exactly how I came to know Friedrich Klingner. He lived in the retirement community in a cursedly small house in front of which blossomed a large number of wild flowers. Reserved and ascetic, he was always dressed in an old soldier's coat, which he wore as a measure of frugality and bore as a silent accusation. Together we read Pindar, and this was not a chance thing for a generation that had just learned to read the late work of Hölderlin in Hellingrath's edition. For mysterious reasons, supposedly on account of my ability to make an abstract conceptual statement, Klingner believed he could draw profit from a general reading. He therefore had the peculiar and for me altogether too pampered habit of preparing the text exactly, with all the ancient commentaries attached. He would read it to me, translating, and then look expectantly to me for what I had to say. It was similar when we read Augustine's *Confessions* together. In this way I became wrapped up in the sound of artistic prose as a poetic form, but only as an entertainment. And this was a kind of symbolic constellation for the whole first period of my studies, in which I had still not learned what real work was and no one really demanded such a thing of me.

All of this changed when I met Heidegger—a basic event, not only for me but for all of the Marburg of those days. He demonstrated a well-integrated spiritual energy laced with such a plain power of verbal expression and such a radical simplicity of questions that the habitual and more or less mastered games of wit with categories or modalities quickly left me.

Paul Natorp

De nobis ipsis silemus. About the self it is better to keep silence. So begins
Paul Natorp's self-description, published in 1920. I hope it is not
inappropriate to commemorate the merits of such a man, who knew
what is was to keep quiet, especially since I can speak only from
impressions gained as a young student, one of Natorp's last doctoral
candidates, immediately after the First World War.

Paul Natorp was a member of the Marburg School. His numerous
contributions to the history of philosophy as well as to systematic
philosophy itself were governed by a concern, shared with Hermann
Cohen, to renew and develop further the critical act of Kant. Within
the shared framework of the Marburg School, one of the most impressive schools in recent philosophy, the question was: What was the
distinctive quality in Natorp's work that broke through systematically
only at a late stage in his intellectual development? To ascertain this,
we must briefly consider the basic idea of Marburg neo-Kantianism.
This was the transcendental method, that is, the generation of reality
by pure thinking. This was how Cohen formulated it. This formulation
was guided by the methods of seventeenth- and eighteenth-century
science and especially by the model of its basic mathematical principle,
the idea of the infinitesimal. The mathematical mastering of the con-
tinuum of motion, and the formulation of the law of generation of
motion, led to the understanding that it was thinking itself that en-
gendered reality. That this kind of generation is an infinite task constituted nothing less than the universal meaning of this principle for
the fact of the sciences. These are methods for engendering objects

and for determining reality. Cohen grounded even ethics in the fact of the sciences, and he understood jurisprudence to be the logic of the human sciences.

But the multiplicity of possibilities in this determination of objects leads inherently to a question concerning their unity. Here Natorp had his first distinctive word in his formulation of the task of a "general psychology" with reference to Kant's transcendental synthesis of apperception and in harmony with Cohen's systematic intentions. Corresponding to the trend toward the differentiation of object determination was the converse trend of integration to a unity of consciousness. The "object" of psychology is not an independent object [eigener Gegenstand], a subjective that stands alongside the objectives of the other sciences, but rather a different way of looking at the same things. It is the same appearance that is at one time grasped according to its objective character, at another time as a moment in the experience of a definite subject. It is clear that if one thinks the totality of all objects and, on the other side, the totality of all the possible points of view one can construct out of the totality of objects, then it is the same world that is thought from two different sides. This had already been brilliantly expressed in Leibniz's monadology: The coexistence of the focal points of all individual perspectives in which the whole presents itself is the world itself. An infinite consciousness comprehends nothing other than the totality of being. But certainly for finite human consciousness, the totality of object determination is an infinite task, and a similar infinity is to be found in the idea of pure subjectivity. The reconstruction of subjective experiences is only a methodical approximation vouched for by the actuality of consciousness, in the same way as it is evidenced by the finiteness of the finite human consciousness in the phenomenon of remembrance and the common spirit among individuals. Natorp moved here along ways that converge with Dilthey's psychology of the human sciences as well as with Husserl's phenomenology. But he applied this psychology not to the task of laying a new foundation for the human sciences or to that of giving a new methodical orientation to philosophical research, but rather to the systematic unity of philosophy itself. This problem of systematic unity presented itself to him in the correlation of objectification and subjectification, and this meant the complete mastery of the concept of method, of the process, of the *fieri* over even the fact of science. In this way, Natorp must be seen as the strictest method fanatic and logician of the Marburg School.

But this was precisely the point at which his difference with Hermann Cohen and the independent way of his late philosophizing began to define itself: the transcendence of method. He formulated this in the idea of a "general logic." The universalization of the transcendental problem, which was meant here, was no longer restricted to the fact of the sciences and its a priori foundations. Life must be grasped as a unity with science, creating in moral action and artistic activity, in *praxis* and *poiesis*, not the objectification inherent in both willing and creating, not its objectification in the human sciences. The unity of theory and practice, sketched out in Kant's doctrine of the primacy of practical reason and implemented in Fichte's doctrine of science, was to reach its full universality in Natorp's general logic. It reached its true completion not in the correlation of objective and subjective methodologies as developed by general psychology but in the far more fundamental correlation of thinking and being that carries and grounds the infinite progress of methodical determination. But even this correlation is not the final one; it presupposes its own primordial "undismembered" unity. That is the meaning of the transcending of method that dominated Natorp's late thinking. The transcendental ideal of Kant served him as a foothold from which to think reality as total determination, as the primordially concrete. Only in this did the idea of transcendental psychology gain its full systematic impact.

The unity of practical and theoretical reason constituted the deepest systematic point even in Kant's thinking. Its implementation in the unity of separation and unification, of the thinking out of existence and the thinking out of the direction, of the should, of the task—this was the key idea of the general logic. It was supposed to achieve the permeation of Idealism right down to the last particular and thereby solve the "most pressing question of contemporary philosophy," the problem of the *principium individui.*

This context first emerged clearly in 1917 when Natorp published a major critical disagreement with Bruno Bauch's book *Immanuel Kant,* a product of southwest German neo-Kantianism. What Natorp found lacking in this book was an understanding of the systematic indispensability of a transcendental psychology. Only from such a point of view could the generalization of the transcendental inquiry with respect to extratheoretical objectifications gain its full impact. The dualism of the logical forms and the amorphous matter of cognition cannot stand up to the idea of a general logic. The idea of an infinite determinability includes the presupposition of a total determination of the particular and with that the complete logicality of the amorphous. Natorp viewed the problem of individual determination as the ruling one not only in the realm of theory but above all in ethics. But right here, in southwest German neo-Kantianism, he found missing the necessary further thinking out of the Kantian move in this direction, which Schleiermacher had had in mind. "Ethics is to be grounded as a logic of action, to be sure from the point of view of form, or *logos*, but for matter in its full individuality, which constitutes its only durable meaning."

The unfolding of the systematic thought [*Systemgedankens*] that had been developed out of the general psychology was of decisive importance for the systematic problem of religion. And here Natorp saw himself at a decisive advantage with respect to Hermann Cohen, whose systematic intentions were similar to his. For in religion the individual meaning is fundamental, not just as a task and methodological aim. Precisely this was the weakness of Cohen's ethicization of religion. It did not go beyond the circle described by the methodology of the determination of existence and will. It was therefore unable to think appropriately the absolute individuality of God. The motive of an absolute individuality, however, already underlay Natorp's general psychology. Elevated to the universality of the systematic principle, it resulted in a recognition of the full meaningfulness of concrete being and therefore in the idea of a general logic (in no respect hemmed in by matter or by remnants of indeterminateness, formlessness, and meaninglessness). Natorp put all this under the motto of Heraclitus: "You would not find the borders of the psyche if you were to seek them, even if you were to attempt this by going every which way— so deep is its *logos*."

The *logos*—that is, the meaningfulness of being, as the undismembered, the primordially concrete—always precedes all determination of meaning, all rationality. Precisely this is the decisive insight of this particular general logic, that it is not limited by the irrational, by life, but rather comprehends the *logos* itself, its sense, in the reality of the tension between rationality and irrationality, between concept and existence, in their *coincidence*. In untiring variations on his thought, Natorp kept repeating that in this ultimate coincidence of diverging and self-contradicting elements, the authentic affirmation of being appears in the "lively act" of pure creation. Now at last the third of the systematic directions of Kantian thinking could attain its systematic share of the general logic. This was the aesthetic, thought of here as *poiesis*, creation beyond all time and process. It is the thought of individuality, which in the individuality of God and of the whole of being surpasses all method, in that it assigns to method the sheer boundlessness of the task.

The systematic concern of his later years with the materials of historical interpretation compelled this masterful researcher of ancient philosophy to further development. And so in a metacritical supplement written in 1921, an aged Natorp himself criticized his much-disputed 1903 Plato book and worked out the perspective of a more appropriate understanding. Natorp's conception of the Platonic "idea" was one of the most paradoxical theses ever presented in historical research. He understood the idea from the point of view of natural law, in the sense in which it is fundamental to Galilean and Newtonian science. The hypothetical procedure of the natural sciences certainly does not ascribe to the law a reality of its own, but rather describes in the law the regularities of natural happenings themselves. It is precisely for this reason that the Platonic doctrine of ideas has been an object of criticism since Aristotle, because the ideas were supposed to represent a world of their own, an intelligible cosmos separated from the sensually accessible world by an unbridgeable gap. For all that, Natorp had hit upon a common ground between Plato and modern science, and in this respect, by the way, he had been anticipated by Hegel, whose dialectic of the "reversed worlds" thinks the "extrasensory world" of the understanding as a "quiet realm of laws." The law here is the "constant picture of the unsteady appearance"—thus the Platonic idea. Right here is the root of the neo-Kantian image of Plato. The idea is certainly what truly is, what as real being is fundamental to phenomena. But this foundation, the hypothetical idea, is as little an existing being alongside existing beings as is the mathematical scheme of the equation in modern science. But this is not because it does not have an independent existence alongside the being of phenomena. It is, rather, the other way round: The being of phenomena has no existence unless it exists in the unalterable self-sameness of the idea.

This was and continued to be a powerful abstraction imposed on Plato's philosophy by Natorp. The later Natorp recognized that not only was the idea a method but that the otherworldly unity of "the one," the primordially concrete, was fundamental to the multiplicity of ideas. Every idea is now no longer a mere looking out onto an infinitely distant goal, a positing of subjectivity, but a looking through to this one that originates in the one of being itself. In this respect, however, it is also the authentic essence of the psyche. *Eidos* and *psyche*, however, do not correspond as do hypothesis and method with respect to the logical unity of the system, but are what they are insofar as they are united with the one, the "primordially living," "primordially concrete," the "*logos* itself." The essential aliveness of the one life lives in the aliveness of its creative expression. The later Natorp no longer maintained the separation of the logician Plato from the mystic Plato, something the early Natorp had carried to extremes.

In an astounding way, this approaches the neo-Platonic interpretation of Plato, as if a century of laborious distinctions within the handed-down Platonic writings (which had become such a tangled mess in the interpretive tradition) had never occurred. What comes to expression in this extreme consequence of Natorp's thinking is more than an individual event of philosophical development. Precisely here is to be found his real, contemporary significance: His thinking attests to the inner belongingness of nineteenth-century neo-Kantianism to neo-Platonism and to the speculative Idealism of the successors to Kant. Already in Cohen's rediscovery of the fundamental idea of critique, there is a Hegelianism that is not owned up to, and it is to Natorp's credit that he consciously discovered the systematic impulses of Fichte and Hegel in the consistent thinking out of this neo-Kantianism.

Let me close with a personal recollection. When we young people, with the irreverent glance of youth, saw the little ice-gray man with the large wide-open eyes and the monumentally plain cape, he was often in the company of the young Heidegger on a walk up the Rotenberg, the younger man's attention turned respectfully to the honorable old man. But for the most part, both men found themselves in long deep silences, and this kind of silent dialogue between the generations touched us as having something of the dark and light sides of the one philosophy. Taken as a whole, Paul Natorp's thinking was in any case an attempt to answer the question Meister Eckhart had posed: "Why do you go out?" Once more the answer sounded as it had with Plotinus, in mysticism, and with Fichte and Hegel: "In order to come home."

Max Scheler

He was completely incredible. But if today you ask a young person interested in philosophy or even an older person, he hardly knows who Max Scheler was. He might know that Scheler was a Catholic thinker, that he wrote the influential *Formalism in Ethics and Non-Formal Ethics of Values*, and that he was somehow connected to the phenom- enological movement founded by Edmund Husserl and rightly or wrongly continued by Martin Heidegger. But Scheler has no presence in the contemporary philosophical consciousness comparable to that of Husserl or Heidegger. How did this happen? Who was he?

It was in 1877 that Max Scheler came into the world, and it is over fifty years since his sudden death, at fifty-four years of age. Is it because of this early death that no one knows him today? Scarcely. His most productive years certainly came late, but Scheler did not belong to those who wait, ripen slowly, and know they have ripened. He was also anything but unknown in his lifetime. He was a star of the first order within the phenomenological movement, which held a high opinion of itself. Disputed? Certainly. The solid craft of the old master Husserl, which many followed equally solidly but with deadly boredom, was not the manner of Scheler. Once when he, as a Cologne professor, greeted his Marburg colleague Nicolai Hartmann, he said: "My genius and you keeping your nose to the grindstone—that's what makes a real philosopher." This was not exactly directed against Hart- mann, but it was a key admission about himself. Husserl and the followers of phenomenology who kept tabs on Scheler looked upon him with undisguised discomfort. His brilliance was overwhelming.

What was to become of philosophy as a rigorous science within the fired-up essence of this man?

I recall exactly my first and only meeting with him. I was a young Marburg philosophy student, and I knew very well Scheler's chief work, *Umsturz der Werte*, a two-volume collection of writings that had been published before 1914 and reappeared just before or during the war. I was greatly impressed by the rich variety and brilliance of this man, who did not command German nearly as well as Nietzsche but who knew how to speak with no less fascination. Ernst Robert Curtius, who was then a Romance philologist in Marburg and who looked after me in a friendly way, was a great admirer of Scheler. When in 1920 Scheler came to give a lecture at the invitation of the Catholic Student Union, Curtius brought us together. Our conversation took place in a trolley car, a portable salon in that small metropolis of thought. The trolley had a single-track mind, it took long stops at familiar meeting places, and it proceeded at its own leisurely pace. In his nobly friendly fashion, Curtius held himself back, and thus I was delivered without defenses to the prying and probing presence of Max Scheler opposite me.

What an appearance! Whoever has been in the faculty lounge at Cologne University knows the portrait by Otto Dix that hangs there. It is an enthusiastic document in the style of the new ugliness. But it is no exaggeration. It is the naked truth. Head sunk between the shoulders, and a nose that I had to keep staring at. Its broad projection—what a masterful drainage system!—overhung a kind of rain gutter that, as I later saw when he gave his talks, constantly leaked. But during this conversation it remained dry.

His dry nose quickly took aim at me. He asked me about everything possible, but not about what preoccupied me at that time, unripe little boy of twenty that I was. This was the Marburg neo-Kantianism of Cohen and Natorp, and the first deviations of Nicolai Hartmann, which I took to be "phenomenological." Instead he questioned me about Rudolf Otto, the famous author of *Idea of the Holy*, the method of which he called "phenomenological"—and to my astonishment about the experimental psychologist Erich Jaensch, the discoverer of "eidetic" memory, which we abstract philosophers took to be fully beneath our dignity. Uncomfortably I stuttered about this or that. In order to find some basis for conversation, Scheler finally said: "Don't you think that philosophy is something like pulling puppets on a string?" I was thunderstruck. So little seriousness in so great a thinker.

But then I was carried away by his lectures. I understood suddenly what he had meant. Pulling strings, pulling on puppets—no, it was more like being drawn along, a nearly satanic sense of being possessed that led the speaker on to a true *furioso* of thought. When I once later told Husserl of the demoniac impression Scheler had made on me, with dismay he replied: "Oh, it's good that we have not just this man but also a few deadpans." (Husserl was the soberest, driest, least demoniac phenomenologist one could imagine.) At this time, in 1923, it had not yet dawned on Husserl who Heidegger was. Later he saw in Scheler and Heidegger two dangerous seducers whose aim it was to entice people from the right way, the way of phenomenology as a rigorous science.

Who was this man up there talking about the eternal in man? A Catholic thinker—hardly. Certainly he was even less a neo-Kantian, although he had been one. He had habilitated with the neo-Kantian Rudolf Eucken, a cultural and political celebrity in those days—after all, hadn't Eucken been a Nobel prizewinner? But then he had had to leave Jena—that upright little town was too tight for his dissolute temperament. In any case he shifted to Munich. He was always a lover of beautiful women (but only three times married). From Munich, as a kind of restless Ahasverus, he sponsored the connection between the Munich psychology associated with Theodor Lipps and the Göttingen phenomenological school associated with Husserl. When I met him in 1920 he had just begun his teaching activity at Cologne.

In between lay years of political, partly diplomatic, partly cultural-political activity, witnessed above all by two wartime books—*Der Genius des Krieges und der deutsche Krieg* (1915) and *Krieg und Aufbau* (1916). One recalls here Hermann Lübbe's curious chapter about the wartime books of German philosophers, unfortunately with a one-sided limitation to philosophy and to Germany. Scheler's books can at least claim that they brought the breadth of his philosophy to bear on the short-sightedness of those times and thus retain their interest even today. It was "left" Catholic politics on the basis of German national tradition to which he lent his spirit and his pen. Finally, with the end of the war came the well-earned success of his *Formalism in Ethics and Non-Formal Ethics of Values*—between Husserl's *Ideas* and Heidegger's *Being and Time* the most significant publication in the series of phenomenological annuals. That brought him a teaching chair in the newly founded Cologne University.

What connected him to phenomenology? This can easily be put in a negative way: an inclination against abstract constructions and against intuitive insights into essential truths. In phenomenological circles, one understood by this the kind of insights that are not empirically won or cannot be verified, that are accessible only in the form of idealike abstractions. To the uninformed these things are easily mystified as "essential visions" and are thereby mocked. Methods here, methods there—but for intuitive gifts Scheler surpassed all so-called phenomenologists, and he was hardly inferior in observational skills to the master Husserl, who with endless energy subordinated his minute descriptive art to the philosophical task of self-justification. And certainly Scheler was possessed of a vastly superior, unrestrained intellectual audacity and expansiveness. A truly volcanic nature. When in 1923 I went to Husserl and Heidegger in Freiburg, the story was told of a recent visit Scheler had made to Husserl. With tongue in cheek, he had asked Husserl whether God could distinguish between right and left. This sounds like a frivolous game, a pulling of puppets on a string. Or was he pulling the arm of Husserl, the defender of philosophy as a rigorous discipline? In the final analysis, the question was a serious one for him.

The catchword "intuition" had already in 1901 become the bridge that connected the two thinkers. It was at one of those early Kant conventions, preludes to the convention epidemic of our century, that Scheler met Husserl. Scheler's natural gift for intuition was truly phenomenal, but simultaneously he had in him something of the vampire who sucks the blood from his victims. At the heart of Kant—and this was, taking everything into consideration, his moral philosophy, his doctrine of the categorical imperative and the sense of duty—there remained not a single drop of blood once Scheler had selected him as his victim. One is never so unjust as when one sets oneself against one's own youthful foolishness. Neo-Kantianism, which Scheler took to be Kant, was his youthful foolishness, and his Kant criticism was therefore blindly one-sided.

But in the meantime, what insights! The hierarchy of values, the status relationships that Scheler had researched in *Formalism in Ethics and Non-Formal Ethics of Values*, were anything but a catholicizing metaphysical doctrine of goodness. Scheler traced back to the value contrast of courage and cowardice the ancient German ordering of laws according to which even manslaughter, not to speak of kidnapping, was a lesser crime than theft. This was an irrefutable intuitive truth, one that perhaps suggests a parallel with the Christian revaluation of the irreplaceability of life against the irrelevance of property. The penetrating lucidity of his intellect laid bare to him a hierarchy of values and goods that in result, not in method, referred back to a medieval arrangement of stages—with the highest dimension that of the saint and the personality of God. Was this his final word? Not at all.

"The reading public is well aware that in certain *higher* questions of metaphysics and the philosophy of religion as in such an essential question as that of the metaphysics of the one and absolute being (where the author remains firm), the author has not only continued to develop his position since the appearance of the second edition of this book but has also so deeply *changed* it that he can no longer identify himself as a 'theist' in the original meaning of this term. . . . Today as then, ethics seems to him important for every metaphysics of absolute being, but metaphysics is not important to the grounding of ethics. The changes in the metaphysical perspectives of the author are not to be traced back to changes in his philosophy of mind and its objective correlates in the acts of mind. They are rather to be traced back to changes and broadenings in his philosophy of nature and his anthropological insights."

I recall that when Scheler's "falling-out" with the Catholic faith was made known many were furious with him—mostly because they had believed in him rather than in the message of Christianity. Curtius defended him with the argument that one should welcome it when a great mind becomes free.

Scheler's personal spirituality had something of ecstasy in it, whose reverse was a sinking back into the dull stress of life. He had been one of the first in Germany to take up and propagate the teachings of Henri Bergson. The *élan vital* that drove him on so powerfully was not a muddying of his high intellectuality but the supporting stream from which he nourished himself. He summarized, so to speak, his chaotic and unorganized nature when he taught the dualism of stress and mind and the impotence of "pure" mind. This did not fall from the blue. Nor was it a mere turning into himself that drove him to this and compelled him to break with the Catholic concept of a personal God. Pure mind really is impotent. In his early writing on sympathy feelings and on love and hate (1912), and especially in the second edition of the 1923 book, he took issue with all reduction of "intellectual feelings" to the driving forces of pleasure and pain (just as from another perspective he criticized reductions of relations of production to an economic basis). He understood that it is the reality of stress that elevates mind to itself, yet the ways of the heart (Pascal) retain their own status. The story is told that Max Scheler wrote a long loving letter every Sunday for the duration of his life to his divorced second wife, the sister of the great conductor Wilhelm Furtwängler.

But our concern is not only with the private breadth of personality that is shown here. It is with the breadth of the problems that are posed to modern thinking. The transcendental ego, "consciousness in general," the absolute knowledge that is mind—these are not the secured points of reference, the *fundamentum inconcussum* of all truth. Kierkegaard's objection to Hegel, the absolute professor, that he had forgotten existence, repeated itself with reference to neo-Kantian transcendental philosophy. But Scheler did not become an *Existenz* philosopher. The pure doctrine of essence, and this was how he understood phenomenology, seemed to him to be only one side of philosophy— the spiritual sphere of deactualized possibilities of essence. The experience of reality itself was not accessible in this way. It provided for Scheler the theme of a type of empirical metaphysics that, behind all the particular realities investigated by the sciences, should be a science of reality per se.

This was no mere speculative adventure in the style of the later Schelling, who had opposed the positive philosophy of mythology and revelation to the negative philosophy of metaphysics. Scheler was a child of the century of science. He certainly had a first-rate speculative head, but what he simultaneously pursued was the collection of the sciences in metaphysics. Gestalt psychology, physiology, and above all sociology came under his scrutiny. The great study called *Erkenntnis und Arbeit*, which appeared in 1926 and critically worked over American pragmatism as well as the sociology of knowledge, contained the idea of a philosophical anthropology. Scheler's last work was a pragmatic treatise, "The Place of Man in the Cosmos," and its focal point was an outline of such an anthropology. This was a vision of a new land into which even then a researcher of the stamp of Helmuth Plessner had already taken a few steps, to be followed later by Arnold Gehlen.

Max Scheler was characterized by an enormous intellectual gluttony. He swept up whatever could nourish him, and he possessed a power of penetration that everywhere pushed through to the essential. The story is told that his reading so devoured him that whenever he met a colleague he would compel his participation simply by ripping pages out of whatever book he was reading and pressing them into the hands of his astonished companion. In this manner he is said to have used up several copies of Nicolai Hartmann's *Metaphysik der Erkenntnis*, which he prized highly. Maria Scheler once told Karl Reinhardt (who related the story to me) how Scheler began his day: With hands flattened on the buttons of his shirt or nestled on his tie, he spoke to himself without pause, trying out possibilities of thinking—rejecting, weighing, pursuing them to their most extreme conclusions—constantly holding his breath, tirelessly homing in on philosophy.

Perhaps he never did justice to Husserl (as little as the latter did to Scheler). Husserl's return to the inquiry of transcendental Idealism struck him as a wrong turn along the way to the thing itself. Scheler was the very opposite of Husserl. But he did recognize the genius of Heidegger early. Witness to this may one day be given from the manuscript he was preparing for the *Philosophische Anzeiger* at the time of his death. It contains his arguments against *Being and Time*. Heidegger, for his part, after he had shed the "school" compulsion of Husserl, clearly saw the philosophical potential of Scheler. The posthumous dedication of his Kant book, celebrating the "relaxed power" of Scheler, bears witness to this. The real dialogue of the fifty-year-old Scheler with the thirty-year-old Heidegger did not take place, but a common foundation for it was present.

The conversation did continue in its fashion, for Scheler's distinction among the different relativities of existence [*Dasein*] pursues no transcendental inquiry but is intent upon the construction of reality itself. Here the conversation with Heidegger could get started and had in fact already begun with the examination of the transcendental self-conception of *Being and Time*. Both were agreed that their starting point was not self-consciousness but rather what had initially made such a self-consciousness and theoretical orientation possible. Scheler criticized the dogmatism in the theory of pure perception. He saw in the adequate stimulus of perception the idealized end result of a great process of disillusionment with which the exaggerated drive-fantasies of human beings had met. He derived from this exaggerated drive-fantasy, penetrating through everything, the experience of empty space and empty time. Heidegger's ontological questioning behind the back of being as presence pointed in a similar direction. But was Scheler in a position to follow Heidegger's ontological inquiry and to manage the dualism of stress and mind? Had Heidegger made Scheler's evaluation of the sciences serviceable for his own ontological inquiry? The conversation continues. When in 1928 Heidegger heard the news of Scheler's death, he spontaneously included in his lecture a eulogy that ended with the sentence: "Yet once more a way of doing philosophy sinks into the darkness."[1]

Max Scheler was a spendthrift. He took and gave. He was infinitely rich, but he held nothing back. He always lived in plans and announcements of new books that would never appear. Evangelist of a philosophical anthropology, he encouraged the expectation that after his early death this *magnum opus* would emerge out of his papers. Committees were formed. A first volume appeared. There were wonderful things about death and the afterlife, about the feeling of shame, about models and leaders and so forth—but in truth all this was preliminary work from his brilliant period of creativity shortly before the First World War. A big new edition of his writings began after the Second World War, carefully looked after and protected by his widow Maria. That edition is said to be proceeding smoothly, but no one can edit papers that do not exist. Unless surprises await us, we shall have to be content with what is well known but hardly known well enough.

1. There are two versions of this quote from Heidegger in this book, and I have translated each one differently to retain the original inconsistency. [tr.]

No One's Years

When in 1923, after an attack of polio and as an immature doctor of philosophy and all-too-young husband, I went to Freiburg for a semester to study with Heidegger, naturally I also attended the lectures and seminars of Husserl. He received me with honors as an emissary of the Marburg School and a pupil of his patron Paul Natorp. To find a thoroughly Wilhelminian man of learning, with beard, glasses, stiff collar, and a gold watch chain on his vest, was no surprise. That was the style of the period. My father dressed similarly. Husserl's presentation was smooth and not without elegance, but it was without rhetorical effect. What he presented sounded in all ways like refinements of already well-known analyses. But there was an authentic intensity there, especially when he really lost himself in a description instead of developing his programs. Something like this occurred when, to demonstrate deceptive perception, he described his visit to the Berlin Panopticum on Friedrich Street. Much to his embarrassment, a young lady at the entrance winked at him. Then it dawned on him: "This was a doll!" I can still hear his soft, eastern pronunciation of the word *Puppe*. Or then again there was the "red apple" that when bitten into proved to be soap! Fyodor Stepun, who once accompanied me to a Husserl lecture, later characterized him as a "watchmaker gone mad." In fact, during his presentations Husserl often did look at his hands, and these were kept busy with the fingers of the right hand circling the flat palm of the left hand in a slow, turning movement. It was a set of concentrated movements that, taken together, gave a "fingertip feel" for the hand-worked ideal of precision in the Husserlian art of description. He always appeared in the seminar with a large retinue: Heidegger and Oscar Becker, among others. His seminars began with a question posed by him and ended with a long statement in which the answer he had given earlier was redeemed. A question, an answer, and a half-hour monologue. But sometimes in passing he gave excellent insights into vast speculative areas that led up to Hegel. In his writings hardly any similarly large vision is to be found.

His presentations were always monologues, but he never saw them as such. Once upon leaving he said to Heidegger: "Today for once we really had an exciting discussion." And he said this after he had spoken without period or comma for the duration of the session in response to the first and only question raised (with some pride, I believe the question came from me). Laced with tension of a different sort were lectures and colloquia with Heidegger. But Heidegger will be described often enough in this book. My meeting with him in Freiburg had nothing noteworthy about it.

Nicolai Hartmann had sent me to Richard Kroner. He greatly admired Kroner's book *Von Kant zu Hegel*. But as a teacher, Kroner found himself in the very difficult position of being put up alongside Heidegger. I confess that the compactness and energy of Heidegger's teaching made everything else that I had experienced, perhaps with the single exception of Scheler, appear to be flat. But I still think fondly of the regular Wednesday get-togethers at Richard Kroner's house, where he, Stepun, and I held discussions. These two old friends of mine had a good rapport with each other, and this allowed us to overcome the shyness that otherwise inhibited Kroner.

I was sent to Julius Ebbinghaus by Heidegger. These men were then good friends, and Heidegger was convinced that Kroner's *Von Kant zu Hegel* would vanish from sight once Ebbinghaus at last got on the move. As everyone knows, the great work then being prepared by Ebbinghaus never appeared. In working out the development that took place between Kant and Hegel, Ebbinghaus in fact and with decisive conclusiveness made a turn back to Kant. *Habent sua fata libelli.* Those acquainted with Julius Ebbinghaus knew that this passionate reversal was something of a return to the good old ghosts of Prussia, whom he had defended all his life with pugnacious courage.

On the return trip from Freiburg to Marburg (this time an immense journey because of the Ruhr War and occupation of Offenburg by the French), I visited Heidelberg for the first time and brought Karl

Jaspers greetings from Heidegger and Heinrich Rickert greetings from Kroner. The people who greeted me were no less different from each other than those who had given me these tasks. Jaspers, very friendly and with a certain world-curiosity, questioned me mostly about Husserl. He evidently perceived as troublesome the "school" mentality of phenomenology—a preliminary to his critique of all "housing" of philosophy. He obviously retained something of the psychiatrist: He sat in the shadows opposite the window and critically observed. Rickert, in contrast, saw nothing at all except himself—a bundle of nerves, constantly twisting his full beard and eyeing the shining tips of his shoes. He questioned me above all about Heidegger and expressed his astonishment that his student had such a low opinion of him. I came away from this visit to Heidelberg with the feeling that I would come back often to Jaspers's apartment at 44 Plöck Street.

Meeting Heidegger, which was the reason I had gone to Freiburg, confirmed for me that what I had pursued with playful passion and only partial satisfaction in the abstract exercises in thinking led by Nicolai Hartmann was still not what I sought as philosophy. Hartmann himself had a clear sense that I was following his thinking mostly in imitative fashion and was secretly striving after the historical way of thinking. When I found confirmation for my contrariness in Heidegger, especially in respect to the interpretive deepening of the historical uniqueness of expressions of thought, my old schoolboy understanding with Hartmann fell apart, and I set myself on the way to Heidegger. But even a second beginning is difficult, and I now had to overcome a second set of beginner's disappointments: What I had formerly pursued was no longer sufficient, yet I could not live up to the standards of what I was newly pursuing. These were years of deep doubt about my intellectual gifts, but they were also years in which I finally began to work seriously. I became a classical philologist under the friendly guidance of Paul Friedländer.

But what still had to happen before I became really clever at this? Heidegger had set us onto his trail. We learned from him what a lecture could be, and I hope that none of us has forgotten. I recall a telling incident that occurred when, as a young *Ordinarius* in Leipzig, I visited Nicolai Hartmann in Berlin for the first time. (After Heidegger's refusal of the call from Berlin, Hartmann had taken the position.) He was very condescending and started by asking: "Well, what's doing with philosophy in Leipzig? Anything happening?" And then he continued soothingly: "Hans-Georg, tell me, what are your four lectures there?" Astounded, I asked what he meant. I did not have just *four* lectures; every one I read was different. He, then, in response: "But Hans-Georg, that's sheer exploitation!"

But back to Heidegger. This Black Forest fellow, who from childhood had grown up with skis on, often participated in our handball games, and in this activity we reached a high level of athletic prowess. Sometimes Heidegger also participated in our bowling tournaments, which we in Marburg held in the Dammelsberg and which he always attended with childlike passion. We also learned industry from him. He began his day very early and gave his lectures at seven in the morning during the summer semester. Naturally, we all hurried to these morning lectures without breakfast, and soon we were all getting together afterward to have a sort of picnic in the rooms of one of our members. This was Walter Bröcker, who lived in the Hofstadt. Bröcker would procure a whole bucket of Liebig's meat extract, and everyone would add something to the breakfast, which would be dragged out until around noon. These were the famous Aristotelian breakfasts in which we talked for hours about what we had just heard. Karl Löwith and his friend Marseille along with Walter Bröcker—they had come with Heidegger from Freiburg—simply pushed in and added themselves to us old Marburgers—Klein, Krüger, and myself—and we constituted a narrow circle of initiates. We took great pride in ourselves and later looked down with condescension on the many who streamed to Marburg to study with Heidegger.

Why should one deny that it is an advantage to have a genius as a teacher? But one should also realize that such an advantage is not owing to one's self. We were terrible. Once we had a thoughtful discussion with Paul Tillich, at that time a young visiting professor in thee theological faculty and the extreme opposite of all that Heidegger embodied for us. He was a highly intelligent and very moving spirit who explained things in terms of the forms of reflective thought and who, so to speak, retrospectively arranged his studies of the great thinkers in the filing cabinet of his reflective concepts (as he himself innocently put it). We were then already so far along the way, having taken the first step in practicing the new mode of working that Heidegger embodied, that Tillich's mode of working seemed worthless to us. Heidegger's mode consisted in making the interpretation of a text as convincing as possible, to a point where we risked losing ourselves to it. That is how things went for us in Heidegger's lectures, and this was especially the case for me with reference to Plato and Aristotle, so that all criticism was lost on me.

More fruitful was the new impetus that Heidegger gave to the theologians in Marburg. The situation there was in any case tense. Marburg has been the leader of the historical school of theology, and the call "Karl Barth ante portas" could still lead to a kind of panic. Especially significant, however, was the circumstance that Rudolf Bultmann, who himself came out of the liberal theology of Marburg, was at the time he came to know Heidegger being moved by the catchwords of dialectical theology. Bultmann's sharp sarcasm, and even more the incorruptible earnestness with which he struggled for clarity and distance from all theological pathos, had led him to a radical internal criticism of theology. In this he was encouraged and strengthened by Heidegger. It led to a true friendship, such as seldom happens between men in their middle thirties and forties, one supported by the community of their spiritual ends and efforts. As a result the student body developed a strong and proud group feeling. First we went to hear Rudolf Otto. Then an hour later we went to Bultmann's sharply gripping exegeses in order to receive weapons to use against the fortified dogmatics we had heard earlier.

But even more apparent was the intellectual revolution that took hold of the theologians and philosophers when foreign guests gave lectures. The most unforgettable for us were the so-called theological slugfests. Everyone streamed into room number six if not into the main auditorium, not only to hear the famous guests but also to be present when they were put up against the wall in the discussion battles. The first of these festivals was not yet a real slugfest but only a prelude. This was the visit of Eduard Turneysen, Barth's friend from Basel, who proclaimed dialectical theology for the first time in Marburg. In the discussion following the talk the whole theological faculty put in an appearance. First the played-out and well-to-do elderly ones, such as Neibergall, Martin Rade, and Karl Bornhäuser (a united front from one end to the other), then Bultmann's pointed questions, and finally Heidegger's weighty contribution, which conjured up the radical self-doubting of Franz Overbeck and called theology (was this its repudiation or its confirmation?) to its task of finding the word, as it was charged with calling to belief and preserving in belief. It was a dense atmosphere that surrounded us in Marburg, and every presentation, every discussion, made its waves. Heidegger especially, but also Bultmann, came back to these events in their lectures. I myself cannot claim to have been a competent listener at these first meetings—this happened only later when I had deepened my own theological studies and learned from Bultmann.

Bultmann was a passionate humanist as well as a sharp theologian, and that brought us together in a different manner at a very early point. For fifteen years I attended the famous "Bultmannsche Graeca" that took place every Thursday, in Bultmann's apartment if I am not mistaken. Heinrich Schlier, Gerhardt Krüger, and later Günther Bornkamm and Erich Dinkler were also part of the little group that read the classics of Greek literature with Bultmann. It was not learned work that we did. One of us was condemned to read out a German translation, and the others followed in the Greek text. We read thousands of pages in this manner. Sometimes a discussion developed and new outlooks resulted; but Bultmann was always calling us back to order to continue the reading. Whether it was Greek tragedy or comedy, a Church father or Homer, a historian or a rhetorician, we hurried through the entire ancient world one evening per week for fifteen years. This schedule was maintained by Bultmann with strictness and perseverance, week after week. We began punctually at 8:15 P.M. and read until the clock struck eleven. Bultmann was a strict man.

Only then did the postmortem begin. One could smoke beforehand. Bultmann preferred black Brazilian cigars or a pipe to cigarettes, and only because of the haze they left did he indulge in what he called "weakling's cigars," wrapped in a leaf of blond tobacco. At eleven o'clock there was something to drink, usually wine. But one was never allowed to forget that one was in a frugal house. When the bottle was about finished, Bultmann would set it upside down and after a few minutes pour out the few drops that had collected in the neck. This cheerful period, which began with the wine, fell into two parts: high-level academic gossip and the telling of jokes. The former was very nasty, the latter very deft, and Günther Bornkamm above all celebrated many triumphs with his talent for telling a tale. Bultmann noted down the jokes that seemed to him to be worthy, and in later years he would fall back smilingly on this long-collected stockpile. In this way, too, he was the classic picture of the truly learned man. One day the first volume of his collected jokes was filled, and we were given the task of suggesting a witty motto for volume two. There were fifteen years of this inner comradeship, lasting until I finally left Marburg in 1938 or 1939. I missed nothing so much as this circle of friends and the form of its life.

The Marburg of the 1920s was not yet the mass university of today. It was completely contained within the little city Marburg then was, and contact among those who belonged together happened easily. Fundamentally, all so-called educational experiences were the same. There was no presentation, no poetry reading, no evening at the theater, almost no concert that one could attend without later bumping into someone and having a conversation in which the experience was referred to. Certainly this was not an acquaintanceship of everyone with everyone. On the contrary, it was a climate and a surrounding in which groups knit tightly together. Also, when I speak of the Heidegger "school," I do not mean thereby all the students of Heidegger but rather that small group to which I belonged. Parallel to this were other groups in which young people got together.

Marburg was especially charming during vacation periods, when the town seemed quite dead. Basically, every fifth Marburger was a student, and even if the sparse economic circumstances of our lives kept us close to home, we still managed to get together socially. Aside from sports, perhaps the nicest of our customs was reading great works of literature in small groups. In the course of the more than fifteen years that I spent in Marburg, we read thousands of pages—the great Russian writers, the English, the French, and then also modern authors like Joseph Conrad, Knut Hamsun, or André Gide. Our reader was almost always Gerhard Krüger, whose clear understanding afforded him a masterly naturalness of speech. He had a special preference for realistic novels, and the famous story of Captain Kopekin became for us a byword: "Man must have his mutton chops." We did not always have ours. These were years of unbelievable shrinkage in the economy—inflation, deflation, rising unemployment, and the like hit us from all sides.

Karl Löwith was a special master of the short story. He was also the involuntary source of innumerable anecdotes because in his pensiveness and abstractness he did not take note of many of the little things of everyday life, or he took note of them in a surprisingly literal way. One day while reading the newspaper he said, chuckling to himself: "Not again! Why here's another of those little organizations. This one's a committee opposed to sleeveless dresses." And he showed us an announcement of the Committee for the Humble Poor, not noting that the German words for "arm" and "poor" are the same. On another day he said: "I never knew that cheese was made out of flies' eggs." It was hard to talk him out of this, because he had seen with his own eyes worms crawling out of some cheese. A very special kind of problem arose when someone put forth the thesis that a three-legged table would not wobble. No mathematical demonstration for this state of affairs found favor with Löwith. Only after hours of verbal combat, when one of our physicists had managed to put up a matchbox on three match legs, did Löwith give in, but with a postscript that granted him satisfaction: "It can still fall over." Löwith was by choice a semi-Italian and spent many years there before he fully returned to Marburg. Even after his return he never stopped gushing about Italy. He encountered his mirror image in an Italian lecturer in Marburg who gushed over Germany in a similar manner. His name was Turazza, and he was a humanist from head to toe. Löwith would say something like: "Italy is too nice. There are no ashtrays there. Every floor is an ashtray." Or our Italian friend would say: "Germany is too nice. Coffeehouses here are quieter than churches are with us." Löwith believed he had found an especially characteristic difference. He maintained that in Italy one ate only the green leaves from radishes, and in Germany only the red root. I was downright disappointed when much later I went to Italy and was not able to verify this story.

The sort of comic situations serious philosophers can fall into is illustrated by the following story. A large circle of us were sitting together when Heidegger chanced by. Someone said that a herring lived up to twenty years. Whereupon Heidegger, the philosopher of the unique *personal* authenticity of death: "What, *a* herring?" He then joined in the general jubilation. Later I consolingly showed him my copy of *Being and Time*: There on the page where Heidegger says about animals that they do not die, only perish, there was by chance enclosed in the paper a small insect that had perished—it lived on as a proof.

Marburg was a citadel of Romance philology. The proud list of names speaks for itself: Eduard Wechssler, Ernst Robert Curtius, Leo Spitzer, Erich Auerbach, Werner Krauss. In fact, the company of these significant philologists and what they radiated, both directly and through their students, was an important element of the liberal education of the Marburg of those days. The philologists also sponsored a lively series of lectures that allowed us to make the acquaintance of many famous names. I recall an elegant lecture by Etienne Gilson; an almost gushing presentation by Jean Baruzi, the Leibniz scholar; and a skeptically cosmopolitan lecture by Georges Duhamel. I myself admittedly lived a cloistered life since I had mounted a rigorous program for the study of classical philology alongside my philosophical studies. It was not yet clear to me whether my scholarly talents were adequate, and I therefore decided to devote myself simultaneously to philological and philosophical studies on the chance that I might become a schoolteacher. The Marburg reader may wonder that I am saying nothing about the famed university jubilee of 1927. Well, I took absolutely no notice of it. I still did not really belong to such things; and despite the title of doctor that I had carried for years, I felt like an overaged student of classical philology.

We read a good deal of Plato with Paul Friedländer. At this time he was preparing his major work on Plato, and his seminar was a hard schooling. There were then only three regular members, and in the prevailing style of philology this meant that every third week one of us had to come forward with an interpretation of his own. One of my seminar friends was Hans Schaefer, later an ancient history colleague in Heidelberg. He was the son of a Marburg physicist, Clemens Schaefer, whose large figure rose to a black fur collar topped by a small head with a flashing pince-nez attached to it—a frequent sight on the Wettergasse. Hans Schaefer was already a well-educated pundit and possessed a rich repertory, especially in respect to languages. Friedländer's style was to use the seminar to support in a sharp-witted manner the invalidity of suspected works or lines of thought. Even if this was seldom convincing, it was extraordinarily useful. One learned how difficult it is to prove inauthenticity and how correct Hegel is when he says: "Arguments are a dime a dozen." Texts did not, however, become more authentic through such demonstrations. But the extreme of such examples only served to make clear the rule, which was that under Friedländer one learned in an incomparable way to discipline one's feel for language, that inner ear without which literary judgment is impossible.

Friedländer was determined to broaden the social life of Marburg, and to this end he set up a regular "jour," a Sunday afternoon gathering, repeated at least three times each semester. These were really to be treasured, even in Marburg where people were always getting together.

(Above all in the streetcar, which ran from the South Railroad Station, one would meet Ferdinand Wrede and Karl Helm, Paul Jakobsohn and most certainly Paul Jacobsthal, the archeologist, for he took it to the university every morning precisely at a quarter to nine, with the punctual sense of duty of a Prussian official.) Friedländer was very friendly to me, and later I was to learn a good deal from him. With his Berlin sarcasm he was a master at stifling all approximate gossip and at distinguishing the few real from the many preposterous claims. Nevertheless, I cut off my studies of ancient philology fairly abruptly because I had not buried my philosophical plans.

I do not think back terribly fondly on my state exam. All the chivalry of my examiners was called upon just to get me through. They were Ernst Lommatzsch, Paul Friedländer, and Heidegger. How would I ever have fared under the "objectivized" procedures of the present? When, after the exam, Friedländer was going home with Heidegger, he spoke with him of the intention to habilitate me in classical philology. The next day I received a letter from Heidegger. He spoke to me about accelerating my dissertation, presumably because he would be going to Freiburg as Husserl's successor and wanted very much to habilitate me before then. I felt very uncertain at this time and was somewhat astounded at this approach. Later I realized that Heidegger was quite right. One had only to think of the words of Nietzsche: "I have long been accustomed to judging philosophy professors according to whether or not they are good philologists." It could no longer be so terribly wrong, now that I had learned something, to open up to me the possibility of teaching. Thus it came, finally, just at the point of Heidegger's departure from Marburg, that the genuine freedom of our Marburg existence came to an end and we began a new chapter as private *Dozenten*.

Martin Heidegger

When Martin Heidegger celebrated his eighty-fifth birthday in the fall of 1974, it may have come as a surprise to many young people. For decades the thinking of this man has been part of the general consciousness, and his place in our turbulent century is, despite all changes in the constellations, beyond dispute. Periods of Heidegger proximity and Heidegger distance alternate, as is only the case with the really great stars that determine epochs. One of these periods was immediately after the First World War, when the effectiveness of Husserl's young assistant in Freiburg began to become apparent. Even then he radiated an incomparable aura. Then, in the five years Heidegger spent as a teacher in Marburg, his academic influence steadily increased, and with the publication of *Being and Time* in 1927 that influence broke through into public view. With a single stroke, world fame was his.

In our times, in a Europe that since 1914 has become provincialized, where only the natural sciences are able to call forth a quick international echo—one thinks of names like Einstein, Planck, and Heisenberg, and to these one would have to add the names of theologians like Karl Barth who, through their churches, are able to exercise influence beyond national boundaries—in such times, it is astounding how the fame of the young Heidegger spread throughout the world. When, after the end of the Third Reich, Heidegger was not allowed to exercise his Freiburg professorship because of his early support of Hitler, there began a truly international pilgrimage to Todtnauberg, the little town where he spent the greater part of the year in his "hut," a modest house in the Black Forest.

The 1950s provided yet another high point of his "presence," even though he was hardly active as a teacher. From this period I can still recall how he came to a Hölderlin conference in Heidelberg, and what a technical problem it was to manage the life-endangering congestion in the large lecture hall of the new university. This is the way it was at his every public appearance.

Then with the stormy development of the economy and of technology, with prosperity and with comfort, there came for young people in the academic world new, sober modes of thinking. Technology and Marxist ideology critique became the determining intellectual powers, and Heidegger disappeared from what he characterized so angrily as "idle talk," until in our times what seems to be a new generation of young people have rediscovered him, as if he were a forgotten classic.

What is the secret of this enduring presence? Heidegger never lacked for enemies and still does not. In the 1920s he had to establish himself in the face of innumerable forms of academic simplemindedness. The ten years from 1935 to 1945, and no less decisively public opinion in the entire postwar period, were not favorably inclined to him. The *Destruction of Reason* (Lukács), the *Jargon of Authenticity* (Adorno), the abandonment of rational thinking to pseudo-poetic mythology, the windmill attack against logic, the flight from time into being—one could considerably lengthen the list of these attacks and accusations. And yet when the Klostermann publishing house announced a seventy-volume edition of the complete works of Heidegger, the whole world certainly sat up and took notice. Even a person who knows nothing of Heidegger can hardly let his eye wander away indifferently when he looks at photographs of this lonely old man, seeing him peering into himself, listening to himself, reflecting beyond himself. And one who takes himself to be "against" Heidegger or for that matter "for" Heidegger makes himself ridiculous, for this is not the way to get around a mode of thinking.

What is this, and how did it come about? I recall exactly how I first heard his name. In a seminar led by Moritz Geiger in 1921 in Munich, a student was giving a passionate speech marked by an unusual mode of expression. When I later questioned Geiger about this, he said in the most matter-of-fact manner: "Oh, he's been Heideggerized." Didn't the same thing happen to me soon enough? It was hardly a year later that my teacher Paul Natorp gave me a forty-page Heidegger manuscript to read, an introduction to an Aristotle interpretation. This

affected me like an electric shock. I had experienced something similar
as an eighteen-year-old when for the first time I came face-to-face
with verses by Stefan George (whose name was then fully unknown
to me). I certainly did not bring a sufficient understanding to Heidegger's
analysis of the "hermeneutic situation," here employed as an introduction to a philosophical interpretation of Aristotle. But then the
discussion in this paper was about the young Luther, about Gabriel
Biel and Peter of Lombard, about Augustine and Paul. That Aristotle
came into view precisely in this manner, that a highly unusual language
was being used, that the talk was carried out in terms like "Um-zu"
[in order to], that it was about the "Woraufhin" [as to what] and the
"Vorgriffs" [preconception] and the "Durchgriffs" [reaching through]—
things like these remain in my memory to this day. They broke through
to me. This was no mere learned doing moved by a historical problematic. The whole of Aristotle then assumed an importance for me,
and when I received my first introduction to Heidegger in Freiburg,
my eyes opened wide.

Yes, it was an eye-opener. Today it is said of Heidegger that he
lacks conceptual precision and has a poetic vagueness. It is true that
Heidegger's language was as distant from the curious near English
that has become modish in contemporary philosophy as it was from
mathematical symbolism or from the playing with categories and
modalities that I had practiced in neo-Kantian Marburg. When Heidegger lectured, one saw things as if they had taken on bodily form.
In a tamer form and limited to the phenomenology of perception,
much the same thing could be said of Husserl. But terminology was
not the phenomenologically productive thing about Heidegger's language. It was not by accident that the young Heidegger preferred
above all other works of Husserl the sixth logical investigation, where
the concept of "categorial intuition" is developed. Today this doctrine
is frequently held to be unsatisfactory, and modern logic is set in
action against it. But Husserl's praxis, as well as Heidegger's, is not
to be refuted in this manner. This was a meeting with live language
in philosophizing, to which the technical precision of logic's tools cannot
do justice.

In the autumn of 1923 Heidegger went as a young professor to
Marburg. As a way of saying farewell to his native Freiburg, he invited
a large number of friends, colleagues, and students up to his house
in the Black Forest for a summer evening's celebration. Up there on

the Stübenwasen a huge bonfire was lit, and Heidegger gave a speech that deeply impressed all of us. It began with the words: "Be awake to the fire of the night . . . ," and his next words were: "The Greeks. . . ." Certainly the romanticism of the youth movement was in the air. But there was more. It was the decisiveness of a thinker who beheld as one our time and old times, the future and Greek philosophy.

It is impossible to exaggerate the drama of Heidegger's appearance in Marburg. Not that he was out for sensation. His appearance in the lecture hall certainly had something of a guaranteed effectiveness to it, but the unique thing about his person and his teaching lay in the fact that he identified himself fully with his work and radiated from that work. Because of him the lecture format became something totally new. It was no longer the "lesson presentation" of a professor who put his essential energy into research and publication.

The "great book" monologues lost their priority of place because of Heidegger. What he provided was the full investment of his energy, and what brilliant energy it was. It was the energy of a revolutionary thinker who himself visibly shrank from the boldness of his increasingly radical questions and who was so filled with the passion of his thinking that he conveyed to his listeners a fascination that was not to be broken. Who will ever forget the acerbic polemics with which he caricatured the cultural and educational goings-on of those times— the "craze for being present everywhere," the "they," "idle talk," and "all this without pejorative meaning"—that too. Who can forget the sarcasm with which he characterized colleagues and contemporaries? Who among those who then followed him can forget the breathtaking swirl of questions that he developed in the introductory hours of the semester for the sake of entangling himself in the second or third of these questions and then, in the final hours of the semester, rolling up the deep-dark clouds of sentences from which the lightning flashed to leave us half stunned.

When for the first and only time Nicolai Hartmann heard Heidegger give a lecture, the initial one in Marburg, he said to me that he had not seen such a powerful performance since Hermann Cohen. Here were really two antipodes: the cool reserved Balt who gave the impression of being a grand bourgeois seigneur, and the small, dark-eyed mountain farmer whose temperament repeatedly broke through despite all attempts to keep his reserve. I saw them once greeting each other on the steps of Marburg University: Hartmann was going to his lecture, as always in striped trousers, a black coat, and an archaic-looking white collar. Heidegger was on his way out of his lecture in a skiing outfit. Hartmann just stood there and said: "Can you really go to lecture dressed like that?" Heidegger's satisfied laugh had a special reason, for on this evening he was giving a lecture on skiing by way of introduction to a new classroom ski course. It was the pure Heidegger who began his lecture with: "Skiing is something that can be learned only on the land and for the land." The typical hammer blow with which fashionable expectations were beaten down, and simultaneously the hope of new expectations. "He who can do a respectable stem turn, this person I would take with me on any ski tour."

Heidegger, a skier from childhood, did have his athletic side, and the Heidegger school was infected by it. We were the second-best handball team in Marburg, always reaching the finals, and for years Heidegger always came to our practice sessions, even if he wasn't as superior to us here as he was in everything else.

Of course Heidegger did not always run around in a ski outfit, but he was never to be seen in a black coat. Instead he wore a peculiar suit that we named the "existential" outfit. It was a piece of clothing designed by the painter Otto Ubbelohde, one that tended slightly to a rural folk style, and in it Heidegger in fact had something of the modest magnificence of a farmer dressed up for Sunday.

Heidegger began his day at the crack of dawn and four times a week in the early morning hours put us through Aristotle. These were memorable interpretations, with respect to both the strength of their illustrative content and the philosophical perspectives they opened up. In Heidegger's lectures we were often so personally touched that we no longer knew whether he was speaking of his own concern or that of Aristotle. It is a great hermeneutic truth that we then began to experience personally and that I was later to justify in theory and to represent.

We were an arrogant little in-group and easily let our pride in our teacher and his manner of working go to our heads. And today one can easily imagine what was happening with the second- or third-rate Heideggerians, those whose scholarly talent or education was not fully developed. Heidegger worked like a narcotic on them. This whirl of radical questions into which Heidegger pulled us became caricatured in the mouths of the imitators. Frankly speaking, I would not like to have been a colleague of the Heidegger of that time. Everywhere there were students who had learned a thing or two from the master, mostly "the way he cleared his throat and the way he spit." These young people could be destabilizing with their "radical" questions, the substantive emptiness of which was concealed by their demanding tone. So when they trotted out their dark Heideggerian German, many a professor in many a seminar must have had the experience, described by Aristophanes in the comedies, of how the students of Socrates and the Sophists broke all the rules of human decency. Just as in those times there was no true objection to Socrates, so now there was none against Heidegger himself because of this situation and the fact that not every one of his followers had liberated himself to do serious work. Still, it was remarkable to see how Heidegger, who had invented the term "liberating care," could not prevent a large number of people from losing their freedom to him. Moths fly into the light.

We sensed it when Heidegger was writing *Being and Time*. Occasional remarks pointed in that direction. One day in a Schelling seminar he read out the sentence: "The fear of life itself drives human beings out of the center." And then he said: "Name for me one single sentence from Hegel that comes up to this sentence for depth." And everybody knows about the first effects of *Being and Time*, especially on the theologians. This was the effect of the existential appeal of the "being toward death," of the call to "authenticity." One heard more Kierkegaard in this than Aristotle. But already by the 1929 Kant book, the talk was no longer about the *Dasein* [existence] of human beings but rather about *Da-sein* [being-there] in human beings. The question about being and its "thereness," which Heidegger had heard in the Greek term *aletheia* (unhiddenness), now became loud and clear. Heidegger was no Aristotle redivivus but rather a thinker led not only by Hegel but also by Nietzsche, a thinker who had thought his way back to the beginning, back to Heraclitus and Parmenides, because the never-ceasing play of disclosure and concealment had dawned on him and also the secret of language, in which both talk and the hiding of truth occur.

Heidegger first realized all this completely only when he had gone back to his home country, to Freiburg and the Black Forest, and began "to sense the power of the old ground," as he then wrote to me. "Everything began to get slippery." He called this intellectual experience "the turn," not in the theological sense of a conversion but in the sense he knew from his way of talking. The term "turn" refers to a bend—a hairpin or switchback—in the path that goes up a mountain. One does not turn around here; rather, the way itself turns in order to continue going up. Where to? The question is one that cannot be easily answered. It is notable that Heidegger named one of his most important collections of later writings *Holzwege*. These are paths that do not simply carry one onward but compel one to climb along an untried way or turn back. Whatever happens, the heights remain.

About Heidegger's Freiburg period, starting around 1933, I know nothing from my own observations. But that Heidegger after his political interlude took up the passion of thinking with a new spirit and that his thinking led him into previously untried regions was soon clear even from afar. There was a paper on the key words in Hölderlin that cut a very strange figure in the journal *Das innere Reich*. It sounded as if Heidegger had disguised his thinking in the clothing of Hölderlin's terminology about the divine and the gods.

And then one day in 1936 we went to Frankfurt to hear Heidegger's three-hour lecture on the "Origin of the Work of Art." Dolf Sternberger's report in the *Frankfurter Zeitung* was headed "The Deserted Landscape." Certainly the strictness of this intellectual excursion was alien to the reporter, the friend of the panorama of human doings. It was also unusual to hear talk about the earth and heaven and the conflict between the two, as if the concern with concepts of thinking was the same as the concern in the metaphysical tradition with matter and form. Metaphors? Concepts? Were these expressions of thought or announcements of a neoheathen mythology? Nietzsche's Zarathustra, the teacher of eternal recurrence, appeared as the new model. In fact, Heidegger was then orienting himself to an intensive interpretation of Nietzsche that would find expression in a two-volume work, the real counterpart of *Being and Time*.

But this was not Nietzsche. There was also nothing of a religious eccentricity here. Even when occasional eschatological tones sounded, when the seemingly oracular talk was about the God who "supposedly suddenly" might appear, these were extrapolations of philosophical thought and not the words of a prophet. This was a strenuous struggle for a philosophical language, which sought to go beyond Hegel and Nietzsche for the sake of retrieving and then "repeating" the beginnings of Greek thinking. I recall one time up at the cottage during the war years when Heidegger began to read to me a Nietzsche paper on which he was working. He broke off suddenly and pounded the table, sending the teacups clattering, while crying out from irritation and frustration: "This is all Chinese!" Here was a need for language as it can only be experienced by someone who has something to say. Heidegger needed his whole strength to hold out against this need for language and to keep himself from being diverted by the temptations offered by traditional ontotheological metaphysics with its conceptualization of his question about being. It was the dogged energy of his thinking that everywhere broke through when he spoke on "Building, Living, Thinking" in the great hall where his Darmstädt "talks" took place. And it broke through in his paper on "The Thing," which swung out in an enigmatic word dance. And it was there in his interpretation of a poem of Trakl, and again in his interpretation of a late Hölderlin text. Often these papers were given in the excellent Kurhaus Bühlerhöhe, where Heidegger was once even followed by Ortéga y Gasset, who had been drawn in by this seeker after the gold of speech and thought.

Heidegger also complied with the routines of academic life. In a regular working session of the Heidelberg Academy of Science, he spoke on "Hegel and the Greeks." He gave a long, difficult presentation on "Identity and Difference" as his contribution to the jubilee of Freiburg University. On another such occasion, Heidegger gave a seminar for his former students, as in the old days, on a single sentence from Hegel: "The truth of being is the essence"—very much his old self. All of this is to say that he was an exiled man in his questioning and thinking, one who carefully put forward one foot at a time to see if there was any firm ground—a peevish, sulky man if one did not grasp where he sought to set foot, and a man not in a position to help others due to the weight of his own effort. I often brought him together with my own circle of students in Heidelberg. Sometimes a conversation succeeded, which meant that we were taken along on the hike through thinking and did not stray from the path. Only he who goes along knows what such a path is.

Today most people think differently. They do not want to go along but rather want to know in advance where a path leads; or better, they already know where one should go. Such people desire only to locate Heidegger as an example of the crisis of bourgeois society in the period of late capitalism. Heidegger represents for them a flight out of time into being or into an irrational intuitionism, a neglecting of modern logic. But perhaps these contemporaries deceive themselves in that they would have nothing to locate and nothing critically to transcend if this philosophy were not simply there, more unreflective than the thinking of other contemporaries, itself shut off to mere reflection. But at least two things ought to be undeniable by anyone: No one before Heidegger thought back so far and thereby did more to make understandable the ways in which the course of contemporary civilization, right up to its present technological stage and the current struggle for world supremacy, has been the immediate result of the thinking of the Greeks, their founding of science and their establishment of metaphysics. And in doing this, no one ventured further than Heidegger out onto the shifting foundations of unconventional concepts, so that the human experience of other cultures, especially those of Asia, would show themselves from afar as modes of our own possible experience.

One day the poet Paul Celan appeared among the pilgrims who made their way to Todtnauberg, and from his meeting with the thinker a poem came to be. Just think about it: A persecuted Jew, a poet who did not live in Germany but in Paris, yet still a German poet, uneasily ventures this visit. He must have been received by the "consolation of the eye" of the small rustic property with the running spring "with the cube of asters on it" as well as by the small rustic man with the beaming eyes. He inscribed himself in the cottage book, like so many before him, with a line of hope that he kept in his heart. He walked with the thinker across the soft meadows, both alone, like the individually standing flowers—the orchis and the orchis. Only on the way home did it begin to become clear to Celan what Heidegger had murmured and what still seemed crude. He understood the daring of a thinking that another—"the man"—could also hear but without understanding it, the daring of a stepping out onto a shifting foundation, as onto beaten paths that one cannot follow to their ends. The poem reads:

Arnica, eye bright, the
draft from the well with the
cube of asters on it,

in the
cottage,

Martin Heidegger

a line is written in the book
— whose names did it receive
before mine? —
a line is written in this book
a line about
a hope, today,
for a thinker's
coming
word,
a hope in my heart

forest glade, unleveled,
orchis and orchis, separated,

crude, but later, in traveling,
clear,

the one who is driving us, the man,
the one who is listening, too,
the half-
followed, trodden
paths in the high moor,
moist,
very.

Rudolf Bultmann

When the order Pour le Mérite voted to make Rudolf Bultmann a member in 1969, he had already reached the advanced age of eighty-three years and could only participate in our activities from a distance. He nonetheless greeted the acceptance into this circle of scholars, researchers, and artists with great satisfaction and devoted his complete attention to us. He had long enjoyed a worldwide reputation as the old master of New Testament research; but the peculiar tension that can exist in the life of a German theologian—to be a historian, philologist, and man of letters while simultaneously occupying a teaching position commissioned by the church—had confronted Bultmann in an especially sharp way throughout his life. Thus the scholarly recognition represented by acceptance into the order was especially meaningful to him because it was conferred by laymen entirely outside the church.

Bultmann came from a Lutheran pastor's family in Oldenburg. Born on August 20, 1884, he spent his childhood and school years there and then pursued his theological studies in Tübingen, Berlin, and Marburg. He was stamped by Marburg's great theological faculty, especially by Jülicher, Wilhelm Herrmann, and Heitmüller. After spending four years in Breslau, where he had his first professorship, and one year in Giessen, he returned to Marburg in 1921 and remained faithful to that city to the end of his life. During his last decade he lived in deep retirement, especially after the suffering and death of his spouse had isolated him. He died at the honorable old age of ninety-two on July 30, 1976, up to the end attentively and actively devoted to his children, students, friends, and to the life of the mind.

Thus for over half a century he lent his presence to Marburg, the oldest Protestant university in Germany. His unique fruitfulness as a teacher of generations of theologians is evident to this day in the lively annual gatherings of Marburg alumni. His pedagogic charisma was inseparable from the productivity of his research, and especially from his untiring, probing energy and his concentrated earnestness. Anyone who heard him lecture, even once, or participated in his oversubscribed seminars, or came upon him in his ecclesiastical office as preacher was seized by the intensity of his presence. There was nothing of false pathos or rhetorical trickery about him. The utmost in sobriety, penetrating insight, sarcasm, and sometimes warming, sometimes grim humor were characteristic of him, but one had to experience it directly to understand what it was like when in an exegetical lecture he read the text of the Bible in Greek and in his own translation as if he were doing it only for himself and only for purposes of reflection. In the air there was a tension that did not let up when Bultmann's interpretations mixed together the most astounding learnedness and the most subtle perspicacity with an often merciless derision of his theological colleagues. And when in his seminar he took the lead in pointed, sharp, polished debate, open to every rebuttal, his own reply lightning fast as it closed in from behind the blue clouds of smoke emerging from his pipe—this was indeed a show. But then again it was not show but exemplary integrity, very much without play and without showiness.

It was this unwavering integrity that in substantial measure protected him from the preachiness, pathos, and routine that so easily come to characterize the ecclesiastical office. It was this unwavering integrity that also lent him strength in controversial times, in the ecclesiastical conflicts of the Hitler period and also in the endless conflicts with ecclesiastical authorities both before and after the Third Reich.

The organization of his intellectual life was one of unprecedented discipline and frugality. More than a small part of his scholarly production was set to paper on the backs of paid bills and letters and even on the unfolded insides of envelopes. But he was most frugal when it was a question of his time. Without reducing his enjoyment of life, his family, friends, and intervals with a glass of wine, he maintained the strictest division of time. Even his free time was meaningfully planned and filled up. Of course every trip was exactly prepared and executed. The annual cure for his hip pains, which he took regularly at the *Schwarzer Bock* in Wiesbaden, characteristically included a detailed reading program from the most varied areas of the arts and sciences. Along with a consistent daily routine of reading, which cultivated both classical and modern literature, there belonged his imaginary travels to the far reaches of the world. He would select the trains he would take, the hotels where he would stay, and with careful historical and artistic preparation, all the sights he would see. This fairy-tale talent of the born scholar was a mixture of fantasy and pedantry. And imagine what a constant collection and accumulation of his own stupendous knowledge was also brought into play here!

And very seriously. Somebody who knows more than me would have to explain how the learned work of this great exegete structures itself. It began with the 1910 *Lizenz* dissertation on the style of Pauline preaching and the cynical–stoical diatribe, and already with this piece there was an enrichment of the formal-historical method of the historical theology of that time. This theology reached a representative high point in Bultmann's 1921 book, *The History of the Synoptic Tradition*, a standard work in its field. And even later Bultmann proved his mastery of philological craft, especially through his innumerable contributions to conceptual history. This brought the New Testament scholar into a productive relationship with the whole great literature and language of ancient Greece. Great exegetical performances, above all the comprehensive commentary on the Gospel of John, which gripped him for nearly two decades, show him at the height of his historical-critical art. And even if he were not an original theological thinker, he was a great philologist and a truly convinced humanist. Greek philosophy and literature were to him forever contemporary, and when he was called upon after 1945 to offer his thoughts on the reorganization of Marburg University, he decisively and radically placed the humanistic tradition at the center of his suggestions.

Still he was not just a philologist but rather a real theological thinker whose reflections constantly circled the methodological problems of theology and their relationship to philosophy. In his younger days, at the time of the First World War, the crisis of historicism was already in the air. Polymaths like Wilhelm Dilthey and Max Weber, great philologists like Wilamowitz, historians like Theodor Mommsen and Eduard Meyer, theologians like Adolf von Harnack and Ernst Troeltsch, had enclosed and subdivided the historical universe with a powerful expansiveness; but this tradition was exhausted. Reflective figures such as Werner Jaeger and Karl Reinhardt, Karl Barth and Friedrich Gogarten, now raised their voices. For a long time the young theologian Rudolf Bultmann had also quested after a way to bring his deepest religious engagement into harmony with his scholarly integrity. In this respect, two confrontations were decisive for him: that with dialectical theology, especially with Karl Barth's commentary on the Epistle to the Romans, and that with Martin Heidegger in their years of fruitful collaboration in Marburg. Just to endure the tension in these relationships posed a challenge. But to the theologian in Rudolf Bultmann, they pointed out his much disputed way.

What united him to Karl Barth, the Calvinist theologian, is clearer in the negative than in the positive. What is available to us today of their sharply expressed and extremely varied correspondence reflects two things. The first is a new commitment to the word of preaching; the second is a turning away from religion as culture, from the claims of a natural, philosophical theology as well as from the social-political activism of a "Christian world" and the mundane activities associated with it. Still more radically than Luther, Rudolf Bultmann knew only one sacrament—that of the word. To bring the word of the prophecy into his own speech and that of others—his whole exegetical effort was applied to this, but in such a way that his obligation to scholarly integrity and the clear rationality of his personal being held off all arbitrariness.

Just as self-understanding was the pedagogical aim of the teacher Bultmann, so self-understanding in belief was the sign under which he placed his entire scholarly work. Everything that did not serve this end he therefore avoided as "mythological." Even the authors of the New Testament, above all the ones closest to him, Paul and John, were for him less witnesses to the holy message than partners in a theological conversation, and with the self-understanding of these partners he knew himself to be in agreement. Thus from the passage about the end of the world in the Gospel of John, he interpreted away the entire dimension of time. The end of time is now, it is the moment of the call in which the formula *simul justus simul peccator* becomes true. In eliminating the moment of time from the eschatology of John, Bultmann went so far in doubting the authenticity of the text that he explained the farewell address of Jesus to be a misunderstanding, a mythologizing addition made by an editor of the gospel.

That the radicality of his integrity brought him into conflict with naive belief and understanding and with church authorities was no wonder. And yet it still came as a surprise to him and his friends when the publication of the paper he had written as an ecclesiastically sponsored teacher on the "Demythologization of the New Testament" raised a real storm. The daily mail that reached him quickly rose to hundreds of pieces. For Bultmann himself and for his students, this paper was only the working out—provocatively presented—of the fundamentals of the exegetical procedure he had always followed. It was a formulation of the hermeneutical principle that understanding must be a translation into one's own language if it is to be real understanding, and that this is a problem of method and not a dogma. It was hardly a matter of heresy.

That Bultmann felt himself called to as well as capable of a simple "coming to terms" by transferring into his own words the mythological speech of the Bible and the Bible's message and, moreover, that he knew how to justify the methodological clarity of his exegetical position—for this he was indebted to the second important confrontation of his methodical thinking, that with Martin Heidegger.

I have already described something of the Marburg atmosphere that surrounded Heidegger and the resultant give-and-take between him and Bultmann. Bultmann appropriated in his own way the existential analysis of human existence that he read out of Heidegger's thinking and out of *Being and Time*. Heidegger's thinking put into his hands the conceptual means to articulate his own self-understanding of his beliefs and his resultant theological work. This was not simply objectivating knowledge, not an operationalization of knowledge bestowed on him as one under the call of belief. The structure of care, the anticipation of death, the temporality and historicity worked out of the existential analytic of existence served him as the elements of a philosophical understanding of existence.[1] For theologians these elements had an unanticipated truth precisely because they claimed to be existential determinations rather than existential ideals.

---

1. To convey a distinction in the German, I am translating *Dasein* as "existence" and *Sein* as "being." [*tr.*]

His approach was contested from the theological as well as from the philosophical side, by Karl Barth and Emil Brunner as well as by Karl Löwith, and beyond a shadow of doubt the Augustinian and Kierkegaardian coloring of Heidegger's existential analytic had become unrecognizable. Even more serious was the fact that Heidegger's own thinking went off in a quite different direction. The first treatment of the question of being, put forth in *Being and Time*, became the starting point for a long series of attempts at thinking that disavowed the anthropological understanding of that first great work. In this respect it had to be of interest to theology how in place of the authenticity of existence, Heidegger's thinking came to be dominated by the mortal and the immortal, mythology and sayings, poetry and language, Hölderlin and the pre-Socratics. Rudolf Bultmann could not follow him on this path.

In the quarrel with Barth that was always flaring up, Bultmann insisted that theology required a clarified body of concepts. Only philosophy had such a thing to offer to the self-understanding in faith insofar as it had elevated the general structure of existence's understanding to the level of concept. He therefore wisely held to his already achieved clarity, unperturbed through all the theological conflicts in which his integrity ensnared him, be it with Karl Barth, Karl Jaspers (whose critique of demythologization he fended off masterfully), or the tendencies of his own students to restore a strong accent on the historical dimension of New Testament research or to draw out dogmatic consequences that referred back to the later Heidegger or even to Hegel. These tendencies he followed with skepticism, but also with the ready goodwill of one who knows about the finiteness and historicity of man only in theory.

The sacramental life of the church, its symbolism as well as its dogmatic, remained always in the background for this tireless exegete. But he protected his extreme integrity and the essential truths of his insights even beyond death. According to his willed decree for his own funeral service, only communal singing and the word of the sacred scriptures were heard: Words of the Old and New Testaments, which lent a quiet reflection to this long and rich life, came to be spoken.

Gerhard Krüger

Gerhard Krüger was born on January 30, 1902, in Berlin, and he received his schooling in the Gymnasium at Friedenau. After a short period at Tübingen, he carried out his studies entirely in Marburg, where he habilitated in 1929. After 1933 he spent a semester as a substitute faculty member in Göttingen and Frankfurt, and it was at Frankfurt that he finally became a professor. But he had already shown his effectiveness as a teacher from 1929 onwards as a private *Dozent* in Marburg. Later, from 1940 to 1946, he was professor at Münster, and from 1946 to 1952 at Tübingen. But, as I have noted, he began his studies at Tübingen, where he showed a historical-political interest and studied under Johannes Haller. He came then to Marburg, and his first appearance there is unforgettable to me.

It was in 1920, at the philosophical seminar. You could look out through a large, churchlike neo-Gothic window onto the chicken coops of the university steward. Paul Natorp sat on the stern side of the horseshoe table and sought, sunk into himself, the way out of the methodologism of the Marburg School into the freedom and wholeness of a "general logic." He also sought the way to the young people who crowded around him. A pale young student who had come out of Tübingen but who was obviously from Berlin got the floor and developed in short, precise sentences the way in which self-reflection is caught up in itself. That was Gerhard Krüger. What struck one about him at this time was not just the sharpness and clarity of his understanding but most of all the great sobriety with which he came to terms with Idealistic philosophy. In this respect he was predetermined to help to its completion the self-dissolution of the Marburg School, which at this time was finding expression in Nicolai Hartmann's departure from neo-Kantian Idealism.

From early on there was in his appearance something decisive and certain, persevering in a rugged way. He could say the most amazing things right to your face while simultaneously and carefully probing himself and his position. But if an imperturbable consistency in thinking, one that swings neither left nor right, is a virtue, then Gerhard Krüger possessed this virtue to a high degree and owed to it his early intellectual independence and self-sufficiency.

We came of age in an atmosphere filled with tension and stamped by strong intellectual models. There was the Marburg School of neo-Kantianism, then in its final stages. Following the departure of Hermann Cohen, Paul Natorp was giving in to long-repressed impulses that originated in mysticism and music. Nicolai Hartmann, more and more seeking and measuring his own departure from Marburg Idealism, drew us all together and brought to a rustic and proper Marburg something of the wild intensity of the endless nocturnal discussions of his Petersburg student life. And then on this map appeared the young Martin Heidegger, stormy and with a magnetic attraction pulling one into the swirl of new and radical questions. It was not easy to forge one's own identity as a student, no matter how gifted one was.

There was also Marburg theology, in these years following the impulses of Friedrich Gogarten and Karl Barth, but above all the figure of Rudolf Bultmann venturing along new ways of historical self-criticism and dialectical self-grounding. Gerhard Krüger distinguished himself in both areas very quickly. He made a special effort to deepen himself in Kantian philosophy, the metaphysical principles of which had been turned against neo-Kantianism by Nicolai Hartmann and Heinz Heimsoeth.

The powerful philosophical impetus of Martin Heidegger, who in 1923 began a five-year teaching period in Marburg, also drew Krüger along in the same direction. What Heidegger put into words was revolutionary for our consciousness at this time, because his thinking went back to primordial experiences of existence in such a way as to replace the workings of science with radical philosophical reflection. Under this impulse, Gerhard Krüger began to work out in Kant's philosophy as well the philosophical meaning of the human experience of life.

Meanwhile, however much Heidegger's genius had seized him, Krüger persevered on the "realistic" countermove to Idealism that he had encountered in Nicolai Hartmann. And in the context of a discussion of Kierkegaard and the new dialectical theology, Krüger gave an early warning of the hidden Idealistic motives in Karl Barth's commentary on the Epistle to the Romans. He did this in a much talked about paper in a journal called *Zwischen den Zeiten*. As a student of Rudolf Bultmann, he participated in the renewal of the theological problematic when dialectical theology subjected liberal history to a passionate criticism. In the recognition of the unavailability of belief and of divine grace, his critical turning away from Idealistic thinking found its positive counterpart. In his logical remarks on Barth's commentary, the philosophical implications of a "dialectical" speaking about God are critically laid bare, and the question of the condition of the believer in historical time is prepared. Didn't the domination of "the concept" repeatedly lead back to the vicinity of that autocracy of thinking against which Kierkegaard's critique of Hegel had been directed? And if the authority of Christian doctrine or the sermon goes against this, how should this be grasped adequately with thinking? Krüger displayed astounding consistency in his loyalty to these early questions. Along with Heinrich Schlier, he soon belonged to the small circle of friends around Rudolf Bultmann. He was something like a philosophical censor in the animated circles of the Marburg Academic Union, where an elite of theological and philosophical young people gathered.

Is it possible today to construct a picture of what it was like to grow up then, in the "golden" twenties? After getting our doctorates, we were very much on the margin of the university, a small group of young academics who prior to habilitation never appeared in front of students as teachers, who lived an impoverished existence on the few grants available, and who were working toward completely uncertain ends. We also did other things: Gerhard Krüger was an inspired reader, and so in an intimate circle of family and friends we read together — thousands of pages of Dostoevski and Tolstoi, Gogol and Goncharov, Hamsun and Dickens, Balzac and Meredith. Alongside this activity was Bultmann's Graeca, where we cultivated Greek literature in a similarly social manner. There for many years we read Greek authors, Homer and the tragedians, Herodotus and Clemens, Aristophanes and Lucien. Heinrich Schlier, Günther Bornkamm, and Erich Dinkler were the theologians, Gerhard Krüger and I the philosophical members of this weekly circle. We were united with Rudolf Bultmann through respect and friendship and a common love for Greek language and culture. All and all it was a comradely period of our lives.

This lasted until the podium separated us and then united us in a different way. Krüger's lectures were given with a superior certainty and had a strong effect, especially thanks to the philosophical interest of the theologians in Marburg. Among Marburg students, it was then said of Krüger and me: With Krüger one learns how everything has come to be exact; with Gadamer one learns how little we know about what exactness is. Krüger was an excellent teacher, and his effectiveness continued after 1933, when our circle thinned out and our situation became difficult. The unwavering persistence with which he sought to draw from the philosophical tradition the answer to his question concerning the being of the believer in contemporary history was astounding, and no less unwavering was his human and political posture in that time of questionable accommodations. This meant a good deal to his friends, of whom I was one.

Meanwhile Gerhard Krüger's brilliant habilitation work, *Philosophie und Moral in der Kantischen Kritik*, was published. Krüger called upon Kant to witness that the creative order, as a reality to be accepted, could by itself serve to ground a moral philosophy; this meant, under conditions of freedom, not so much self-determination as a self-commitment to the moral law. This was an unusual reading of Kant, not without significant contradictions, but today it is an established way station in Kant research, partly at least because of the excitement brought about by Eric Weil's French translation. What a novel Kant this was! We all certainly learned a good deal from this book, especially from the interpretation of Kant's moral philosophy. But the richest learning material was not the convincing argumentation of this interpretation but the decisiveness with which the author's personal philosophical interest came through. This was done by making the founder of critical philosophy and the evangelist of moral autonomy and practical freedom appear to be very nearly the defender if not the renewer of Christian metaphysics. The autonomy of practical reason was interpreted as unconditional obedience in respect to moral law, as a submission to the claim of moral law. The metaphysical impact of Kant's critique, the creative theological background of his doctrine of the faculties, and his controversial doctrine of the passions came together with the indicated lines of a moral teleology to form a highly unusual figure.

It was not long before the philosophical intention that guided Krüger would free itself from this first contribution. Krüger became more and more absorbed in the aporias of modern enlightenment. In a significant essay on the origin of philosophical self-consciousness, Leibniz and Descartes gave Krüger the opportunity to work out the problematic of modern self-conscious freedom in all its sharpness. With this he was able to pose the question of whether "the ways of our old philosophical tradition, the possibility of theological thinking, are not after all the correct ones."

What distinguished Krüger's way and simultaneously assigned him his rank was that he did not simply return to the Christian synthesis of ancient philosophy and the Gospels and find his satisfaction in the connection with scholastic thinking. He sought rather to put new life into the philosophical motives that had formed the classical tradition of philosophy. In this way his own questioning oriented him toward Plato. His Plato book, based on a full command of the available scholarly and philosophical research, was a kind of grounding of the natural knowledge of God. This was what he sought to recognize in Plato, the critic of heathen polytheism who nonetheless stayed with the religious traditions of Greece. A new passion for insight—*eros* philosophy— allowed Plato to overcome the passionate worldliness of archaic Greece while simultaneously preserving its religious foundations. The modern counterconcept of a sovereign thinking, whose aporias Krüger unremittingly pursued, lends to classical philosophy its outstanding characteristic of being an accepting reason. From this perspective, Krüger oriented himself to the global order of things, which the Christian doctrine of creation had grounded on the basis of revelation, and sought with philosophical means to show it to be a teleological universe of goods. At the center of this excellently researched book entitled *Einsicht und Leidenschaft das Wesen des platonischen Denkens* was Plato's *Symposium*. In the introduction, Krüger developed in a sovereign manner the religious background to the Greek concept of reason. These seventy pages may be counted among the master performances of philosophical conversation with the Greeks.

The basic meaning of moral experience in life is to set an absolute limit to all arbitrary action in an unmistakable evolving natural order. Such a moral meaning should, in the end, also take the disturbing violence and sharpness from the dark riddle that history has become in modern thinking. "In spite of our modernity we remain human beings, just the same as all human beings who have ever lived, and we are therefore able not only to understand Plato and other past thinkers historically but also to repeat them substantively. We meet ourselves in all those who in the recognition of a unified world have also looked out over the borders of their historical situation." In these sentences of Gerhard Krüger we have an excellent summary and the end result of the unique style of his philosophy and teaching.

Krüger's early self-sufficiency led him into critical disputes with his teachers. Thus he wrote a very thorough criticism of Nicolai Hartmann's *Theorie des geistigen Seins*, and after the Second World War, when Martin Heidegger's *Holzwege* publicly bore witness to the change in his philosophical thinking that he called "the turn," Krüger sought in a critical observation to establish that Heidegger's thought experiments could not free him from Hegel's spell. Here Krüger returned to his early doubts about Idealism. That in the famous quarrel of the ancients and the moderns one can be a child of modernity while also taking a reasoned position on the side of the ancients was an insight that closely tied him to Leo Strauss, whose early Spinoza book strongly influenced him. But it also made it necessary for him to take a position that would decisively repulse and criticize contemporary thinking, a position that was occasionally hardened by the features of his character. Certainly he did not easily carry this decisiveness to which he saw himself led. But precisely for this reason his voice became loud and clear.

The most important collection of his minor writings, written before he became ill, bore the title *Freiheit und Weltverwaltung* [Freedom and world administration] (1958). I recall that this title baffled me, although I was well aware of the content of the volume and of the author's philosophical position. But didn't he prove to be right? Doesn't one read this title today without the least astonishment? Must one not feel an inner sense of agreement that what is brought to a formula in this title is what constitutes all the unsolvable contradictions of our moment in history: In an ever more carefully and consistently administered world, how should we accommodate the inexhaustible resources we have in the human condition and the freedom that is entrusted to it?

It was thanks to the Klostermann publishing house and the help of his friends, especially the selfless generosity of Wilhelm Anz, that Krüger's lectures were published as an introductory text. Entitled

Gerhard Krüger

Grundfragen der Philosophie: Geschichte, Wahrheit, Wissenschaft (1958), it once again gave to broad circles of people the voice of this now-silent teacher and the sterling quality of his thinking. It is a voice that to people today may sound "between the times." But is that not what thinking means—to be between the times and to question beyond all time?

Teaching Years

"We" at that time meant Löwith, Krüger, and me.[1] Löwith was the first to habilitate. At bottom he agreed with Schopenhauer. That is, he did not have a high opinion of the academic style of philosophy, and he felt himself more at one with moralists like Schopenhauer. Heidegger later told me how Löwith, with whom he had once had a close connection, had read the proof sheets of *Being and Time* and become increasingly gloomy as the book progressed. This was because in the final analysis Heidegger, whom Löwith took to be a radical critic of philosophy in the style of Schopenhauer, Kierkegaard, and Nietzsche, was himself presenting a "philosophy"—and one with a transcendental signature at that. Precisely because Löwith was such a strong individualist, his entrance into the teaching body of the university, and thus into a social position, meant a fundamental change in his feel for life. It also became apparent that Löwith was not only a superior writer but in his own way, and at the highest level of style, a very effective teacher.

Heidegger had foreseen this. Löwith's habilitation was celebrated in Heidegger's house, and Heidegger gave a lengthy talk—much to the despair of his wife as we were sitting in front of full dishes. But the talk was well worth listening to. Heidegger had borne the torch of revolution in the academic world, and this was his first noteworthy recognition of the institution of the university. With grim energy and certainly from a real tension that supported his spiritual daring and

1. The reference here is to the teaching assistants of Martin Heidegger. [tr.]

his resistance to tradition, Heidegger had earlier given critical polemics center stage and had often knocked about the brilliant Max Scheler. But now he made some acknowledgment of Scheler. In his talk he openly generalized the authentic experience that enabled him to find in Scheler a significant advocate of his own cause. Heidegger then turned this into a good luck wish and an encouragement, so to speak directed at the three of us, that we should fruitfully use the newly acquired community of the collegial life. When, shortly before Heidegger's departure for Freiburg, Max Scheler died, Heidegger came to the college in a black tie and gave a beautiful five-minute eulogy. It closed with the sentence: "Yet once more a way of doing philosophy sinks into the darkness."

My habilitation proceedings found their way to a conclusion only after Heidegger had already left Marburg. It was in the record winter of 1928. I was sick with a strong case of flu when, hardly back on my feet, I wanted to break out and hurry to my test lecture. But my winter coat was frozen fast to the wall of the vestibule of the modest rustic house in which we lived. The spiritual baptism of fire that a habilitation was supposed to be could not be performed with real water. The underground main on Ockerhäuser Avenue remained frozen right into July, and we had to haul our water from a nearby spring.

The tempo of our life now began to change. The beginning of every semester was filled with anxiety: Would the chosen theme prove seaworthy? And would I prove able to sail it to the opposite shore? And every semester the well-known experience of Til Eulenspiegel repeated itself for the *Dozent*: Paradoxically, one had to commit to paper the announcement of courses for the next semester before one had given one's first lecture and had had a chance to measure the success of the ongoing semester. And in the final analysis a good deal depended on this. A summer trip, for example, would not be paid for out of our minimal base salaries but only from the tuition money that would come to us if we found listeners. There was a keen competition among us, but we three Marburg *Dozenten* all earned good reputations. At that time an investigation of German universities was published by the *Vossische Zeitung*, and I have never forgotten that when Marburg was discussed, "three reputable private *Dozenten* for philosophy" were singled out for praise.

We were good comrades, despite our being so different from each other. Löwith's brilliant style of delivery, his art of interlacing original quotations into the contemplative progression of his lectures in such a way that they worked like a strengthening of his own voice, the certainty of his appearance, the immovability of his face, his sarcasm and his sometimes hardly audible irony—these qualities drew in many listeners. Among the theologians it was customary to say of him: "Löwith, my sweet poison." Gerhard Krüger was a born teacher, clear and consistent in the construction of his lectures, strict and superior in his seminars. He had an especially strong influence on the theologians, and he sometimes acted as the philosophical censor of the Academic Union, which in the 1920s constituted an academic elite of which Heidegger and Bultmann and later Krüger and Bultmann were the spiritual protectors.

My own style was very different. At the podium I was very shy, and I heard later that people occasionally characterized me as follows: "Oh, there he is, the one who never looks up." In fact, I never read my lectures—often I spoke more or less freely, although avoiding any eye contact with my listeners. Certainly I sometimes spoke over their heads and put too many complications into my train of thought. Even earlier my friends had invented a new scientific measure, the "Gad," which designated a settled measure of unnecessary complications. A joking observer, a student of Löwith, once expressed it as follows: With Krüger everything would be laid out clearly; with Gadamer everything would once again be confused. And even he found the latter style productive. So there were three different styles of teaching. All three had their advantages, especially because they were personal products of thinking and research that flowed over into our teaching. And at bottom it was Marburg that had put its common stamp on all of us.

That was brought home to us once when we were driven to Frankfurt to hear a presentation by Kurt Riezler at the Kant Society. Erich Frank, Heidegger's successor and our paternally friendly *Ordinarius*,[2] had taken us in his car, and we felt the way a farmer might feel coming for the first time into the big city. Paul Tillich shined, Max Horkheimer pro-

2. The *Ordinarius* is a tenured full professor who is authorized to take on research assistants and teaching assistants and is thereby able to pass along or "reproduce" his thinking through a group of paid and loyal followers. How this works out in time is often fascinating. Löwith and Herbert Marcuse (a later assistant of Heidegger) were both Jews and therefore broke with Heidegger on the issue of the latter's Nazism. But Löwith retained much of Heidegger's thinking in his own writings, whereas Marcuse went over to Marxism, bringing a strong Heideggerian influence into the early Frankfurt School. [tr.]

voked, Wiesengrund-Adorno seconded, and Riezler replied in the style of a thoughtful cosmopolitan. The whole style of the debate was such that we felt as if we had just come from a cloister. And indeed this was the case. I recall the first time Max Kommerell visited me in Marburg, on the occasion of a vacation course. He asked me whether I knew some book. I gave him a pointed but not altogether unfounded answer: "I basically only read books that are at least two thousand years old."

Of course we were not alone. Each of us cultivated his own special relationships: Löwith to Hermann Deckert and Rudolf Fahrner, Krüger to Heinrich Schlier and many others, and I related above all to the music historian Herbert Birtner, who would later die in the war, to Georg Rohde, the classical philologist, and to Günther Zuntz, with whom I thoroughly studied many classical texts (to name only those relationships that were productive for scholarship). Added to this there was for me the Graeca that Paul Friedländer had put together with a few young *Dozenten*. A capable philology was constructed in this journal, but when Friedländer moved to Halle it went with him.

Then there was the famous 1929 Naumburg Conference on classical studies. It was a military demonstration on behalf of the *New Humanism*, chaired by Werner Jaeger in the manner of a Church Father. Paul Friedländer took me with him, and it was a significant occasion for me, since I had just begun my Marburg teaching duties. For a long time I had gotten along very well with Jaeger. He had been friendly to me despite my abstract philosophical style and the immaturity of my philological efforts, which later found expression in a critique of his developmental construction of Aristotelian ethics. He even let me have my say in Naumburg, naturally as a strange horse in his stall. On this occasion I first met Karl Reinhardt, with whom I would later succeed in becoming good friends. He was clumsy and cumbersome like a Saint Bernard puppy, with flabby cheeks that slapped around like dog ears. I passed a beautiful afternoon in the Naumburg Cathedral with Rudolf Pfeiffer, who like me had escaped "behind the church"— that is, into the Cathedral—rather than attend conference sessions. I got to know Richard Harder there, in opposition to whom I made a vehement attack on a paper given by Wolfgang Schadewaldt—whereupon Harder introduced me to Schadewaldt, then still very young and immature, like me. He understood my point immediately and defended himself in a merely tactical manner. We would also later become good friends. And during a midday break, Werner Jaeger introduced me to Helmut Kuhn, who immediately entangled me in a long conversation about Heidegger. My attitude was very much that of a camp follower, this being the first conference I had ever gone to (as a follower of the party lines of Husserl and Heidegger, one stayed away from philosophy conferences on principle). What astonished me about the scene at Naumburg was Werner Jaeger's immeasurable authority. Brilliant philologists like Eduard Fraenkel or Friedländer looked up questioningly after every sentence of their papers, concerned about Jaeger's opinion, though he hardly looked like a despot. But Naumburg was a scene set up for a despot. Heinrich Gomperz, an elderly gentleman, always leaning on the wall, his cane held in his crossed legs, his other hand tugging on his patriarchal beard, was arrogantly dismissed by the New Humanists gathered there. I was more impressed by the way in which Johannes Stroux put forth a few remarks in reference to a paper given by Helmut Kuhn that had proved to be a little too formal-abstract; in the discussion Stroux spoke first, apologizing to Kuhn in every possible way, and thereupon put his critical remarks in the most courteous fashion possible.

One must clearly imagine what the first years of a young *Dozent's* life were like then. It was nothing less than an initiation into teaching itself. There were no positions for assistants at all, just as there were no teaching positions for those not yet habilitated, and so we were forced to learn how to teach by teaching. It was not the worst procedure. When the Nazis tried to accommodate the periodically recurring claim that what is essential in academic teaching is teaching quality and didactic talent, they brought an unwholesome emphasis on rhetoric to the training of young academics. The old criterion was not so bad: Pay attention to research above all. He who knew what he did not know could learn something, and he who had learned something had also learned how to pass on that learning. The few exceptions who did not succeed in this program certainly constituted a smaller quota of failures than is found among those who become teachers through a premature evaluation of rhetorical-didactic capabilities. I was the least didactically gifted of our group of three. More accurately, I needed the longest period to develop this side of my talent. But what an adventure it was to be always applying oneself to new themes and new objects of research and to be probing new perspectives as well as one's self. Once I was called upon to lecture on the "History of

Concepts of the World" in two back-to-back periods. On the day I was supposed to present the prehistory of Galilean physics, I suddenly recalled as I was walking up to the podium that I had left my manuscript at home. I did not let on, and by chance I had a few volumes for quotation in my briefcase, so I constructed a lecture from scratch in the spontaneity of the moment. One of my colleagues, a natural scientist who had heard the lecture, said in a very complimentary way that this time I had been excellently prepared. This was a good experiment in the direction in which I was later to develop my style. But such a way, of course, is not for everybody. There is a well-known story about Paul Natorp, who one day upon stepping up to the podium found that he had forgotten his manuscript. In great haste he hurried home, shoved into his pocket the manuscript he had left lying on the desk, and rushed toward the door. There his wife stopped him and said: "But Paul, you have on your house jacket!" Whereupon Natorp quickly changed his coat, only to find when he arrived back at the podium that the manuscript was still missing. But by this time the period was over.

At Easter of 1933 we made our first foreign trip (and the last we would make for a long time) to Paris, with the little money we could get together and were allowed to take. I mention this trip because of two meetings. The first was with Leo Strauss, whom I often saw. He was in Paris as a Rockefeller fellow, and of course he would not return to Germany. At that time he was working on his Hobbes book, which he later sent me, thereby continuing a good intellectual communication that the war would abruptly break off. I would not see him again until 1954 in Heidelberg, but after that I would often meet him in the United States. The other meeting was with Alexander Kojeve, who at that time still called himself "Koscheffnikow." He was a wonderful storyteller and a socialite. Also, an experience that had much to say was a visit to the cinema in Paris. In the "News of the Week" was shown a German gymnastic festival with a well-organized parade. It did not have anything to do with the Nazis, but it had an overwhelmingly comical effect on the French, no doubt because they were not yet able to imagine how masses of people can be organized. With the French it was still called—and this was funny for us—*le nudisme allemand*. How harmless these misunderstandings all seemed, grotesquely being rehearsed at precisely the moment—Easter 1933—

when the new political "style" of Hitler and the art of organizing the masses were finding their unmistakable voice.

After about four years and after our first books had appeared, we were still as poor as church mice. We had just reached the point where we were supposed to be getting job offers — and occasionally an inquiry from somewhere was indeed made about us — and then the year 1933 broke in. It was a terrible awakening, and we could not absolve ourselves of having failed to perform adequately as citizens. We had underrated Hitler and his kind, and admittedly we made the same mistake as the liberal press in doing this. Not one of us had read *Mein Kampf*, although I had paid attention to Alfred Rosenberg's *The Myth of the Twentieth Century*, which according to the *Frankfurter Zeitung* was the philosophical presentation of the intellectual center of National Socialism. That I had failed to see any danger in this pale instrument is easy to understand. It was a widespread conviction in intellectual circles that Hitler in coming to power would deconstruct the nonsense he had used to drum up the movement, and we counted the anti-Semitism as part of this nonsense. We were to learn differently. Especially the theological faculty and the newly formed Confessional Church came out openly against anti-Semitism, but until June 30, 1934, we all believed that this gutter politics would soon disappear.

Things were becoming grotesque in Marburg. The faculty was for the most part conservative or liberal, and what suddenly hatched itself as National Socialist had up to now passed unnoticed. In this context there arose in the spring of 1933 at the usual academic ceremonies the question, ticklish for the university leaders, of what to do about the Hitler salute. A rather obscurely worded announcement was made to the effect that for reasons of style the Hitler salute could not be established for those wearing academic gowns, and this was officially given out as the watchword. It was an elevating spectacle to see how the overly zealous among us nonetheless still elevated their arms. A half year later the refusal of the Hitler salute would become an immediate cause for dismissal. Soon enough there developed a kind of stylization of the German greeting from which the student could very easily recognize the conviction of his teacher. There were very discreet forms of saluting with the hand, but there was also the terrorist opposite. At that time there was a fanatical student leader, ceretainly a psychopath but a striking figure. Once he gave us *Dozenten* a speech in which he shouted with a thundering voice: "He for whom blood has never pulsed through the brown shirt has no idea what the greatness and power of the National Socialist movement is." He was quite certain that for him, too, this was only a rhetorical metaphor, but the man disappeared soon enough. Certainly it remained difficult to keep the right balance, not to compromise oneself so far that one would be dismissed and yet still to remain recognizable to colleagues and students. That we somehow found the right balance was confirmed for us one day when it was said of us that we had only "loose sympathy" with the new awakening.

In the summer semester of 1934 and the winter semester of 1934–1935 I was sent to Kiel to replace the suspended Richard Kroner. For me this was a rich teaching period. I had been friends with Kroner since 1923 and had always found him to be a dignified and composed person. In 1923, when he did not receive the expected call to Marburg, he was crushed. At that time he wrongly took it to be anti-Semitism. But now, in 1934, that it was anti-Semitism—and a militant form at that—that confronted this convinced Christian, it was the common fate of his "race," and this made it lighter for him. Kiel was then a sort of outpost of the Nazi cultural revolution. My colleague was Kurt Hildebrandt, as fine and innocent as he was naive. The people who were then called to Kiel, above all the jurists and the human scientists, were in general gifted young scholars seduced by the political situation and by their own ambition, but never so much that they spouted Nazi nonsense from the podium. The inaugural lectures of the Germanists Gerhard Fricke and Otto Höfler, as I recall them, were of a thoroughly scholarly character. Thus for the moment I felt myself quite comfortable, especially thanks to the friendly philological association with Richard Harder, who kept a clear head in all political situations. I then learned from myself and from others how easily one makes illusions and is prepared to take the situation as not really so bad, as long as it is not one's own goose that is being cooked. One never learns this lesson well enough.

Yet another learning experience: In my Plato seminar there was a young woman student who always gave very good responses, even if they led to nothing. I came to hold a high opinion of her, especially of her industry and talent, only to learn at the end of the semester that she had never read a line of the Plato text. She had read it only in her imagination. No doubt here was a source of danger in non-objective examinations. There is such a thing as a talent for adaptation and adjustment. If only the dangers of objective examinations—these adaptations to robots—were not so much greater!

Kiel was just starting to be reorganized in line with Nazi university policies. Exactly as had been the case in Marburg, the new party organization was a wild bunch of "Johnny-come-latelies" who rapidly learned their roles. I was dispatched home in all haste, and thus shifted from presenting philosophy before empty lecture halls in Kiel back to the better-attended lecture halls to which I was accustomed in Marburg.

Soon enough the fronts became clearer. The Nuremberg Laws put to an end any illusions one had with regard to the demise of anti-Semitism. Our Jewish friends had to leave us or to live quietly like Erich Auerbach and Erich Frank, who were only able to continue private associations with reliable friends. Parting was bitter. When Löwith, for example, went abroad to an uncertain future, one felt ashamed to remain. Soon, though, even the question of one's own status became precarious. The consolidation of the Nazi revolution was spreading. It brought a distortion even to quite harmless areas. There was the University Tennis Club, which when brought under the *Führerprinzip* expelled its Jewish members. It was also required to change its "academic" character by opening its membership to "the people." It was similar in the Marburg Chess Club, where we suddenly noticed the absence of an old gentleman who was usually there and thereby learned that he was a Jew.

The university constitution was also reconstructed according to the *Führerprinzip*, and for a few years this change brought me a good deal of distress. I had been in Kiel and hence had missed Papen's famous Marburg speech, but when I came back I was to get a good taste of it. A National Socialist organization for university teachers was taking shape, the so-called *Dozentenbund*, and in its eyes we were politically unreliable. In a certain sense the *Dozentenbund* replaced an earlier professional organization, the *Nichtordinarienverein* or "Nonprofessors' Union"—a wonderful title to describe a wonderful situation. Each of the members had no higher goal than to get a job as soon as possible, and thus the self-dissolution of the union was basically its highest ambition. But it ought to have happened differently. It began suddenly with a scandal, just like before 1933. One of our colleagues had slipped into debt, and in response his nearest friends beat themselves on the breast, singing all the while, "I fast twice weekly." We simply did not want to defend this colleague, but we also prevented our union from taking onto itself the right to act as a tribunal. I exposed myself a good deal, and when the new National Socialist *Kampf* organization replaced our self-serving union, I was severely slandered. Needless to say, the pharisees were then in the leadership positions of the new organization. So it was that the objections of the *Dozentenbund* prevented the sought-after title of professor from being bestowed on me, and later also on Krüger. It was clear that in the short or long run this sort of action would play to the disadvantage of the *Dozenten*. I negotiated with my colleagues in the *Dozentenbund*—unforgettable and outrageous conversations in which what was held against one were the private friendships one continued to have with Jews. One noticed this kind of thing on the street, too. All kinds of people began to look away when one ran into them. The deputy leader of the *Dozentenbund* once put me under a great deal of pressure and was then disingenuous enough to say as he held his hand eight inches above the table: "Remember how much material we have in your personal files."

These circumstances were destroying the traditional forms of academic sociability, and only a few public facilities offered any room for such gatherings. Among these was the Circle of Friends of the Humanist Gymnasium, which Bultmann chaired and whose guest lecture programs continued unchanged. Bultmann himself gave a learned presentation on "The Light." Karl Reinhardt presented in an unforgettable manner the enigmatic sayings of Heraclitus. Max Kommerell often came from Frankfurt to visit me, accompanied by a troop of young friends, and once after long hours of socializing he gave a presentation at the circle on the failure of Faust's experiences with Helena and Greece, a thrilling improvisation. I myself spoke on Plato and the poets, a piece that has been printed under the motto: "He who philosophizes is not at one with the premises of his times."[3] This was well camouflaged as a quote from Goethe and thus not quite a heroic act. But it was also not an accommodation.

So in the 1930s my little ship had run aground. How I was to get it afloat again was a difficult question. Of course I wanted to save my

---

3. Gadamer is here paraphrasing. P. Christopher Smith's translation of Gadamer's talk reads: "He who philosophizes is not at one with the previous and contemporary world's ways of thinking of things. Thus Plato's discussions are often not only directed *to* something but also *against* it." See Hans-Georg Gadamer, *Dialogue and Dialectic* (New Haven: Yale University Press, 1980), p. 39. [*tr.*]

academic existence in Germany, but without making political conces-
sions that could cost me the trust of my friends in the outer or inner
emigration. Therefore I did not consider entering any party organization. Finally I found a way, one that in the end had success. There
was a sort of political course for active *Dozenten* that was being required
for habilitation. I registered for my "rehabilitation" voluntarily at one
such "camp" [*Lager*] called a *Dozent*'s Academy, and so in the fall of
1936 I went for a few weeks to Weichselmünde, near Danzig. I was
lucky. The director was a count from the Steinmark, active in criminal
justice, who perceived himself to be a *Grossdeutscher* and viewed Nazi
Germany essentially from a foreign-policy perspective, certainly with
some pangs to his sense of justice. He proved to be extraordinarily
tolerant and discreet and demanded lip service from no one (and
when this came from a questionable side, he always seemed to be
embarrassed). Every participant had to give a paper presenting his
discipline and then discuss it—this was all that was demanded of us
(aside, of course, from morning gymanstics, competitive games,
marches with nationalistic singing, and all that kind of paramilitary
nonsense). The majority of the "comrades" with whom one had to
go about were very nice people, approximately my age; I was the
only one who was there voluntarily and who had already had a number
of years of teaching experience. The latter, of course, represented an
immense advantage. Given the traditional German interest in philosophy, there was finally something like an experience of comradeship,
about which former soldiers no doubt know and which happened here
quite effortlessly. I found many a good friend there, learned a good
deal, and was able to avoid all unpleasant contacts. I was also able
to gain a political grasp on a number of things—but unfortunately (or
was it fortunately?) not enough to see the inevitable coming of war.
There was a horrid "political" excursion to Danzig, where Rauschning
was to speak, but he was unfortunately replaced by what struck me
as a barren and cold functionary, Greiser by name. Another intermezzo
was my participation in a celebration at Tannenberg, where we saw
Hitler from a distance. He impressed me as being simple, indeed
awkward, like a boy playing the soldier.

By means of this rehabilitation camp I won an influential friend in
Count Gleispach, who intervened for me in Berlin in my attempt to
attain the title of professor. That it went well in the end was a consequence of high politics. From a historical distance, it is today quite

clear that the decision to seek a military solution to Germany's situation in the East forced the National Socialists to declare the hunting season over in the German universities. A war could not be won without science, and so they had to spare scientists, at least until the war had been won. At Marburg, this shift occurred during the rectorship of the jurist Leopold Zimmerl. He was impartial toward people and had a certain interest in philosophy—especially since he was involved in scholarly polemics with what was then the Kiel School of criminal law (Georg Dahm, Karl Michaelis, etc.) and sought a philosophical following. I recall a study group on the theme of "wholeness" in which this practical concept had to rest content patiently with the most contradictory interpretations. But at least the sycophantic adaptations that had poisoned the first years of the consolidation of the Nazi revolution were tabooed in this circle. This was the special merit of Zimmerl, and he interceded a good deal on my behalf.

There was also the special reason that I nearly went to Halle as a classical philologist, at least to substitute, and the intervention of Zimmerl had made the point that I was indispensable in Marburg. Thereafter he took it upon himself to canvass everywhere on my behalf. Then in the spring of 1937 I finally got the professorial title. This was an outer sign that those in power would be more tolerant. Thereafter there would not be much more waiting for a call. Very aptly Gerhard Krüger quoted Goethe's *Faust*, "It takes a title to gain your confidence," and soon after my call to Leipzig I started work toward getting my somewhat younger colleagues positions.

All in all, this long (ten-year) period of being a private *Dozent* bestowed on us by the political situation proved to be a burden easier to bear than would have been the case under earlier, more normal conditions. It was so obvious that politics were decisive here that one did not engage in self-doubting—indeed, a lack of success became something of a mark of honor. The private *Dozent* who was left behind at this time was supported by the sympathy of nearly everyone. We had many friends and like-minded colleagues. For some, Marburg was something of a penal colony, as it certainly was for Kurt Reidemeister, the mathematician. Also there was Guido von Kaschnitz and a man a little too elegant for Marburg but nonetheless thoroughly humane—the Gymnasium director Steinmeyer. And there were the mathematicians Franz Rellich and Arnold Schmidt, and present as teachers were the historian Otto Sell and the Romance philologist Kalthoff.

Later Wilhelm Anz, who had participated in my first seminar, came back to the Gymnasium. There, too, was the equally brilliant and absurd Werner Krauss and the Romance area assistants. But if I hope not to exclude any like-minded colleagues, I shall have to present a list of nearly all the philosophical faculty.

Above all we had students. We had all begun as heirs to a great teacher, and each worked in his own style. With Krauss and Kalthoff we read Maurice Scève and Paul Valéry. I deepened myself in Hölderlin and Rilke, and above all my lectures in Greek philosophy served to form a small circle of excellent students, among whom were Karl-Heinz Volkmann-Schluck, Walter Schulz, Christoph Senft, Harry Mielert, and the young Arthur Henkel.

A Hölderlin seminar in the winter of 1937 was my last duty in Marburg. For Hölderlin our whole circle came together once again, and many of these people would not survive the Second World War. I went to Leipzig in 1938, and therewith a Marburg existence of nearly two decades came to a close, like a dream dreamed to its conclusion. When a little later, after the deaths of Erich Jaensch and Dietrich Mahnke, I was called back to Marburg with the offer of a position in philosophy, I refused the call. Dreams are not realized outside of themselves. Their realization lies in themselves.

Richard Kroner

When the first volume of Richard Kroner's major work *Von Kant zu Hegel* appeared in 1921 (followed by a second volume in 1924), the crisis of the ruling neo-Kantian philosophy moved for the first time into full public view, even if in the form of a philosophical-historical inquiry. The southwest German school of Wilhelm Windelband and Heinrich Rickert had long been aware that its own center of gravity, which lay in the cultural rather than the natural sciences, would find its confirmation by going beyond Kant and renewing Hegelianism. Windelband had proclaimed this new watchword as early as 1910, followed by his circle of students. The young Julius Ebbinghaus wrote a brilliant dissertation that carried out the programmatic word. Emil Lask, the strongest speculative talent of this circle, took the step to Fichte and beyond. But after Lask's death in the First World War, Kroner's work came to signify the indirect historical continuation of the task.

In those same years new shifts were becoming apparent in the neo-Kantianism of the Marburg School. The aged Paul Natorp was seeking a systematic reconstruction of the primordially concrete [*des Urkonkreten*] in a style that was nearly neo-Platonic. In Ernst Cassirer's history of the problem of knowledge, the signs were pointing toward a third volume in which Hegel was to be at center stage; and Nicolai Hartmann, fascinated with the phenomenological "realism" of Max Scheler, was looking for distance from the great system constructions of Idealism. Nonetheless Kroner's work made a deep impression on him.

When I went to Freiburg in 1923 to deepen my studies under Heidegger and Husserl, Nicolai Hartmann sent me immediately to Kroner, who also taught there as a private *Dozent*. Out of this emerged an enduring friendship, one that was especially enlivened by Fyodor Stepun, an old friend of Kroner's from the prewar period. Kroner himself was of a nearly suffocating sensibility—soft, tender, quiet— and this discretion nearly closed him too much within himself. It lent a certain strained, troubled, helpless quality to every effort to come out of the protective inwardness that prevailed in the academy and in philosophical conversation. But when his childlike, beaming blue eyes lit up, and especially when they nearly disappeared in the quivering folds of friendly laughter, a controlled flow of goodness enveloped his whole being, and this was very touching. Even then his name was known. He was the founder and editor of *Logos*, the leading German philosophical periodical, and in this function he manifested the multiple ways in which he had been drawn into the educational culture of the times. Only later, when he had clothed his first teaching position (at the technical university in Dresden) in a homogeneous circle of friends, did his bright dialectical and performing talent achieve its full brilliance. When I was ordered to Kiel in 1934 to fill Kroner's teaching post temporarily, I could sense from my own experience how strong his effectiveness as a teacher had been. It was my last meeting with him before his emigration, and it was filled with the unclouded cordiality that had always existed between us.

Only many years after the Second World War did we see each other again. It was a special occasion that brought Kroner to Heidelberg—the inauguration of an international society for the study of Hegelian philosophy. This was a revival of the Hegel Society that Kroner had founded in the 1920s with Koyre, Calogero, Tschizewsky, and other internationally known Hegel researchers. It had not stood the test in 1933, but now Kroner became honorary president of the new group and directed words of greeting and satisfaction to us.

All of this reads so easily today. We know of course that an injustice beyond compensation had thrown our Jewish friends and colleagues, philosophers included, off the track and that success in their new countries could not be a simple carrying-on. But in Kroner's case, his personal life was tightly woven together with the ardor of his preference for and cultivation of the educational culture of German Idealism. To the best of my knowledge, he had converted to Protestantism as a young man, and if this was in fact the case, then it was basically this decision that he was concerned to justify to himself in his life through his way of thinking. The decision for Hegel, brought to fruition in his two-volume work, was in the final analysis religiously and ethically motivated. This motivation was expressed in his whole mode of presenting himself. In this respect, his emulation of Hegel was not totally without limitation. He was no Hegelian in the manner of the first Hegel students, modeled along the lines of a Gabler or an Erdman. He was also not an *anima naturaliter Hegeliana*, as in our century Wilhelm Purpos and Otto Cloos were, although he did become completely submerged in Hegel's peculiarly powerful language. Kroner sought much more to repeat the synthetic achievement that he saw in Hegel, namely the unification of the Greek and Protestant inheritances of our tradition. He sought this not just as a critical continuation of neo-Kantianism but also as a descendant of the historical school of the nineteenth century.

Nonetheless, in his major work he is through and through a Hegelian. His own unfolding of the problems and aporias that had driven philosophical thought onward to Fichte, to Schelling, and finally to Hegel remained completely captive to the Hegelian perspective, no matter how completely everything was thought out and newly formulated. What determined Kroner's entire presentation was the schematic of subjective, objective, and absolute Idealism that was introduced by Hegel and was supposed to distinguish the viewpoints of Fichte and Schelling as well as his own, but that frankly was not appropriate to the subject matter. Not for a moment did Kroner weigh the possibility that Hegel's synthesis limited whatever moment of truth might be hidden in Schelling's essay on freedom and in the unsatisfying theosophical successors to that essay. Kroner did not actually develop the inquiry of more recent Hegel research, first formulated by Paul Tillich and Erich Frank and since the book by Walter Schulz discussed in terms of the perfection of Idealism. Kierkegaard never entered into his point of view.

Needless to say, in those times he was unable to bring about a systematic presentation of his thinking. The programmatic essay of 1928 called "The Self-Realization of Spirit" was not carried out, but as the title already tells us, the program repeated with determination the thesis of absolute Idealism. Then fate intervened to throw Kroner off track.

It would take a separate investigation to trace the consequences that forced emigration and gradual assimilation to America had on Kroner's thinking. It could not have been easy for a man so deeply formed by the Protestant and metaphysical traditions of Germany to hold out and then go on to make his mark against the antimetaphysical passion of his American surroundings. On the other hand, it must have meant something to him that in America, Christianity and especially Protestantism had a much stronger social impact than did German cultural Protestantism, whose deep weakness became so terribly apparent in the religious struggles of the Third Reich. After some years of silence and reorientation, Kroner once again raised his voice, this time in the New World, and it was the voice of the man he really was.

A major series of publications in English began in 1941, and it was immediately apparent from the themes of these writings that the Hegelian synthesis of belief and knowledge, religion and philosophy, was no longer taken for granted by the lonely refugee driven from his homeland. "*Versöhnung des Verderbens*" [reconciliation with the catastrophe] could hardly have been expected from the synthetic strength of this concept alone. Thus the religious function of the power of imagination found in him an advocate in respect to the claim of absolute knowledge. "The Primacy of Faith," the theme of Kroner's Gifford Lectures (1939–1940), was characterized by a decisive accent of opposition. And in a similar manner, the small German booklet called *Freiheit und Gnade*, in which the octogenarian Kroner laid out before German readers the results of the religious philosophical work that had previously been published in English, showed with great emphasis the limits of human freedom: namely, the power of fate and the grace of belief. Anyone who reads these pages today recognizes in them a clear critique of the secularized modern world's ideal of autonomy and of the industrial period's universal deconstruction of tradition. Simultaneously one senses, as in the earlier Kroner, a moving closeness to the Idealism of freedom, that religious liberalism of the first hour, to which he appealed with the help of a number of quotes from Schiller and Goethe.

When Kroner came to us as a guest in 1962, he was surrounded by an aura of the most urbane German educational air, which in recent times had been scattered by blasts of colder air. He who had suffered the hardest of personal fates now appeared to us almost as one who had been spared by the storm that had raged over us. What a tragic paradox! An impressive calm had settled over him and now accompanied him into a ripe old age. He died in 1974 in Switzerland, where he had gone for medical care soon after his ninetieth birthday. On that birthday the German ambassador had presented him with the great merit cross of the German Federal Republic, a small sign of our gratitude.

Hans Lipps

I must say a few words to introduce Hans Lipps to the contemporary reader. From him the expert has two not very extensive books, hardly enough. With disturbing directness the talk is about metaphysical, logical, and above all speech-phenomenological questions. To these may be added two posthumous collections of writings.

All of these books bear an unmistakable stamp. They do not introduce themselves to the reader. They prepare no one for what they will discuss. They simply begin. Only rarely does Lipps refer to the specialized literature of philosophy. Thus it is not easy to learn about his thinking. There is only one way: to allow oneself to be drawn into conversation with him. "In philosophy one's position can only be transformed through argument."

Anyone who knew him will recall the impetuous manner with which he applied himself to his conversation partner: without restraint, without flourish, totally concentrated. His large eyes nearly left his head when he said what he thought. And he always said what he thought without reservation. What he said was always clever, but it was not always clever that he said it at all, as he periodically had to learn the hard way during the Third Reich. He was a resolute original. When in 1936 he was called to Frankfurt as an *Ordinarius*, he took an apartment in Bad Homburg. If one tried to visit him in the middle of winter, one was received into an unheated room by a Lipps clad in coat and blanket. He possessed a huge rubber tree, given to him by his family, and it spread its branches across the broad front window. He was convinced that the rubber tree could stand no heat. . . . He had a tiny automobile that he could steer through the streets of Frankfurt in staccato, breakneck fashion and from which he emerged as a true giant. "I am a six-footer. That is my measure."

The reader will find this staccato style in his prose as well. Short, hacked-up sentences, with abrupt insertions and sharp endings, themselves following the compulsion of an intensely internal logic, piling up on each other. Never have I seen handwriting comparable to his. Only a few words, each written in huge brushstrokes, filled each page. One could decode them only from a distance. It is difficult to work with such monumental writing gestures. At the podium he followed the inner dictate of thoughts that spun out on their own accord. But his personal behavior was anything but arrogant. He was totally without self-absorption, fully to the point, and driven by a broadly sweeping, jerky manner of gesticulating. A one-in-a-million. Anyone who knew him closely speaks of him with uninhibited reverence.

How should one describe his philosophical position and his philosophical status? One can talk about the obvious. He was born in 1889, was a pupil at the famous Kreuz-Gymnasium in Dresden, and was richly gifted for the arts as well as for the sciences. After a few false starts, he dedicated his studies to medicine and philosophy, and this he did before the First World War, in Göttingen. He worked as a physician during the war and in 1921 became a *Dozent* in Göttingen.

I shall follow the sequence of his writings and begin with the first: *Untersuchungen zur Phänomenologie der Erkenntnis, I: Das Ding und seine Eigenschaften* (1927), a title that already reveals a good deal. He was a pupil and admirer of Edmund Husserl, who had taught until 1916 in Göttingen. Husserl's Göttingen phenomenology circle was an intensive group of young researchers to which people like Max Scheler and Husserl's Munich admirers, including Alexander Pfänder and Moritz Geiger, added themselves. It was a true school of the new way of thinking, oriented toward descriptive care and observation. After the premature death of Adolf Reinach, the young Lipps became the strongest representative of this fruitful Göttingen phenomenology. But his own works have nothing of the school manner. He distinguishes himself clearly from Husserl himself as well as from all of Husserl's followers.

He did share one thing with Husserl and Scheler—the power of observation. The sharp and subtle distinctions through which the analyses progress observe a high degree of abstraction. At the same time they overwhelm the reader formally with concretely envisaged phenomena, which step-by-step illustrate and articulate the mode of questioning. What does it mean, that a thing "has" characteristics? Does it really have them? Is the thing something of itself, or does it come to be from its characteristics? This question, propounded by Johann Friedrich Herbart, to which Husserl had dedicated some well-known analyses, is transposed with a jerk by Lipps out of its logical and epistemological abstractions into the most concrete of questions. Already in this early book, contemporary with Heidegger's *Being and Time*, the world of praxis has an unconditioned methodical priority. "That which is 'of itself' [*an sich*] can be conceived first and foremost on the basis of such an intercourse with things." "That which is called 'Being In Reality' [*In-Wirklichkeit-Sein*] does not only have the function of an argument for a truth in the sublimated sense, as it constitutes itself in the sphere of pure consciousness. So it would be an autonomous reason that had been placed in a brutal reality." One could continue to recognize motifs taken from Nicolai Hartmann's *Metaphysik der Erkenntnis* (1921), which Lipps did not quote; from Max Scheler's *Die Formen des Wissens und der Bildung* (1925), which he did quote; and from the "re-cognition [*wiederzuerkennen*] of Martin Heidegger, whom at that time he could not quote. But what a tremendous lack of concern is evident in the manner with which the book's foreword characterizes his turn to "motifs not yet revealed." "In this there is a transformation of some of Husserl's formulations. But I believe that in this also I remain only a pupil of Husserl."

In fact he doggedly went his own way for the sake of using his own formula: "between pragmatism and *Existenz* philosophy." Certainly he did not remain uninfluenced by what happened in philosophy, especially by Heidegger's preparation of the question of being. In the first work of his mature period—the *Untersuchungen zu einer hermeneutischen Logik*—the influence of *Being and Time* showed itself clearly. There we find a return to Aristotle and the roots of Aristotelian logic, done to prepare the background from which language lets itself be abstracted as the living context of things and as the completion of existence. The fourth section, "Word and Meaning," is the true contrast to the famous first logical investigation of Husserl. Neither "expression" nor "sign" nor any firm arrangement of word and meaning do justice to the function language serves for mankind.

Lipps prepared a second book for printing but did not live to see it appear. He was killed on September 10, 1941, while serving in Russia as a regiment physician. The book, *Die menschliche Natur*, spans a colorful set of phenomena from psychology and moral anthropology. Behind the short pointed statements with which he presents his phenomenology, the author is betrayed, but one must also say that he succeeds in hiding his extraordinary knowledge of the world and the breadth of his education.

Under the beautiful, telling title of the *Die Verbindlichkeit der Sprache* [The obligation of language] and the somewhat colorless *Die Wirklichkeit des Menschen* [The reality of man], the thoroughly concentrated work of the prematurely deceased Lipps is completed in two volumes. It would find a good reception even today. For the explorations of the foundations of language undertaken in England in the wake of Wittgenstein, Austin, and Searle have not only a predecessor but also a tremendous counterpart in Hans Lipps—and one that is without a program. Lipps wins a nearly inexhaustible supply of information from his interrogation of language, its words, usages, modes of expression, proverbs, and practical functions. It is language and not an epistemological a priori that reflects the relationship with things and allows us to grasp them. This ear for language and this eye for its gesture are what distinguish Hans Lipps among phenomenologists. One learns to look language in the eye with him.

Leipzig Fears

After almost twenty years in the small world of Marburg, the last five under tremendous pressure, the move to a big city and to a university outfitted in a grand style was a great change. Of course the political situation threw its threatening shadow over the scene. But it is understandable that the new beginning in Leipzig, partly with older colleagues and partly with contemporaries who had already made names for themselves, pushed the gloominess of the world situation into the background. Compared to the moral terror that had made the Marburg atmosphere so repressive, the Nazi party hardly put in an appearance at Leipzig University. With some anxiety I undertook a visit to the leader of the *Dozentenbund*, the representative of the party, and it passed surprisingly simply. Max Clara, an anatomist, explained to me that Leipzig was a work-oriented university, and to that I could respond with conviction and without hesitation that if that was the case, I would certainly feel at home. Somewhat less encouraging was my first visit to the dean. I had been ordered to Leipzig on a temporary basis, and when I introduced myself, he responded in a somewhat sour manner: "So the Reich has sent you to us." The Reich's Ministry of Education had just been created, and the local patriotism of Saxony was taking it hard. But this was not directed against me personally. In truth, Leipzig was an astounding university. A few years later, already well into the Second World War, the psychologist Hans Volkelt complained to me that he had *not* become *Ordinarius* in Leipzig *because* he was a Nazi. (He was the *Extraordinarius* in the Institute for Psychology and a zealous party member.) One might think that this was an absurd claim that stood all the facts on their heads, but the absurd thing was that he was correct. I myself worked with the faculty personnel committee and can confirm this. This was Leipzig. Some excellent men—including the rector, a longtime party member who must have imagined that the Third Reich would develop in a very different way and who insisted on scholarship as the highest academic value—surprisingly came to our aid in holding off the more militant Nazis. In Marburg my friends and I had felt ourselves to be a minority viewed with hostility, but there was none of this in Leipzig. The question of scholarly quality seemed to be absolutely determining. And so I was still able to experience what formerly counted most among the charms of German university life—that leap from the outsider's position as *Dozent* to the full authority of a colleague with equal status.

But Leipzig presented philosophers with an unusual situation. For political reasons Theodor Litt was pushed into retirement, although he stayed on in Leipzig as a private citizen. As the successor to Hans Driesch, Arnold Gehlen had worked for a number of years alongside Litt, and as the successor to Gehlen, I found myself suddenly alone in a large field. All the stranger was the response that I found in the faculty. In it the unchallenged leadership belonged to classicists like Helmut Berve, Friedrich Klingner, Wolfgang Schadewaldt, Bernhard Schweitzer, and their friends, and I was close to them. Precisely at this moment, the scholarly prestige of Leipzig psychology—impressively and brilliantly represented by Wilhelm Wundt and later Felix Krueger—was exhausted with the retirement of Krueger, a major personality. This was due to politics, since Krueger had publicly defended Spinoza and other leading Jewish philosophers. Philosophy quickly won respect, especially the mode of working founded in intellectual history, in which I was adept as a pupil of Heidegger and a trained classical philologist. My inaugural lecture, "Hegel and the Spirit of History," had a large and friendly audience composed mainly of German historians, who were then holding a conference in Leipzig. This was a lecture I could later print unchanged; political bending was not expected in Leipzig.

The war broke out a few weeks later. I recall the moment: I was in the Café Felsche with acquaintances when the news was announced over the loudspeaker. An unforgettable moment, especially for someone who had experienced the outbreak of war in 1914, even if only as a fourteen-year-old. Then a fever of patriotic enthusiasm had overshadowed everything, including the ridiculous delirium of spy hunts and (especially nice) the hunt for the automobiles carrying gold from France to Russia, which were supposedly picking their way through Germany and were to be stopped at all costs. How different it was now. The war news was received in Leipzig like a report of death. Depressed quiet all around, grim faces on the street. Since it was all well planned, the transition to the war economy—in which each according to his coupons received the same portions—was smooth and without a break. I myself was shattered. I still held to the illusion that such an insane thing simply could not happen. Friends helped me get myself together. One did so by means of his own bracing sobriety: "Now it's all a matter of survival." Another by means of his fantastic capacity for illusion: He offered to bet with me that we would have peace by Christmas, saying that the war with England/France was in his opinion a mere comedy, all well calculated by Hitler. Even such optimism as this, the absurdity of which was clear, had something curiously consoling about it. What a power there is in nonsense! But sometimes it all came together in a terrible way, as when I visited a colleague I had thought of as a friend and found on his table a map upon which the forward progress of the German armies in Poland was indicated with little flags. I suddenly felt myself very much alone. In the course of time, though, this flock of lonely people came together and multiplied more and more.

Immediately after the capitulation of Poland, Leipzig University (together with Halle and Jena) was reopened, and in the great hall of the faculty lounge, decorated over the centuries with old faculty portraits (all of this was later destroyed by fire), one suddenly met new faces, famous names sent to Leipzig to take the place of drafted professors. I recall, just before the outbreak of the war, having a long discussion about Plato with a somewhat elderly gentleman, and it brought us nearer to each other. This turned out to be Andreas Speiser, a mathematician from Basel. Or a meeting with Rudolf Smend—strict, stiff, and self-assured. Or a few good hours with Franz Beyerle—open, fun-loving, and effusive. Also the historian Peter Rassow was there for a while—all very odd. There was certainly no one in this group who did not add himself to the lonely flock I spoke of earlier.

In 1938 I became a professor at Leipzig. The first pleasant surprise after the outbreak of war was an invitation to a Hölderlin Conference at the Goethe Society of Florence. Italy was still not in the war. It was Christmas, and at home everything was snow, ice, and darkness. The

weather in Florence was by chance of the softest mildness. Everything
was fragrant with aromatic wood fires. People were certainly worried,
but they were not without hope of staying once again on the sidelines,
as in the First World War, and later coming in on the right side. I
was put up in a Swiss cottage, and for the first time in my life I drank
instant coffee. The German colony was very receptive. Among my
audience were some semi-emigrants, who had displaced themselves
only as far as necessary from a fatherland grown hostile—tragic symbols
of the disaster. Among them I met Percy Gothein, the young friend
of Stefan George who was later murdered in Holland. He struck me
as wooden and very German. Such is life.

In Florence I saw much that was beautiful—that is as expected. I
took with me another memory: There were still all sorts of things to
be bought, so I acquired a cowhide briefcase. In 1939! And it still
exists today—used for decades by me, as the schoolbag of my daughter
from my first marriage, as the schoolbag of my daughter from my
second marriage, and now once again by me—a memorial to crafts-
manship in a still not completely industrialized economy.

Another unusual thing happened to me on account of my position
in Leipzig and despite my being otherwise unworthy. No doubt for
the sake of foreign propaganda, a small congress of Dutch and German
Hegel researchers was scheduled for Weimar, with the support of
Leipzig University. It was to be held during Pentecost, 1940. Of course,
the Dutch could not come since in the meantime the offensive in the
West had rolled over Holland. Just as I barged into the small gathering,
which was meeting in a place called "The Elephant" in Weimar, the
chairman, Hermann Glockner, was starting an argument by asserting
that the absence of the Dutch was from a scholarly point of view an
advantage. Perhaps he was correct, but. . . .

The meeting opened with my paper "Hegel and the Dialectic of
the Ancient Philosophers," an assemblage of the studies of many years
that would become the first chapter of my little Hegel book. Now I
certainly did not count among the leading Hegel scholars, but still, it
was not forbidden to try to understand something of Hegel. Or was
it? In any case, the gathered colleagues attacked this *homo novus* as
they would any upstart, challenging everything—for example, an error
made by Hegel in translating Plato (as if I did not command Greek),
or an obvious allusion to "old times" that allegedly did not refer to
the Greeks but rather to the eighteenth century. I had not brought

the Plato text along, but fortunately I did have Hegel's *Phenomenology*, so that I was at least able to convince the non-Hegelians that I understood something of Hegel.

The remaining papers were more or less orthodox, more or less unoriginal, harmonizing, offering a general recipe—on the whole giving evidence of a sad sterility and a ghostly unreality, not that of political propaganda but merely that of self-propagation. I recovered from this spiritual strain by means of a visit to the graves of our great poets in the Weimar cemetery and a visit to Rilke's daughter and her husband Karl Sieber. The remembrance of this visit accompanied me during all my further studies of Rilke.

One must be clear about the situation. The wave of revolutionary consolidation (of evil memory) had long since ebbed. From the point of view of the regime, a critical and more than unreliable youth now filled the lecture halls. My first "war" lecture was a presentation on Plato, and when I came to the chronology of the Platonic writings and said of language statistics—quite without ulterior motives, but who knows all his ulterior motives?—that this method was indeed primitive, but that like a lot of primitive things it had had a good deal of success, I was given a thunderous ovation. My unconscious had no doubt become more courageous than I had realized.

The extent of a general solidarity is shown by the following anecdote, which I had forgotten but which was later retold to me by the protagonist himself. I was giving a Plato lecture. In the discussion a soldier on leave asked what Plato might have said when a criminal tyrant became the *Führer* of a state. I answered: Of course he would have approved the murder of such a tyrant. There was no follow-up to this.

On the whole one may say—and this holds equally for all German universities—that the provinciality and petit-bourgeois character of Nazi party ideology and its representatives could not for long penetrate Leipzig. The Nazis were certainly capable of despising the universities, but in the end that meant underrating them. The surveillance of the faculty that no doubt occurred was a pitiful thing. When a female student, questioned by the Gestapo about my lectures, once explained that there was never any discussion of politics, she received the embittered answer: "That we already know." Unmolested, I was able to hold exercises in the philosophical seminar on Husserl's *Logical Investigations*, and the standing requirement to designate writings of Jewish authors with a little star was never observed in Leipzig. Only Nazi professors were recognizable by such means.

Once there was a dangerous complication. In a seminar I had used the logical example: "All asses are brown." Uproarious laughter. A female student excitedly reported this to a friend in a letter that was read by the friend's parents. There followed a denunciation, and the poor girl was put to work in a factory. I was ordered before the clever and well-meaning rector, who with satisfaction concluded that it had after all been only a logical example.

The story shows how the surveillance of students was manipulated and how dangerous the terror and the business of denunciation were. In many other areas the principle of terror consisted essentially in the promotion of the *presence* of the state's power in the consciousness of the citizen. Charity benefits, the struggle against corruption, soup Sundays—we professors, too, "collected" under the watchful eye of small and petit-bourgeois party members.

But this is all well known, and I am suggesting that these events be read merely as typical. Take, for example, the following experience in a bookstore. A student comes in and asks: Have you anything by Heidegger? No. By Ernst Jünger? No. By Guardini? No. Thank you and good day. For these were the authors we read. And of course Rilke. This was the high point of his popularity. If there ever was anything that flatly contradicted the bombastic phraseology of the Nazis, it was the highbred mannerism of Rilke's language. I repeatedly interpreted the *Duino Elegies*, for the last time in 1943 as Leipzig was being bombed. Ten days or so after the nearly total destruction of the center of the city (on December 4, 1943), I sat in a still sound building—but without heating, light, or windowpanes—and continued with the third elegy. Students were there—of course not all of them— each heavily bundled up and with a candle. Darkness.

When the Stalingrad catastrophe opened even the blindest of eyes to the outcome of the war—only the deluded would never see—the situation became generally more dangerous. The politically active resistance was gaining strength then. The mayor of Leipzig, Karl Goerdeler, regularly sponsored presentations in his house. Once I spoke on Plato's state, and I recall Goerdeler's all too frank reaction—a comment on the kind of intelligence we would need "then." One could feel that something was brewing, even though one did not know anything. This fundamental mood, which spread with the looming defeat, was given appropriate expression by Anton Kippenberg when he got in the habit of saying: *Et illud transit.*

Aside from the trip to Florence in 1939–1940, I went abroad twice during the war. I did not fully recognize that thereby one was being used for purposes of foreign propaganda, for which a political innocent was sometimes suitable. Such instances were an escape with mixed feelings. The first undertaking was a 1941 lecture on Herder in Paris. The paper was published as a monograph and was available for a long time after the war. It was a purely scholarly study. Of course the same thing meant, from the point of view of the sponsor, a misuse of academic work. But I think that one could correctly assume that among the listeners there were at least some people who knew how to abstract from the circumstances and all ulterior motives and who were still interested in the scholarly aspect. There was still such a thing as a literary public, no matter what they say. During this trip I met some old acquaintances: Marie Albert Schmidt, who was always repeating "this is not my war," and Jean Baruzi, the passionate mystic and researcher of Leibniz. But admittedly one does not sit comfortably at the point of a bayonet and does not come away with a good conscience.

Much more charming and favored by circumstances was a trip in February 1944 to Portugal. I owed this trip to a former Leipzig colleague, the Romance philologist Harri Meier, who at that time was director of the German Cultural Institute in Lisbon. He had put me, certainly a hopeless case due to my political unworthiness, on a list of desirable speakers. But then a bomb fell on the Berlin office. The newly established replacement office had an empty desk, and Meier was clever enough to induce me to resubmit my papers immediately. No bureaucratic office is going to reject out of hand the first proposal on which they have to work.

So it happened that out of the rubble and ruin of Leipzig and in the middle of a dirty half-winter I took the first flight of my life to the Iberian south. After the ghastliness of the incineration of Leipzig, of the trembling when one got into the bomb carpet, of the strains of the night-long attempts to extinguish the fires and then of the efforts to repair windows and roofs all around—the contrast was so great that I still know every detail. I recall the evening before departure at the dining room of the Hotel Fürstenhof in Berlin's Potsdam Square, where at a neighboring table a silent delegation of Finnish officers was dining. They were a circle of lonely men, between whose chairs stretched the expanse of the tundra. Then in the morning the pseudo-internationalism of the Hitler super-empire with the departure from Tempelhof Airport. Then the impression of a first flight above a carpet of clouds and fully on the other side—today a perfectly common feeling but at that time exciting for me in the way an astronaut's flight must be. And the slowly opening doors of peace and prosperity: Barcelona, Madrid, Lisbon, and the whole colorful landscape of Don Quixote and Sancho Panza, whom I met on many a Portuguese donkey.

The temporary release from the universal jail being erected by a war-threatened Germany conferred a strange unreality on everything we saw in "freedom." The natural and the normal of reality can have such an effect if one exists in unnatural and abnormal life circumstances, as we then did. There were other unusual happenings that helped make the entire experience seem unreal. After a long flight with two refueling stops in our good little Junker airplane, we arrived toward evening in Madrid. But it was Saturday, and the last leg of the trip had to be put off until Monday. So we were brought to Lufthansa's contract hotel, the Palacio, right near the Prado, and were exposed to the imaginary splendor of this sort of old luxury hotel. At that time I spoke not a word of Spanish, and also in Portugal I could only use my French. Even worse, I did not have any Spanish money. Should I admire the Prado from the outside and only peek into the cafés? On Sunday morning I wandered into the German consulate, where I was received in a friendly manner by a cigar-smoking, newspaper-reading official. He outfitted me with the little money I requested for the Prado and a café. The Prado itself: What it meant, suddenly after years of horror, to be able to see this world of beautiful things—this is indescribable. Since then I have seen the Prado often and explored it more thoroughly. But this one Sunday in February of the war winter of 1944 was like a demonstration and a denunciation of world history.

The weeks in Portugal, often together with Carl Friedrich von Weizsäcker, who as the son of a diplomat was terribly pampered by the Germany embassy and who always took me with him, continued this trip into fairyland. Suddenly we were surrounded by the blossoming flowers at the Lisbon airport, and then a whole pastoral scene. Only one detail reminded us of the war: All the windows were covered with a latticework of white paper strips. This was supposed to protect the panes in case of an errant bombing attack or a sudden violation of Portugal's neutrality.

Thanks to the sympathetic understanding of my Lisbon colleagues—Harri Meier, Wolfgang Kayser, Joseph Piel, and others—one presentation and one week became several. The first draft of my Prometheus paper took shape in Kayser's home. And the curious ways of this old culture! After my presentation in Lisbon to an endless number of female students (far fewer male students: the young men had to make money), there waited in the lobby a mighty host of mothers, there to pick up their carefully protected daughters. A very German and festive promotion to the doctorate in Coimbra in which I took part was a fully medieval scene, with gowns and ceremonies, an exchange of speeches, and brotherly kisses. In Lisbon I met not only German intellectuals like Willy Andreas, who to my embarrassment tended to lapse into propaganda tones, but also Ortéga y Gasset. He was living there in the circles of the high aristocracy, since he was not on good terms with Franco. He was a vital figure. I tried to persuade him to follow up the *Revolt of the Masses* with a book on the revolt of the middle class, but he of course did not do this. Instead world history has taken up precisely this choral refrain and shouted its theme in unison into our ears.

On my return to Leipzig I continued my classes amidst increasing destruction. We read our lectures in emergency rooms set up in the university library, from which the books had been removed and which had so far been spared bombing. The audience for these lectures shifted gradually. The temporary predominance of female students was soon overcome by the wounded, the convalescent, the invalids. News of the invasion was whispered to me in front of the library by Goerdeler's daughter. Then came the failed attempt on Hitler's life of July 20, 1944, and a new wave of terror, during which one held one's breath. Unforgettable to me is the smell of burnt paper, which I perceived one February morning in 1945 and just as quickly diagnosed. The Central Security Office, which had been moved from Berlin to Leipzig and installed in a castle in the vicinity of my house, was burning its files. This was a breath of fresh air. We had survived.

Then came the *Volkssturm*, in which everyone who could crawl was ordered to serve, from almost-children to the totally gray-haired. Just as with the alternating weeks of air-raid watches, the *Volkssturm* had no serious military character in this area far from any front. For our dilettante's game there were in any case no longer any weapons, and if one acted fairly reasonably and inconspicuously, survival was not difficult. The real function of this pseudo-military service organization was political surveillance, and one simply had to be prudent about avoiding conversations in groups of more than two people. Soon enough American tanks approached and rolled threateningly all day long around the outskirts of Leipzig.

Leipzig Illusions

The American occupation passed undramatically, and the preparation for the reorganization of the university fell for the most part to me. This was because I was uncompromised and had never been active in academic administration during the Nazi period. We had to choose a rector. Since Theodor Litt had responded to my inquiry with a refusal on the clever grounds that only someone who had constantly belonged to the university's life could become rector, the choice fell to the archeologist Bernhard Schweitzer. With dogged energy he negotiated with the Americans and with the denazification officer, and in endless meetings with us—I had become the dean of my faculty—he prepared a well-thought-out set of new university statutes. We Germans are born with a preference for these fundamental questions.

Did we take ourselves seriously? At the very least, the passivity of the American authorities should have taught us that their stay in Leipzig would not be very long. In fact the Russians took their place in the fall. By the way, the changeover was carried out in flawless fashion, and now of course everything began anew, but with different aims.

The Russian program—then also that of the communist functionaries with whom I had to work—was to initiate a phase of "democracy" that was supposed to prepare for the later transition to a socialist state. Living in my house at this time was Berlin's later minister for industry, Fritz Selbmann, an old-school communist who had worked in the mines, survived the Third Reich in a civilian prison, and devoured the entire prison library, a mighty arsenal of semiliteracy. He declared publicly with an honest pathos: "We didn't take off the brown strait-jacket in order to put on a red straitjacket." Similar illusions were embodied by the newly founded *Kulturbund*, which was supposed to bring together "antifascist" intellectuals for free cultural cooperation. There were "free" elections for officers of the *Kulturbund* in Saxony, and through some slip-up I received the most votes and should have become president. But this did not sit well at all. This democratic it was not supposed to be, and a motion of acclamation was used to elevate the politically reliable Ludwig Renn to the presidency. No use was made of my vice-president's position. I tell this to illustrate the orchestration of the operation. Slip-ups often offer the best insight into the way plans are supposed to work.

Preparations for reopening the university did not make headway. In the end we had to admit that the new authorities were not prepared to tolerate Bernhard Schweitzer, the rector we had elected in the American period. Schweitzer disclosed to me one day that I would be the rector chosen to reopen the university. I was duly elected and now began the exhausting, interesting, illusion-rich, and disillusioning work of construction—or was it deconstruction?—of Leipzig University.

In this period I learned a good deal, and not only about the game of politics. There has always been something like this in the small world of academia, and the rules of the game have been known since Machiavelli and are everywhere the same. What I learned above all was the unfruitfulness and impossibility of all restorative thinking; and when I went over to the West two years later, as a professor at Frankfurt, I was more than a little perplexed by the illusions I still found in the academic politics there, at whose peak stood Walter Hallstein. It is difficult to talk about my two years as rector in Leipzig because there is too much to tell. Above all I now belonged to the political "elite" of the Soviet zone. Thus I often met Wilhelm Pieck and Walter Ulbricht, Paul Wandel and Abusch and Gysi. I also later met Gerhard Harig and Ackermann, to mention those who later fell from grace but who were the first to enlighten me, and not to mention the small and smallest gods from Dresden and Leipzig.

In another sense the entirety of the immense Leipzig University was now brought into my horizon for the first time. My experience here had essentially been confined to the war years, which had loosened all contacts. For example, the medical faculty with all its personnel and institutional problems was completely new to me. But precisely this faculty immediately laid claim to a large part of my political-administrative activity, for the truly imperial structure of these famous clinics was especially ruffled and shaken by the revolutionary seesaw. What was happening here was not a matter only of university revolution but also of the woes and well-being of sick people. For this reason the medical faculty fell under the aegis not of the Ministry of Culture but of the Ministry of Health, and it took its responsibility seriously.

The sought-after "socialist" reconstruction of the university was set in motion as a process of social upheaval from both sides. Children from the "lower" classes were given preference in admission. This selection was very systematic, and highly gifted children of professors could often not be gotten through in the face of opposition from the Russians. On the other side, they sought to rid themselves of as many professors and assistants as possible; this was simple to do in that the laws of the occupying powers provided for the release of all who had been members of the Nazi party, even if only formally. But it was not so simple to fill the gaps. Fortunately the full professors of the university had for the most part kept their distance from the party (and were for that reason in Leipzig and not in Berlin or Munich). But into the open position the revolutionary wave sometimes washed up really questionable pieces of driftwood, and it was no simple matter to get rid of them. An essential part of my activity consisted in being on the lookout in the East, the West, and overseas for researchers with socialist convictions who could fill the gaps without endangering the level of quality. But of course questions about qualifications are precarious and often undecidable.

In the field of medicine things were sometimes different. I recall the case of a surgeon whose lack of abilities our excellent pathologist Werner Hueck (with whom I was becoming increasingly friendly) had to establish for the Russian authorities in tiresome procedures. Fortunately they were from the Ministry of Health. This division between two Russian ministries, and the corresponding division between the Dresden ministries and the central administration in Berlin, which was gaining more and more influence, was the basis of much of the academic politics of the rector's office. I learned then that only in balance-of-power situations is it really possible to steer a course, and every political intention must in the end create a balance-of-power situation if it is to be effective.

A consistent policy of "legalization" was implemented by the occupation power and the SED, which was forcibly united through a surprise attack on the SPD.[1] They left the self-administration of the university formally untouched and began their socialist reconstruction through institutional additions and an infiltration of personnel. In this manner a new faculty for the science of society was constructed, and later a new faculty for the science of education. These were intended to shift majority power in the faculty; and similarly in student politics a new grouping called "worker-students" was created. But such procedures could only be effective in the long run, and the early student elections brought the communists clear defeats. In the university senate, a skilled handling of negotiations brought about complete solidarity, without exception, and this included the newly constructed faculties and their representatives, who belonged to the SED. The substantive problems with which the leadership of a university must deal are of course unambiguous. No academic teacher can withdraw from these problems and still be true to himself. I had, with the backing of the Russians, successfully resisted the addition of student representatives in the senate, and in difficult situations I could depend on the shrewd advice of my colleagues, especially that of Otto de Boor, the dean of legal studies. Hence the warding off of the ceaseless, irrelevant attacks of the local, ambitious, and self-important SED activists was on the whole very successful—something that would have stigmatized me as a "reactionary" in the later development of Leipzig University politics and in the cultural politics of the German Democratic Republic.

I had to devote a good deal of time to a task that proved to be melancholy in the end, namely, making it possible for all my excellent Leipzig colleagues—Theodor Litt, Karl Reinhardt, Friedrich Klingner, among others—to emigrate to the West. It was predictable that with this continuing emigration, which was not matched by a correspondingly large reverse movement of good people from the West, the scholarly rank of the university would increasingly decline. It was for this reason that I myself finally accepted a call to Frankfurt University, which the then rector Walter Hallstein personally offered me one day when I was on summer vacation at the "cultural spa" at Ahrenshoop in Mecklenburg.

1. The SED, the ruling party of the German Democratic Republic, is simply the Communist party by a different name, but since there is also a Communist party (KPD) in West Germany, it is convenient to retain the initials SED. [tr.]

Conducting this rector business was in any case a galling task. Since the radicals were constantly attempting to get power over the university I led, one had to be constantly on one's tocs. It soon proved necessary to reserve to myself the opening and distribution of incoming mail. This was the only way to suppress the purposeful indiscretions and the misdirection and interception of mail that followed from the side of those functionaries who had been smuggled into the administration. From early morning until late evening I was in the office, insofar as I was not in Dresden or Berlin or at all-German rectors' conferences in the West.

This constant presence brought me the special esteem of the Russian cultural authorities, by the way. They loved to make surprise visits, for purposes of control, and in Leipzig the rector was always immediately available. Also, I never had anything to hide or cover up. It was clear to me from the outset that the Russians were distrustful people, and I therefore always confronted them with absolute openness and with decisively clear opposition. When I did not get my way with them, and that was of course most of the time, the Russians could at least be certain that I would carry through their directives exactly, even against my own convictions. An interesting example, unimportant but symptomatic, should be told: According to an old custom, the catalogue of the university listed the most famous Leipzig students— such as Camerarius, Altdorfer, Christian Wolff, Leopold Ranke, Richard Wagner, and Friedrich Nietzsche—and this was kept as a kind of honor roll. The Russians demanded the elimination of Nietzsche's name. I refused—it was not possible to leave out a name of such international rank. The Russians affirmed that "at some later time" such an acknowledgment might again be possible, but for political reasons Nietzsche's name was at this time not admissible. With that I decided that the entire honor roll had to be eliminated, and the Russians respected this decision. (The directive that they themselves had to carry out was clearly obeyed: The name of Nietzsche did not again appear.)

On the whole, communication with the Russian cultural officers was not very difficult. They had directives to give because they had been given directives. Of course, they were not officers but rather professors in uniform, thus giving us much in common. In contrast to this, the German agents in this first period—before the excellent chemistry professor from Dresden, Arthur Simon, took over the Ministry of

Higher Education—were narrow-minded doctrinaires who were just bursting with self-importance. In order to prevail, I had to resort to the threat of resignation, which always worked since the Russian authorities had placed their trust in me. Of course, that did not make me beloved in the eyes of these people.

The standard was higher in the central administration in Berlin. There clever people such as Paul Wandel and Rompe had the say, and I had many friendly conversations with them. Aside from politics, we were certainly separated by an entire world. What philosophy was in my eyes was in their eyes something completely beyond comprehension. "Scientific" socialism and dialectical materialism as well as perspectives and measures taken from physics (Rompe was a physicist) were not applicable to philosophy, and when one day I was especially convincing in discussion with Wandel and Rompe, they came to the conclusion that it would be better if philosophy were transferred to the fine arts academy. This was in my eyes a crushing result of this attempt to reach understanding. But who knows? Today, perhaps, many in West Germany would also be of the opinion that what I called philosophy, what I taught, belongs in a fine arts academy. That in the past few decades Heidegger has more easily found a response in the art academies in Berlin and Munich than in the universities is food for thought.

Still another illustrative story. Theodor Litt, an inspired speaker, had such great success with his lectures, which did not spare Marxist ideas from criticism, that the Russians finally suspended him. I was outraged. This was just what the Nazis had done, a kind of eternal recurrence. This had to destroy all trust in our newly acquired freedom of research and teaching. I traveled to Berlin and brought this before the highest Russian authority (Solotuchin was the minister). Fortunately I had an excellent interpreter. I learned at this time that when translators had to be interposed, the real dialogue was not between me and the addressee but between me and the interpreter. I had to convince him so that he could convincingly represent my case. In this case I succeeded. The Russians gave in, although adding that I "bore the responsibility." That was perhaps a hidden threat, but nonetheless it was also a declaration of trust, and I was able to prevent further mischief. Of course by the next semester Litt had exchanged Leipzig for his hometown of Bonn, so that this responsibility was one I no longer had to carry.

With energy and full of illusion, I tried in those times to defend the scholarly status of the university. Without illusions one cannot even try to hold such an office. Special problems in this respect were the so-called worker-students. Sent from the factories to the universities without sufficient schooling, these young people had it hard. With all their zeal and even in cases of real theoretical talent, they were seriously disadvantaged from the outset, and their possible failure threatened the university with the charge of being "reactionary." In truth this experiment did not succeed and rapidly had its day, and frankly it was meant only as a transition. Above all, these were for the most part not children of the working class but rather middle-class children who had not finished high school and had gone to work in the factories. There they stood out as intellectually endowed and were now sent back to school. Perhaps they did not come back to the rows of the lecture halls with the right enthusiasm, but they did pursue their studies with tremendous zeal. There were tensions between such differently prepared groups of students, but on the whole one could successfully compensate for their shortcomings. I remember once, returning from a rectors' conference in the West, I found everything in an uproar. This turned out to be nothing more than an artificially incited confrontation, and I mention it only because the party functionary I met on this occasion was the then general secretary of the Central Committee of the SED, Walter Ulbricht. I did not notice then in his obsequious face the special political talents that he undoubtedly possessed and later demonstrated.

In academic instruction I was for the first time successful in making the sort of transition I had sought from lecture to subsequent discussion, as I would again in the late 1960s in Heidelberg, and both times it was for the same reason: Marxist schooling gave many students self-confidence and a certain dialectical skill. Even if it was nothing more than a downright dogmatic attitude that came out in the discussion, this was why we were there—to overcome all dogmatisms through schooling in critical thinking. Even if one did not convince every discussion partner, by this means one could still bring an entire lecture hall to reflect on a subject. It seems to me almost more difficult to lead toward critical thinking listeners who have a patient, schoolboyish readiness to learn. I felt similarly later in Frankfurt, by the way, with the students from St. George's who had been trained in neoscholastic dogmatics. Here as well, of course, it was a matter of a minority of articulate dogmatists serving as a foil for the authentic teaching and learning process.

Aside from the numberless negotiations I had to conduct, as rector I also had to give speeches. These were sometimes political, sometimes philosophical presentations, with Marxist discussion partners who were in my eyes trite Enlightenment thinkers and philosophical dilettantes. More and more I was brought to the realization that a neoscholasticism was being prepared here. People like Ernst Bloch, who would be my successor in Leipzig, and Hans Mayer must have experienced this later.

That the Russians never felt comfortable with the peculiar connection between teaching and research in the German university was not surprising. They treated professors as not very different from high school teachers. They could not see why I could not transfer the history courses (by chance we no longer had a single historian at the university) to the orientalists, of whom we had several outstanding representatives. From an "academician," that is, a member of a Russian academy who only performed research, they would have demanded nothing of this sort.

On the whole the Russian authorities were much less narrow and schoolmasterish than the German communist functionaries, although admittedly they carried out their political assignments unswervingly. Some experiences left a lasting impression on me. One day I had some business at the Russian post headquarters. There was at this time a Referendum for the Expropriation of Aristocratic Properties, introduced by the SED, and I was asked by the Russian town-major what I thought of this. I criticized the whole thing very sharply, essentially from the point of view that in the twelve years of the Third Reich we had had enough sham plebiscites and fake elections (this plebiscite was of course also a sham because the princely properties and indeed all large properties had already been appropriated). There resulted a long conversation on the authenticity or inauthenticity of elections, and the whole command structure heard me out. The next morning a Russian jeep pulled up before my house and a Russian soldier rang and said he wanted to speak to the rector. I was terrified. Too much had been said, and it had been said too freely. With a good deal of cool and a resolute determination, I urged the man into my study, had him take a seat, and asked him what he wished. He sprang up, his hand outstretched, and said: "The commander sends

you Pentecost greetings"—and then wine, sugar, and flour was un-
loaded from the jeep! That was very Russian: For sincerity one could
also earn their gratitude, as long as this did not go against a contrary
set of orders.

The decision to go to Frankfurt was in my situation not so simple
to carry out, for my departure was quite possibly a prestige question
for East German cultural politics. Even if I had bitter opponents in
Leipzig and Dresden, I had very good relations with the central administration in Berlin, where some capable people sat, and with the Russian
authorities. I had to avoid giving a political color to my decision to
leave. That I was no Marxist was clear to everybody. But they themselves believed in their politics and were convinced that the change
in social reality would of itself lead me over to the right side. Being
determines consciousness.

So I faced a difficult task, above all with the Russian administration,
in explaining my departure. I was questioned about my reasons, and
it was pointed out that they had always put their trust in me, that
they had protected me against foolish disturbances that originated in
Leipzig, and that they valued my work highly. I answered in terms
of a love of my home country. I had been born in Marburg, and for
twenty years I had belonged to Marburg University, the university of
the Hessian land, and Frankfurt was also Hessian. "And do you know
what Hesse is? It is the home of Grimm's fairy tales." Saying this
turned out to be a real inspiration. There was no more resistance but
instead best wishes for a good trip. Of course, the decision to let me
go followed from other reasons, but my argument had also struck an
understanding chord in the Russian soul.

A third experience with the Russians was more complex. I had
already begun my lectures in Frankfurt but had returned to Leipzig
for the official transference of the rector's office and also for the
organization of private legal matters related to my move. Everything
had gone flawlessly. The transfer of the rectorship occurred in the
best of form—with a friendly press and my picture in the newspaper
as I hung the rector's chain around the neck of Erwin Jacobi, the
famous expert on constitutional law. Then suddenly one evening at
eleven o'clock I was arrested in my apartment. Living in my house
just then was the Romance philologist Werner Krauss, who had just
been called to Leipzig. Like myself, he saw in this catastrophe a political
failure. No one could have guessed that in the end it would prove to

be a misuse of power by local bigwigs who wanted to take revenge because they begrudged me an escape from their doctrinaire corner into the freedom of the capitalist world. The story of my four-day incarceration in the Leipzig jail on Bismarck Street would make a novel in itself. For someone who had never been in prison and had never been a soldier, it was utterly instructive, serious and comical at the same time. Belts and shoelaces had to be given up right at the beginning so that one could not take one's life. I assumed that anything could happen—being left in prison forever, for example—but I was determined to survive. Of course, it is impossible to say how pressed one would be in the long run in strict solitary confinement. My four days were of course nothing and could not seriously bring a person to the breaking point, and I found most of the things that happened to me unusual and comical. This was over and above the routine treatment of a prisoner charged with civil offenses (and I later had to pay money for this!). I kept myself going by calling to memory all the verses I had ever learned by heart. That was like a slow penetration into forgotten wells of the past. At the same time I found myself extraordinarily tense. This showed itself in the following: All day long and into the evening names were being called out through the hallways of the prison, which had been built according to a model well-conceived for easy surveillance. Obviously these people were being summoned to interrogations. But with nearly every one of these announcements, I fancied for a brief moment that I had heard my own name being called.

I was finally called on the fourth night, around ten o'clock. Everything began to go backwards. I even got my shoelaces back, and was driven in a Russian car to a Russian interrogation. My arrest and imprisonment were done, of course, on Russian orders, and this is the context in which I would like to tell something about the Russians.

I was led before a polite Russian colonel in a former SS barracks, which lay in a forest. He demanded that I hand over my briefcase and proceeded with a thorough search of the rich but innocent contents, periodically asking me: "What is that?" This would be something like a coat check. During this "work" he suddenly offered me a cigarette. I thanked him but said: "So long as I am not free I do not smoke." He snapped together and excused himself for his tactlessness! While he was still in the midst of his work, there suddenly entered a strikingly unpleasant major who whispered something to him, and with that the colonel silently repacked the half-emptied briefcase and gave it back to me. I had to follow the other one, who could not speak German. Then came an interrogation with an interpreter. After the usual questions about personal things came the first and only but endlessly repeated question: "What kind of work did you do?" With this I would describe in detail my activities as rector. Stubbornly the question kept repeating itself: "What have you been working on otherwise?" Finally I lost my patience and told him that my day did not have any more hours. "If you answer me in this way, you are going to sit here for a long time." In fact the interrogation was broken off in the middle of the night. The interpreter was reading the newspaper and asking every half hour whether I perhaps now had something to say. The Russian officer had gone away and there was much walking about, looking around in a safe, and so forth. This new scene was as much a riddle to me as the first one. Only later did it occur to me that I had simply fallen in with a bad interpreter, one who should have asked: "What have you done?"—in the classic method of the secret police designed to provoke self-guilt. And in just this manner I later guessed what they were really looking for behind all this. It was my files which were not to be found! I suppose this is the way it is with all bureaucrats. But there are also dangers for the person caught up in this tangle. Bureaucrats are liable simply to forget a person, and this is equal to a death certificate.

In my case it was fortunately otherwise. I was once more taken away and now led into a large room for an interrogation at a long table with lots of high officers. An excellent interpreter, but once again a highly unusual interrogation. After the usual questioning followed some intensive questions about my activity as a professor. What kind of students had I had? Did I also have female students? Where did they come from? I said many were from Leipzig, many from Dresden. "None from Chemnitz?" Yes, also from Chemnitz. It continued in this vein for a while. Then the general chairing the meeting offered a speech to inform me that there had been an oversight, an encroachment by the German police, which they regretted. This last had been simply a seeming interrogation, and the order for my release had already arrived. But then I was stoical. The incident had not really destroyed my composure. In any case I was free. Should they have a taxi come for me (something which of course did not exist for German civilians then)? I thanked them but said I preferred to return home on foot through the night woods. Upon leaving I murmured to the interpreter: "Evidently a denunciation done as an act of revenge." He nodded his agreement and added: "But don't say that." Well, this kind of thing you could probably say to no secret police in the world. But the warning nonetheless sounded sinister to me. It had been just like this in the Third Reich, that one was not allowed to say many things. And the general had also mentioned that I had "expressed myself carelessly several times." That was no doubt what was in the denunciation. I had seen enough.

Despite all this, taking leave of Leipzig did not come easily. Years later I dedicated a commemorative address to that unforgettable university, which sank beyond reach after I left. I would like to quote a bit from that address:

Less than any other of the old German universities does Leipzig owe its establishment to a prince. It is noteworthy that Leipzig has no secondary names, neither that of a ruling prince—as the Heidelberg, Marburg, Göttingen, and Berlin universities have—nor that of an illustrious intellectual figure. From the very beginning Leipzig was an establishment of scholars and doctors themselves, even if with the permission and recognition of the landed aristocracy and the church.

In the year 1409 at the University of Prague the influence of the "German nation"—this is what the corporation that made up the university was called—was reduced in relation to that of the Czech nation. This German nation then unanimously seceded and chose Leipzig as a new location. On December 2, 1409, the festive opening of the university took place in the refectory of the Thomas Seminary. And even if the landed princes were present, the Margrave Friedrich the Warlike and his brother Wilhelm, nonetheless the statutes then enacted were expressly legitimized through the acceptance of the teachers or "masters" of that time. From its establishment, therefore, the University of Leipzig has been determined by the autonomy of its corporate essence. The university has sustained its autonomy in a unique and magnificent way in the face of increasing sovereign power and even in the face of the centralized modern state and its interests. The university owes its distinction not only to the establishment of the significant endowment that devolved upon it in its first century by a decision of the sovereigns, but also to its intellectual independence, which has rested upon its close relations with the city and the citizenry, and to its position within a field of forces that can be represented on the one hand by printing and publishing concerns, theatrical and musical culture, and on the other hand by the existence of the high courts. In this field of forces the University of Leipzig also had its place. Until recent years, right up until our period, the university has owed its position to its ability to defend the freedom of its intellectual unfolding even in oppressive circumstances.

One of the major barriers to reaching an understanding with the Russian occupation power was our differing conceptions of the division of labor between research academies and universities. We, too, were a state-supported institution, but the services that we rendered to the state were only a consequence of our freedom to pursue independent research. In contrast, Russian educational policy confers this particular function on academies rather than universities.

This gap in understanding has had its effect in the reconstruction that is still in process in Leipzig. The research and teaching strengths that are still alive within the university today have a new task. They must guard against a definition of the institution that would serve only the building of the new state and would have academic instruction thoroughly determined by reasons of state, as defined by those in power.

In those decisive first years of reconstruction during which we defended the traditional ways of our university and in which we were naturally the underdogs, the portraits hanging in the office of the rector were for us a powerful reinforcement—not only the picture of Joachim Camerarius but also and above all the extraordinarily alive portraits by Anton Graff of Gellert, Ernesti, and Garve, as well as the portraits of Hornung, Beck, and other great men of the university. The weight of the historical tradition that stood behind us gave us our sense of worth. It is a legacy upon which we may yet build the future of the University of Leipzig.

Frankfurt Intermezzo

I had been sitting on an offer from Frankfurt University since the spring of 1947, but my removal to Frankfurt had its peculiar difficulties. First there was the actual move. I had all the necessary papers from the Russian authorities, and eventually the railroad made available to me a freight car large enough not only for my household goods but above all for my library. But customs remained a problem. What if the Russian customs officials undertook an examination of my library? In this regard they were entitled, indeed obligated, to carry out the law of the occupation authority that no National Socialist literature could be transported anywhere. Although such things were not to be found in my scholarly library, who could guarantee that a swastika would not surface in some book, or maybe on the page of a newspaper in which a book had been wrapped? Such a discovery could lead to the confiscation of all my goods. I therefore decided to travel in the freight car with my belongings. The trip lasted five days, with only instant coffee and a supply of bread, numerous stops, rearrangements with "roll-offs"—a comical feeling, when one is rolling somewhere on one's own power until one finally bumps up against something in more or less ungentle fashion. It took four such days to get to the border. There, with the help of carefully stashed schnapps, cigars, and cigarettes, I was successful in moving the German railway authorities to manipulate the Russians for me, thereby sparing myself all the border checks. I landed, not without a sigh of relief, in Marienborn/ Helmstadt, from which point it was easy going to Frankfurt.

A couple of stories may throw some light on the nature of the two worlds between which I was traveling. In East Germany, whenever I wanted instant coffee I got hot water up front from the locomotive. When I tried this on the western side of the border, I was sent to the waiting room. One was not allowed to drink water from the locomotive. And then this story from Frankfurt: I do not want to describe the layout of the inner city, which was mostly rubble. But I do want to mention one extraordinary initial difficulty I had. I had gone to the Frankfurt city authorities to apply for the usual residence permit— and it was denied to me! Hallstein, then the rector, intervened. It turned out that while I was waiting in the anteroom, I had not given the expected black/white answer to the German secretary, who had asked how it was "over there." For this she had described me to her commander as "a communist." This called for a special trip to the American authorities in Wiesbaden, who stood up for me with strong words based on their own intelligence reports. The Frankfurt commander gave in, and he said with a snarl: "You must have very powerful friends among us."

Starting up in Frankfurt, in the winter of 1947, was troublesome in many ways. The provisions for living were in general very poor. Heating was short, and there was nothing to buy. It was thoroughly a continuation of war conditions. And no doubt this was all planned. On the one hand, the Germans were supposed to get acquainted in their own bodies with the deprivation they had imposed on other peoples, a reversal of Göring's words: "If there's hunger anywhere in Europe, it won't be here." On the other hand, the system was supposed to replenish the supply of goods up to the day of the currency reform, and in this regard it functioned excellently. But the winter was hard. Truly overwhelming were the students. Since the end of the war there had been no philosophy courses given in Frankfurt, and so I had to deal with a large number of students in the auditorium of the university. And there were almost no books. The refurnishing of the philosophical seminar had only just begun. There was a good deal of work to be done, but there were also good helpers to do it. The assistant, Norbert Altwicker, especially proved to be a true gem and rapidly became something of a "den mother" to the seminar. Our parties later achieved a certain fame, and I shall not forget how Theodor Adorno, who had returned to Frankfurt with Max Horkheimer, was pantomimed: On the basis of his extraordinary knowledge and his tendency to provocation, Adorno had always claimed that it was repressive to perform music straight and simply instead of reading notes like books. The metaphor was taken literally. A silent choir, under Altwicker's masterful direction, performed with open mouths and expressive head movements an irresistible, imaginary music.

In Frankfurt I found good friends from Leipzig, such as Karl Reinhardt and Otto Vossler. Nonetheless, the philosophy faculty, although it comprised excellent people, made a very different impression than did the academic bodies in Leipzig, as I remembered them. How sluggishly things moved in Frankfurt! How one got excited and fought over the smallest things! In the end I had to admit to myself that the barrenness of our faculty meetings fundamentally reflected the normal order and that the beautiful solidarity of our Leipzig meetings bore witness to the pressure we were under there. I held back completely because I very quickly noted what counted here: One lived in the illusion of a kind of innocent power, dreamed up out of the growth of academic independence from the state. And one cultivated a mistrust against those who had come over from the East who knew a little more about the social problems of the postwar period than was visible from a western vantage point.

There were meager times before and after the currency reform in which every bit of attention had to be given to economic problems. Moreover, the state of Hesse was newly established and without tradition, and the creation of the Wiesbaden ministry was a difficult undertaking. Administration lives on the principle of doing things the way they have always been done. But where was the "always" in Hesse? Aside from exercising a little influence in favor of the Socialist party (SPD), the Department of Higher Education behaved correctly; but this correctness peaked in a crippling craze for objectivization. They collected innumerable pages of material for every decision to hire a new professor—the more they had, the better, the more just. For those who appreciate academic ways, this was a great amusement, but in the end it proved to be a preview of later reforms—for example, "objective" exams, on the basis of which the last vestiges of human adaptability and the conducting of genuine verbal exams (the only proper type of scholarly exam) were offered up to the new robot ideal. As everyone knows, the reconstruction of the destroyed cities and federal states proceeded at an outrageous tempo after the currency reform. But this benefited the "cultural" sectors least of all, and so the representatives of culture here and there kept about them something of a ghostly air.

I had been asked by the city of Frankfurt to serve on the award committee for the Goethe prize. There I supported Albert Einstein, because had Goethe lived in our times he would have seen more of himself in this great physicist than in a major writer such as Thomas Mann, to whom the prize was eventually given (and no doubt with good reason). The bicentennial of Goethe's birth in 1949 was celebrated in Frankfurt in manifold ways, and the task fell to me to organize an appropriate congress. Under the theme "Goethe and Science" we were brought together for the first time since the war with a large number of foreign scholars—Swiss, French, Dutch, and others. I functioned as president of the congress, which Franz Böhm, as rector of the university, opened with a very polished speech. The congress report, which was published a year later, did not mention my name because I had by that time moved from Frankfurt to Heidelberg.

I made a few other contributions to the Goethe year, especially a small piece on Goethe entitled "Vom geistigen Lauf des Menschen." It was tastefully and lovingly adorned by Helmut Küpper, but in that year's flood of books not much notice was taken of it. Only in the second volume of my *Kleine Schriften* did it gain recognition, especially in relation to the theme "Der Zauberflöte anderer Teil." The work was based on Leipzig weekend diversions from my period as rector, and it still seems to me to give the first true interpretation of this small Goethe piece.

Serious personal work was not even to be considered in the demanding circumstances of those times. What counted was satisfying the needs of the moment. So for Klostermann I brought out Dilthey's *Leitfaden zur Geschichte der Philosophie*, with a supplement on twentieth-century philosophy in which I sought to work fully in Dilthey's style of thinking and thereby discovered that such strict historical reporting is terribly easy. Klostermann had given me and my family shelter during the period before we could move into my modest apartment. A student text came out as well at this time, the twelfth book of Aristotle's *Metaphysics* with translation and a brief commentary. It was not really representative of my decades-long Aristotle studies, on which it was based, but it proved to be a useful text, and after a printing by Klostermann of 5,000 copies it was produced in a new and more expensive edition. I mention this only as a symptom. Most certainly it bears witness to the restorative tendencies of our culture at this time and especially to the influence of the Catholic Church, but it is also an example of the effectiveness of modest prices on the sale of student books. From long association with the publishing committee of the German Research Society, I am familiar with and thoroughly agree to the principle that the policy of subsidizing the production of books must not entail interference with their price structure. Nevertheless, this example poses the question whether ways should not be found to subsidize the *consumption* of books. This would counter the corrupting tendency of the present time of offering inexpensive student editions consisting of selections, readers, etc. Could we not find a way to publish bilingual texts or at least unshortened classical texts? The Scholarly Book Society in Darmstadt was the first consumer organization to take this route. Meanwhile paperback book production has jumped into the gap, as have the reprint companies; these companies have affected the price structure only indirectly but have nonetheless performed a function by introducing general improvement in photographic printing techniques. Yet it is difficult to register all of these technical advances on the positive side as progress in popular education and the spreading of book culture. Doubtless xerographic reproduction is something of the uttermost practicality, but Goethe was right when he said that "what one has in black on white [i.e., on paper] one takes home with a false sense of security," and the present generation of students illustrates very well the false magic of such an inclination. Xerographic copies are as unfavorable to reading as are radio and television. This is the experience that we have had with it.

During this period I had to organize in Marburg the vacation courses of the Hessian universities, and I could not do this without taking a deep interest in my alma mater. This was a difficult venture immediately after the currency reform, but it led to some good meetings, among which was a thought-provoking public discussion with Paul Tillich based on Heidegger's recently published *Letter on Humanism*. The suggestion had come from a small group of students, and Tillich and I were fully surprised when at the appointed hour we found the large auditorium of Marburg University filled to the last seat and everyone waiting expectantly for us. As would soon become clear, it was a sensation for a Marburg sworn to Kant—this was the work of Julius Ebbinghaus and Klaus Reich—that Heidegger would be taken seriously in these holy halls. In a relaxed improvisation, Tillich maintained a very respectful attitude toward Heidegger and directed his comments to the relations between his work and the Franciscan metaphysics of light. My own introduction and participation in the discussion won for me a number of my later Frankfurt and Heidelberg students.

The Marburg of the postwar years was already somewhat known to me through the so-called Marburg Talks, to which I once went as the Leipzig rector. These were discussions about academic politics, and they had had an astounding response. As far as their correspondence to reality was concerned, they certainly did not merit this. Their function in this period when Germany was divided into zones, each of which was developing along its own lines (evident above all, of course, in the East Zone), was to maintain an exchange of ideas in reference to common problems. The arrangement was soon outmoded, as were most things from this transition period.

Similar considerations applied to the core curriculum—a notion, taken over from the Americans, that had proved a success against the departmentalization of the universities, especially in Chicago. It was not fully grasped that in Germany there were, even then, philosophy faculties and also the so-called *Publica*—"public" lectures, without cost—a nice old arrangement in consequence of which one was obliged as *Ordinarius* to present for listeners from all faculties a one-hour lecture on something of interest from one's own discipline. Today, in the face of the fragmentation of the giant universities, such interdisciplinary efforts have a new significance. My own experience tells me, however, that they should be undertaken as interdisciplinary work circles rather than as mass lectures.

Once in Frankfurt, also because of an American initiative, I had occasion to speak to the question: "How does the German professor conceive his educational task?" My answer was unambiguous: He doesn't, because he doesn't have one. He comes on much too late for that. Home and lower schools possess the continuity necessary for this relationship of educators to young people. There one may rightly speak of an educational influence. A professor who sees his students for a few hours a week and at best comes into contact with them during office hours can mean something similar only for his closest students and co-workers, and above all for the next generation of researchers.

Also falling into my Frankfurt period was the return of the "old Frankfurters," Horkheimer and Adorno. They rebuilt the Institute for

Social Research and initiated a new tradition of the "Frankfurt School," whose representative would later be Jürgen Habermas.

Between my activities in Frankfurt and my beginning in Heidelberg there was an unexpected excursion into the Southern hemisphere. The occasion was Argentina's First National Congress for Philosophy, which Juan Perón outfitted with pomp. For German professors this was a first postwar excursion into the world and also a first contact with old friends who had come to live "over there." I published a small newspaper report about my impressions of the trip, and I would like to quote from that document here. A trip back into the past casts new light on the present. In Argentina everyone lived in expectation of the outbreak of the Third World War and in an amazing certainty of being able to survive once again.

In the spring of 1949, eight German professors and numerous foreign colleagues took part in the First National Congress for Philosophy in the Argentine city of Mendoza. A modern trip taken in an airplane offers little in the way of unusual adventure or varying experience. It is comparable, rather, to the fabulous tales of the thousand and one nights: The next morning one rubs one's eyes, astounded and startled to find oneself in a very different place than that of the night before. The adventure of modern travel consists in the speed with which one changes places. One must first slowly find one's way and grasp where one actually is. But a philosophical congress at which are gathered one hundred and fifty professors from all over the world does not ease the orientation problems. The learned of all nations doubtless stand in a close relation to each other, nearer to each other than to members of other professions in their home countries. But their coming together creates a kind of Babylonian never-never land. And the country into which the magic means of modern technology had so rapidly deposited us—it, too, was of an unusual sort.

This is because Argentina is for Europeans very nearly *terra incognita*. The trip there is not only 12,000 kilometers from Europe, it is also a trip into the European past. Argentina's industrial development and associated social changes have now assumed an accelerated tempo. Nonetheless, it is a country that was very much unaffected by the two world wars. Argentina's progressive spirits may have shared the experiences of the rest of the world, but they comprise a thin layer in a colonial-agricultural people that is entering the whirl of the twentieth century only slowly.

Mendoza is a prosperous, sprawling city, built of one-story buildings because of the danger of earthquakes. Streets and plazas are fully symmetrical, as if they had been laid out on a chessboard, and the city is encircled by endless vineyards, to which the towering curtain of the Cordillera Mountains forms a backdrop. It was an artful landscape. The rain shadow of the Cordilleras created a desertlike scenery, from which the fruitful fields of Mendoza are wrested by artificial means. An irrigation reservoir, built by the Jesuits and fed by the melting snows of the mountains, had transformed the landscape into a blooming garden paradise, in which we now gathered for a philosophical convocation.

For the German participants in this congress it was moving to observe how strong and enduring the influence of German thinking on the thinking of other peoples still is. Argentina is a country within the Latin cultural sphere, not at all American but rather Mediterranean in spirit, deeply rooted in the traditions of Catholic thinking. Simultaneously, however, and to a surprising degree, modern German thinking in its most radical and daring form has gained entry into Argentina. The development of our philosophical thinking was known in detail there. Thus the actual theme of the congress was the quarrel between Christian thinking of the Thomist tradition and that variety of thinking determined by modern German philosophy. At this congress, Husserl and Heidegger were quoted no less often than Aquinas. Metaphysics was the dominating theme; the resolute positivism and pragmatism that are directed against all metaphysics found no followers here, since the congress was attended by only a few Anglo-Saxon philosophers. Although the two opposing fronts were called Thomism and existentialism, the latter was actually a collective designation for everything "modern," meaning thinking that had departed from the dogmatic context of the Church. Authentic existentialism, as the French and above all Sartre have developed it in the last ten years, played only a secondary role at the congress.

The decisive questions were: What is the relation of traditional Christian thinking to this modern way of thinking? Can Thomism, with its traditional methods, grasp the existential riddle that modern thinking has taken hold of with such tremendous earnestness? Or must the attitude of modern to traditional thinking be unconditionally antithetical, in much the way that a methodical atheism (which knows nothing of holy truths) conducts itself toward revealed religion? Both possibilities found representation here, and indeed from quite different sides. In this way the problem came to a head in the unspoken question: Is there a natural theology, or is all knowledge of God necessarily keyed to revelation and all natural knowing by definition without God? Is modern thinking right when it demands a metaphysics of finitude in opposition to the metaphysics of the infinite God or the infinite spirit?

The representatives of German philosophy found an open ear not only among Argentinians; they took it as a special benefit that they could now break the ice with representatives of Italian philosophy and also with the philosophers of other foreign countries. But when I am asked what was the deepest impression that I took from the philosophy congress, I answer that it was the return trip from Mendoza to Buenos Aires. We traveled sixteen hours in a luxury train over a stretch that was as straight as an arrow and went through a vast emptiness at high speeds with only five short stops. When evening came and the sun sank low over the pampas, for a short moment filling the evening sky with a powerful play of colors until finally dark receded into night, with a strange necessity the thinking consciousness felt itself confronted by itself. Are we really what we had so recently been presenting and testing in philosophical exchanges? What are we at all in the face of this strange, indifferent, grand power of nature? The boundless breadth of this land we were crossing in our racing train was of a truly superior reality. One had only to imagine what would happen on this free stretch if the train stopped and a passenger were to step out and erroneously stay behind. In this loneliness he would find no human accommodation. Perhaps what modern thinking teaches is true: Man is nothing but his own possibilities. But what are his possibilities?

After the congress we remained for a period in Buenos Aires as guests of the Argentine government. Some of us gave talks at the university. The hospitality of the Argentinians, both official and private, was of an overflowing generosity. Europe is not a declining part of the earth as long as its culture attracts the noblest of spirits on the other side of the ocean. We returned home in the consciousness that what concerns humanity is everywhere the same, and everywhere the same life is being lived.

Karl Reinhardt

It is not easy to give a picture of Karl Reinhardt that tells what he was like as a teacher and researcher and how he especially belonged to the Frankfurt University. There was something inimitable and un-graspable about him. Hidden behind the harsh strictness of his sarcasm and his lightning scorn was the guild strictness of philological schol-arship, which he always upheld, and the professional exactitude of his parents' home in Frankfurt, where he had been educated. How should his form be presented in words to those who never knew him? How should it become once again recognizable to those who did know him and who honored him? To his essence belonged inaccessible reserve just as much as the beaming magic of his presence. Those who as students heard his lectures will know how helpless his ap-pearance at the podium made one feel. What one experienced was an ongoing improvisation, a troubled, halting speaking, dumbness, silence, and the sudden divining of a perfected mimesis, whether it presented a scene from Aristophanes or a gesture of Socrates. Everyone knows that his lecture preparation was not a fitting in of completed manuscripts or their repetition in the cycle of years. Rather, he was concerned to give the author he was dealing with a new reading from first to last word and to take what he found in the new reading, as it came up, and to pass it on. When I look back on my own experience as an admiring young student and later as a respectful colleague, a similar image presents itself to me—the way he avoided matter-of-fact conversation, the way he held back from the unambiguity of judgment and the taking of positions, obviously uncomfortable with their presumptiveness, and the way he would suddenly light up in mimetic presence. Even my last meeting with him, as he lay near death in great suffering, was suddenly filled with that kind of mimetic presence as he sketched out with a last beam of enjoyment comic observations from many occasions.

Let me describe the state of the discipline whose brilliant representative he became so that I may then ask what it was that made him unique and inimitable among his contemporaries. He belonged to the great Berlin School of classical scholarship, and he himself always admired the tremendous measure of knowledge and ability associated with the name of his teacher, Ulrich von Wilamowitz-Moellendorff. Wilamowitz represented the high point of the historical classical scholarship that had grown out of the demolition of humanistic classicism and its permeation with historical meaning. His encyclopedic spirit pushed classical scholarly research forward on all sides and simultaneously stamped it with his individual, somewhat unkempt historicism. Then, with the change in epochs represented by the First World War, the generation to which Karl Reinhardt belonged was confronted with a new task: from the broad and nearly global scattering of historical-philological research, to seek a return to those authors upon whose validity the very magic of the classical world depended. The task, however, faced the constant danger of a regression into previously established forms of classicist thinking. Wilamowitz's distinguished successor in Berlin, Werner Jaeger, did not remain untouched by this danger. Jaeger's confident historical vision into all areas of research, matured into an admirable body of knowledge, was threatened by regression into a programmatic humanism characterized by a bland educational reality. The central theme of Jaeger's research, *paideia*, the idea and first embodiment of which dominated the period of Greek Sophism, implied a systematic mediation of the classical tradition with the programmatically postulated spiritual "presence" of the Greeks. But this did not harmonize with the sense of Karl Reinhardt's work. However much he sought and ventured to meet once again with the great authors of the ancient world, with Heraclitus and Plato, Sophocles and Homer, he did not want to be a programmatic humanist. What saved him from a regression into classicist educational values in his coming to terms with classical authors was the unique immediacy with which he raised them to the actuality of thought and the presence of the image.

From where did he derive this immediacy? Wherein lay the special quality by which thought and picture became a pure presence for him? It lay in the peculiar character of historical scholarship, in which the cognition of its object entails and presupposes as an ultimate hermeneutic principle a recognition of the self. Therefore, starting from the objectification in scholarly cognition that stands before us in Reinhardt's work, it must be possible to read backwards, as it were, and from this known thing to know and make present the person who recognized himself in this. To begin with, there is style, and style is the man. What a peculiar German Reinhardt wrote. It was a German free of the dust of the school but also without the moderation of an Alexandrian historical justice. The stormy cascades of words with which he expressed himself were of a tense dynamism and suggestivity, as is only the case with the true artists of language who know how to win something from it. The accumulating, the mounting, the contrasting, the flood of exclamations, the flood of questions that poured forth made him the most individualistic writer among the scholars of his time. God help us if ever a computer should count up the exclamation points and question marks at the ends of his sentences—the number would be astronomical. What did this expressive bent of his style express? On what was it based? Precisely this: that the interpreter at every moment was aware of the inner distance that separated him from his objects. The insufficiency of every word, its modesty in the face of the concrete fullness of what might be said, allows a growth as well as a breaking off of speech to be generated within itself. Beyond this there was an unusual, knowledgeable power of imagining the possible at work in Reinhardt's interpretation. Its visible expression was his ability to question. Questions raise possibilities to consciousness. The unique presence that his interpreting work won was based on his work in questioning and on his consciousness of the ambiguity of every answer.

Let me now try to read his work as the mirror reflection of his essence. With decisive clarity, Reinhardt's books are oriented to the immediacy of the thought and the immediacy of the picture. He began with interpretations of philosophers, only to turn his attention in his mature years to the pictorial in poetry. His first important works dealt with the pre-Socratics. What he did in his Parmenides book was truly path-breaking. Only today are we beginning to grasp how the inner affinity of Parmenides and Heraclitus uncovered by Reinhardt opened up a whole dimension of questions. Because of him, research on and philosophical interpretation of the pre-Socratics have gained a new life. It was reserved to him, the philologist, to scatter the fog of religious history and among the early thinkers to recognize the Greeks as the great definers of the world who determined the shape of Western civilization. His second great contribution to the history of Greek philosophy, his Poseidonios book, also received its accent from this ability to ask questions. What led him to this theme was in the final analysis the vital question of all humanistic research—that of the transition from Greek antiquity into the Christian age to which we belong. In Poseidonios Reinhardt sought the traces of this transition. "In the unified form of the world there occurs a leap, only a small tear at first, hardly noticed, then there comes a flowing in, an undercurrent. . . ." Reinhardt sought to show that Poseidonios did not stand on the other side of this border but was the last of the circle of great explicators of the world that had begun with the Ionians. What determined his inner form and distinguished him from all late echoes was the new concept of force, which for one last time was able to bind together the cosmos of the Greek thinking before its concepts changed their reference points and became pointers to the transcendent.

The last book that Reinhardt devoted to a philosopher focused on Plato's myths. Here for the first time he comes into his own and becomes accessible to the reader of the mirror writing of his work. What his Plato book makes clear is his sense of irony. Irony for him is not an occasional appearance or a physiological peculiarity of the Socrates figure of the dialogues. It is rather the universal means of Plato's written work. Incomparable are the pages in which Reinhardt describes Attic society and the power of ridicule in it. It is as if he were describing something from himself, something of the unforgettable attitude that characterized the master of the hospitable Reinhardt house on Hans Sachs Street, in Gohlis, in the Niedenau, and finally on Schumann Street. There is the unity of an awkward big bear with a loving care when Reinhardt writes: "A member of society possessed by pure seriousness is deplorable." More to the point is the loud and clear self-expression that he, coming at it from the outside, recognized in the medium of irony in which Plato immerses all things. Not only in respect to Plato does irony demand "that one have access to more than one level of the soul." And it is key for understanding the equivocal attitude, evasive to the point of being indeterminate, that Karl Reinhardt identified in scholars as in all human beings when he said of the true ironist that he sought "to get through to himself, either by going through himself or by going through others." What he recognizes in Plato is a reflection of himself: the irony of dealing with the self and, arising from it, the irony of exuberance. The mimetic presence that makes Plato's word and work so unforgettable emerges from this doubled and tense irony. At the same time Reinhardt made a genuine contribution to the field of Plato research that should not be forgotten. In the foreground of Plato interpretation it places what he calls the categories of the soul as the origin of *logos* as well as of *mythos*. He thereby displaces the direction of understanding, which since Aristotle and Hegel seeks to find a way to the doctrine of the soul from the doctrine of ideas, insofar as he orients himself from the perspective of the "soul" and thereby makes experienceable the ironic medium in which Plato's work comes together as a unified art. In this way, Reinhardt drew from the immediacy of his knowledge of irony and gave back to the Platonic achievement of thought the ambiguity that distinguishes it.

The second phase of Reinhardt's creative work is dominated by the interpretation of poetry. But only apparently does the philosophical theme thereby leave its beginnings. Poetry is for Reinhardt picture and scene. The dubious reality of theater gives him his philosophical theme, initially deciphered in the didactic poem of Parmenides—the theme of being and semblance and of the inescapable entanglement of human beings. This is the theme that he acknowledges in Sophocles and that his Sophocles book makes into such a tremendous achievement that all memory of classical drabness is banned. Just as Reinhardt brings to bear the present of world literature in each confrontation with Greek literature, so the confrontation with Sophocles was for him a bursting through into metaphysical depths. He knew about the enduring formation of Western theater and about its shaping of human beings through the tragedies of Euripides. Like all members of his generation he was not unmoved by the magic of the archaic beginnings that were dissolved in the age of psychology but lent a new presence to the drama of Aeschylus. But just how the tragedy of Sophocles draws beyond all the charms of the late or the early into the depth in which human existence has its permanent yet fragile home—this he recognized and showed especially in his interpretation of the Oedipus dramas. Just as Sophocles brings to the action of the drama a breathtaking tension, in that he makes "the riddle that Oedipus will dissolve the very thing that draws Oedipus in," so, too, the terrible and unique fate of Oedipus is made into a picture of the human condition. "The demonic, continual reaching beyond, without knowing, out of the realm of semblances into the realm of the true"—it is not the singular tragedy of the blinded king that is disclosed here but the human condition itself. "Here is man entangled in being and semblance." The way in which semblance and being swallow each other up, the way in which the grasp after the unambiguousness of truth shows itself to be a human presumption—this is as much present in the tragedy of Oedipus as it is in the drama of thinking that has been called philosophy since its Greek beginnings. "The ascription of truth to semblance or to the night"—this is indissolubly bound up with the human condition, as Reinhardt expressly says.

When Reinhardt considers Aeschylus, it is not simply the case of a festive master of liturgy being rediscovered by a century grown weary of psychology. Reinhardt never loses sight of the scene, of the mimetic presence and its means. His Aeschylus book has a subtitle rich in contrast: *The Theologian and the Director.* Indeed, the eye for scenic technique in Aeschylean theater is the concern of one who knows about possibilities. The interpreter recognizes himself in his object. For this indeed locates the director as well as the interpreter, and is not the director the first interpreter of a dramatic poem? Is he not the person who sees one among several possibilities, selects it as the convincing one, and raises it to a unique and decisive presence? Even in the title of the Aeschylus book one reads the disguised signature of its author.

And on top of this there was Homer, whom the industry of the humanists and the layered school dust of centuries have made the most worn-out of classical authors. Even he now wins a place in the immediate presence of the scene. Reinhardt understands how to resolve situations out of the epic endlessness of the hexameter and to bring to light the reference points that offer a human recognition. The delayed return of Odysseus, the ever mounting tension until the liberating solution—what correspondences there are between epic composition and human characterization in this poem! And on top of this the *Iliad*, to which Reinhardt devoted years of study, the fruits of which were formed into a major study by Uvo Hölscher out of the papers Reinhardt left behind. Reinhardt showed convincingly that the incomparable charm of this epic is the one that schoolchildren sense when one of them takes sides for Achilles the victorious and doomed and another for Hector the brilliant and conquered. It is the balance of sympathy, which the primal form of epic genius applies to the heroes in combat at the Trojan walls, that keeps us in suspense and continues on right into the Olympian world of the gods, up to the highest point.

When one seeks to read the mirror writing of Reinhardt's work, who can fail to recognize in the irresolute Zeus the traces of that which with unerring self-assurance has deciphered in the balance of sympathy the law of composition of the *Iliad?* And as if the being and semblance of the stage were at work even in the goings-on of the Olympian gods, Reinhardt appreciated the mock vehemence of divine battles as events in which there was fighting without danger of death and intrigue without the deadliness of hate. It is not a giant step from this insight into the "sublime unearnestness" of the Olympian gods to the depths of human self-recognition, which Reinhardt's eye for human and dramatic situations had made so sharp and transparent. Perhaps his most personal effort is to be found in his collected papers as a lecture entitled "The Crisis of the Heroes." This is a not fully worked out but charmingly improvised revision of the piece Reinhardt presented at the Darmstadt Academy for Speech and Poetry in 1953. It seems to be a mere literary theme being dealt with before a literary audience, the point of which one can immediately guess: In the poetry of our time, not only has the hero of high pathos become incredible, the very form of epic poetry as well as the unity of action and the coherence of heroes, even if only as bearers of action, seem to have been lost. But the conclusion of the essay is surprising and revealing; it shows modern poetry, in its form of transitions and the dissolution of the conventional, as a shift from a crisis *of* the hero to a crisis *in* the hero himself. Now the oldest appears as the truest: the anxiety of Hector, the rage in Achilles. The crisis in the hero rests on the "burden of self-knowledge," without which the hero would not be a human being.

Karl Reinhardt succeeded in making the classical objects of humanistic veneration as vividly present as they are in Proust, Joyce, Kafka, Nietzsche, and Freud. Otherwise Plato, Sophocles, and Homer would have been condemned to the ever blander didactic ceremoniousness of humanism. Here they are presented not for the exemplary qualities of their heroes but for their humanity. And yet if we want to grasp how Reinhardt represented himself in his knowledge, must we not say that he did so as a humanist? To vary a phrase that he once spoke at a grave site: "He was so very human."

Heidelberg

When I returned to Frankfurt after my several weeks in Argentina, two pieces of news awaited me. First was the death of my friend Oskar Schürer, to whom I had said farewell a few weeks earlier in the Becker Radiation Clinic in Heidelberg. He was already marked for death at that time. The other news was that I had been called to be the successor to Karl Jaspers in Heidelberg. I arrived just in time for Schürer's burial in the Augsburg Cemetery. On behalf of his numerous friends, I dedicated words of thanks to this man who had had a true genius for friendship. Then in a gloomy mood I traveled to Heidelberg for my first contacts. I happened into Stuttgart late in the evening and wanted to stay overnight, but there was not a single bed in the few hotels that were available to the German population. So I went on to Heidelberg, where I arrived after midnight. The same situation. I wandered fruitlessly from door to door. At one point—it was already after two o'clock in the morning—I seemed to have luck. A door opened for some guests to leave, and I hurried up to it happily—but it was a Red Cross pension for women only. I was completely at a loss. One could not stay in the railroad station, an old building in late Biedermeier style, which conferred upon it a near romantic charm. The waiting room was filled with suspicious figures, for, after all, these were the chaotic postwar years in which every trip was like an adventure in some primal world.

What to do? It was a mild May night, and so finally I stretched myself out to sleep on a bench in Bismarck Square, my little suitcase as my pillow. I slept the sleep of the just until at about seven in the

morning I was suddenly shaken by a rough hand. A straightlaced
police officer stood before me and explained that one was not allowed
to sleep here. Order is, after all, something beautiful. Finally I appeased
myself and succeeded in appeasing him, after he had extensively
studied my papers. Anyway, I was already awake, and so I sauntered
slowly through the waking old town, walked past Jaspers's house at
44 Plöck Street, well known to me from earlier visits. I was still feeling
sad at the loss of my friend and depressed by some other things as
I walked to my inauguration at Heidelberg University, where I would
teach for a quarter of a century. In the seminar building I was led to
Jaspers's office, which was adorned with an old sofa on which later,
in numerous meetings of the publishing committee of the German
Research Society, Dr. Springer, Lambert Schneider, Dr. Knecht, and
Dr. Hanser—the representatives of the publishing world—would sit
harmoniously. Then I was shown the seminar library, whose rooms
Jaspers was said never to have entered but which, thanks to Ernst
Hoffmann's learned care, were not at all badly kept.

Jaspers had already been in Basel for more than a year. Nonetheless,
my beginning in Heidelberg was determined by the contrasts in manner
and style of our teaching. I was later told how at the outset persons
from the old Jaspers circle were put off because I so often answered
seminar questions by saying that I did not know. Jaspers's style had
evidently been very different. To all questions that were thrown out
he gave pointed answers, and this was what students missed with me.
But finally one gets accustomed to everything, and so the young people
got used to me and I to them. Only in one point did I remain an
enduring disappointment: I made no attempt to enter into the rage
for Heidegger that was then taking place. I had learned enough with
Heidegger to know that this, too, was mainly "idle talk."

Once, in the second year of my Heidelberg activity, Jaspers came
up from Basel at the invitation of the student body to give lectures
on the theme of "Reason and Unreason." It was my task to greet
him in the name of the rector and the senate. Naturally, the old
auditorium was filled beyond capacity, and there was a certain tension
in the air. Now it so happened that in my words of greeting I mistakenly
kept saying "Leipzig" instead of "Heidelberg"—I had given too many
such greetings as rector of Leipzig University. Finally the calling out
of "Heidelberg" broke through to me, and I could only save myself
by the following turnabout: "But it does not take someone from Leipzig

to tell you people in Heidelberg who Jaspers is." That was met with friendly applause, but it was precisely this that did not seem right to Jaspers. Humor was not his strong point. I hardly ever saw him laugh. He took everything, even himself, very seriously.

In any case, it was not difficult to grow accustomed to Heidelberg. I was given a cordial reception, and old friends like Viktor von Weiz-säcker were there, although all too soon misfortunes forced him into a terrible isolation. The most important and by far the greatest help in settling in that I gratefully received came from the theological society. It rapidly drew me in, and alongside old friends like Günther and Heinrich Bornkamm I found excellent men like Hans von Campenhausen, Gerhard von Rad, Peter Brunner, Wilhelm Schlink, and the Catholic theologian Richard Hauser. In the thick smoke of theological debate that enveloped this growing but only just then unifying faculty, I found my first inner support. Once again I experienced the fact that the *logos* is common to everyone.

The philosophy faculty in this period was not similarly homogenized. There were some older colleagues who had lost their positions in the Third Reich and were now resuming their activities. On the other side, there was the reinstallation of "nominal party members," to whom the occupying powers had to grant permission, less from a weighing of the justice of the case than from momentary need. This created tension and resentment, and worse still were the cases in which formally charged persons simply were not readmitted because the faculty did not stand up for them. In my experience, this was above all the case if those concerned had maintained no real contacts with those who had been forced into involuntary retirement. An understandable standard, but often unjust. Especially in my own discipline, I had trouble putting things in order because it was difficult in the face of this kind of provincial prejudice to get to the bottom of things at all—but once one got there the charges often proved empty.

At that time Heidelberg swarmed with Americans. They filled all the best hotels but generally did not interfere in the life of the city or of the university. Especially those American officers at the university who took an interest in academic life knew their own American high schools too well to be able to take seriously the notion of "re-education" at this level. In the student body of that time, as veterans were slowly fading out, there was an unappeased longing for an independent intellectual and social life, and we professors tried to be helpful in this respect. Some regular circles took shape that consciously tried out new forms of communal student life, thought little of traditional fraternity life, and were keyed to one or another professor. The university leadership supported this. The student fraternities were still not readmitted, and the showing of the colors was also forbidden. But in the end all such efforts at reform shattered on the fact that these spontaneous groups opposed the unreasonable demand for institutionalization and for the admission of newcomers into their circles. If one tried to persuade the older, riper people who still bore the traces of the war experience, who had nothing in common with the "green" boys and girls, that they had to build up traditions and eventually take over the elite-building, protectionist function of the fraternities, they indignantly rejected such "immoral" demands for protectionism. Thus there was little that could be done, and a feeble revival of the old fraternities was not to be held off for long. Often they took on an unwanted traditional form, because once again the fraternity alumni prevailed and had their way. Even the carrying of the colors, restricted to the fraternity house itself and to formal occasions, was reintroduced when it was championed by the Swiss and Catholic fraternities.

These young people had grown up with war and bombs, and the extent to which they had been drained of strength is illustrated by the following story: Once after a seminar session I was together with a large group of students drinking a glass of wine. Just then the sensational news of Truman's decision to dispatch American troops to Korea arrived. In this everyone saw the first act of the next world war, and the general discussion of the young people revolved about the question how one might somehow manage to "become thin," as they put it. This "without me" spirit was their single unifying characteristic and the one connection they had with what was happening in the world.

Anyway, what I found in Heidelberg was a band of passionate young seekers, fully dedicated to philosophical studies. They blended in nicely with a group of earlier Frankfurt students. All of them wanted philosophy and nothing else and very nearly held it against me if I asked about their career plans.

At this time in Baden there was no special section for philosophy (philosophical propaedeutic) in the examination for higher teaching positions. Therefore, whenever anyone intending to study philosophy came to me, I had to ask myself whether this might be my successor. There simply was no other career goal along this way. Thanks to the obliging nature of the registrar's office, I was able to stipulate at the time I took the position that I would not be asked to administer the so-called Philosophicum, the little obligatory tests given to all future teachers. There were sufficent private *Dozenten* who would gladly do this. Thus I was not compelled to deal with large numbers of students in my classes but only with volunteers. (Since then Baden-Württemberg has eliminated the Philosophicum and reintroduced the philosophical propaedeutic as an elective. I had always aspired to this, for now a professor can wait and see how the written part of a student's state exam turns out before committing himself to that student's dissertation plans.) Even so, it was still too much for any one person to come to terms with the large number of students, and only after I had succeeded in winning over Karl Löwith to return to Germany and specifically to Heidelberg could I again to some extent coordinate my classes and my own work.

This is in any case not easy for an academic teacher, and even in those times it demanded a consistent budgeting of personal time, although the number of students and the whole style of the university were not yet comparable with those of today's mass universities. I resolved to work into a book my lectures on art and history, which I had begun in the 1930s and had continued to try to deepen. This was possible only if I held myself as far away as possible from academic politics. And so I resisted the attempt, made immediately after my return to Heidelberg by Gerhard Hess, when he was elected rector, to get me to take over as dean of the Faculty of Philosophy. I withdrew as far as possible.[1] That the completion of the planned book nonetheless claimed many years should not be astonishing. Basically only vacations were available for consistent work. The semesters were much too draining because of the constantly changing lecture materials and, above all, because of the multiplicity of tasks confronting the academic teacher charged with guiding new generations of scholars. During my twenty-five years of teaching in Heidelberg I strove to create an arrangement that served this purpose of guidance, and with it I followed the model Nicolai Hartmann had established for me when I was young. This was the so-called home circle. At most, twelve persons were

---

1. Gadamer later accepted the position. [*tr.*]

invited to participate, and with these twelve I discussed classical philosophical texts once a week for three hours. Sometimes it was an
Aristotle circle, sometimes a Hegel circle. Fichte, Nicholas of Cusa,
and Spinoza also provided focal points that held us together, often for
several semesters. There was no "teacher" among us; it was always
a free exchange, and we all learned a good deal from it.

Another feature that I introduced into the Heidelberg seminar was
that of regular guest lectures. I did this because I wanted to give the
philosophy students an opportunity to get to know other teachers,
and the discussions that followed were good tests for both participants
and listeners. On the whole I believe that the dialogical style of philosophical discussion before a large circle of participants remains meaningful. For this reason I myself have always given introductory courses.
The usual practice of leaving this to assistants seems to me fundamentally mistaken. In his own area of expertise, a budding *Dozent* can
more easily lead others who are already prepared to do research than
he can lead beginners to clarity from the helpless vagueness of their
mostly incomprehensible questions. On the other hand, it is informative
for everyone, and constructive in unexpected ways, to see how popular
ideas predetermine as well as block the questions of philosophy. Also
beneficial from a pedagogical point of view is the attempt to peel out
the real questions from the bumbling attempts of the beginner, and
this is not just beneficial for the individual with whom one is having
the exchange. It can also happen that someone who is only following
the conversation becomes a partner and a questioner in the conversation, just as happens with all of us when we read the Platonic
dialogues.

I had seen much the same style in the young Heidegger and had
sought to follow him in this: No answer is meaningless, but what it
often needs is a long clarification of the possible meaning that stands
behind the answer as a motive. The young Heidegger, as long as he
did not try to put a literary fix on the fundamental shape of his own
art of questioning, understood this masterfully. We noted this very
clearly in Marburg when Heidegger, in the midst of writing *Being and
Time*, suddenly lost the patience and the openness that makes fruitful
discussions possible. The stimulating impression of such exchanges is
due to the fact that even the leader of the conversation cannot envisage
where the attempt at clarification is leading and what in the end will
be left of the antagonistic position. And only when such a conversation

is conducted in public is it a real discussion with real questions and real attempts at answers. My own nature was well suited to such a "dialogical existence," and I attempted to develop this into a teaching style, despite the danger that the attempted clarification of provisional answers sometimes pushes the sought-after goal of the inquiry off into the distance.

One of the first foreign guests to speak in the seminar was Jean Hyppolite—impressive because of his commitment but incomprehensible because of his poor German pronunciation. This excellent translator of Hegel estranged the German language beyond recognition. What remains of his visit in my memory is that I had to conduct a radio conversation with him. A French intellectual in Germany in 1950 was still a sensation. It said something about the political situation in France at this time that for the "political" conversation we were to hold, Hyppolite insisted that the word "Europe" not be used. For intellectuals of the French Left at that time, this was a taboo; they would have compromised themselves as "imperialists" in the eyes of the French communists if they evinced even a subdued belief in "Europe."

Another among the initial guests was Oscar Becker, a former student of Husserl and Heidegger who at this time was not allowed to teach in Bonn, not because he had been a Nazi or even a party member but because of his well-known freethinking and his racial theory, which was thoroughly free of anti-Semitic intentions. I had great respect for him, above all because of his studies in the history of mathematics but on the whole because of his profound learning. His presentation on this occasion was certainly not compelling: He sought to locate mathematics and psychoanalysis beyond the historical-interpretive dimension as a "para-existence" and then to program a meta-existence that united the two. I was not convinced. But without doubt he did not deserve this proscription. His later return to teaching in Bonn, which I helped bring about by putting him in the number one position on the list for the other Heidelberg chair, was an important moment in the development of a new philosophical generation. Many who were then students in Bonn—such as Karl-Otto Apel, Jürgen Habermas, Karl-Heinz Ilting, Otto Pöggeler, and Wilhelm Schmitz—have convinced me of this. Becker was of a thoroughly tender, even fearful nature. As we awaited him at the seminar table, the stairway of our small "genius" barracks at 40 Ufer Street exploded in an ear-splitting noise.

A usually fearful small dog from one of the other professorial apartments in the house had discovered his lion's heart upon catching sight of Oscar Becker and was preventing our guest from climbing the stairs.

From the large list of those who were guests in this seminar over the years I shall limit myself here to discussing those few who have since passed on; and so I would like to add only two names: Richard Kroner and Theodor Adorno. Kroner, who had had to leave Germany in the 1930s, now returned as a visitor at my invitation. I believe that his paper was on *Hamlet*. This fine, sensitive, and tender man, with whom I had been friends since my Freiburg period, had the effect of a being from another world. This is not to say that he seemed Americanized. On the contrary, in a way that is difficult to describe, his presentation, whose moral and spiritual earnestness was apparent, was like a voice from the past. Certainly he had in the meantime become an old man, but it was not this. It was rather that he was still surrounded by the aura of the educated German bourgeoisie. This was his origin, and despite decades of exile and despite the destruction of the old German cultural tradition, he movingly and strangely embodied it like a late witness.

Adorno's visit came later. He was already nearly a legend. For his presentation he read a tormented but well-styled text that deviated a bit too much from what we were used to in our seminar. He and I presented extreme contrasts in style, appearance, and behavior. Nonetheless, I think back warmly on this visit. My polite and friendly direction of the session sat so well with him that afterwards he very nearly thawed. Years later, when his *Negative Dialectics* was published, at the urging of my students I resolved to take a detailed position on it. Occasionally during my reading of the book, I had noted to my students how curiously the attempted construction and critique of Hegel converged with the line of thought of Heidegger—except that the adherents of the Frankfurt School fall victim to a curious blindness whenever they hear the magic word "ontological." They then fail to see where they really are. I wanted to put this idea forth in hopes of producing a fruitful discussion. And so I stood in the railroad station at the beginning of a vacation trip, the book in my luggage, when my student Reiner Wiehl happened by and told me that the radio had just announced Adorno's death. I was a little too late.

In 1953 Karl Löwith came back to Germany from the United States and became my Heidelberg colleague, as he had been my Marburg colleague before 1933. Here, too, there was not exactly philosophical harmony. Löwith was, as ever, a person committed to his singularity. Ripened after all those years in Japan and the United States, he was certain of his ability and well aware of his publishing successes, which were not meager. Yet philosophy and Heidegger still provoked him to the point of bitter protest, and this protest was enhanced when after the war Heidegger rode a second wave—much like his global success of the late 1920s and despite official proscription—and elicited an astounding response among academic youth. At this time Löwith wrote a sharp polemical pamphlet called "Thinker in Dark Times" but then slowly, as the Heidegger wave subsided, found a calm and worthy relation to his onetime teacher and friend.

When Löwith's opposition to Heidegger was at its high point, he and I teamed up to give a seminar on Heidegger's "On the Essence of Truth." We pulled eagerly in our opposed directions, and this resulted in more than a little tension. Löwith's chief argument that nothing is to be made of "Being" is certainly as unacceptable to me today as it was then. This argument was the untranslatability of Heidegger's conception into other languages. If this were correct, then nothing is to be made of any philosophy that breaks with familiar tradition, not just Heidegger and "Being." Even then I held up to him that it had taken a hundred years to create a halfway understandable English translation of Hegel. Thus Heidegger still had time. New attempts to think often do not come through in their own language and meet with rejection—until gradually much that is strange seems natural and much that is natural seems strange. An example: With good intentions, Eduard Spranger once said of the manuscript of *Being and Time* that there was nothing new in it if one could manage to disregard the willful language! Löwith interpreted the matter differently. He had discovered the young Heidegger for himself and had not mistaken the status of *Being and Time*. But "the turn" and the talk about the Being that was not the Being of beings—this he took to be mythology or pseudo-poetry. But it is not mythology and not poetry but rather thinking, even if the poetic similes and the poetic attempts stemming from the expressive need of novel thinking often present confusing evidence. I have attempted in my own manner to deal with Heidegger's thinking, but that does not belong here.

The reconstruction of Heidelberg University, which was extensively damaged at the end of the Third Reich, even though it was spared bombing, proved to be very troublesome. Economic reconstruction commanded all our attention. The means for schools and universities were very modest, and to that were added endless administrative difficulties originating in the interpretation of legal directives with special regard to the universities. One of these involved the problem of denazification. Here there was an unhappy mixture of attempted political justice and technical necessity. Many of the "accused" had been let go very early, others had to wait a long time, and all of this was to a large extent a matter of chance. Not exactly the conditions for a good climate. A second difficulty originated in the peculiarly narrow application of legal directives in favor of the inclusion of refugees. Of itself this was a real achievement of the politics of the first years—I mean that the inclusion and recruitment of those who had come from the East was legally enforced. It was left to the Swabians, however, to interpret the legal requirement to mean that for every professor who was supposed to be hired, they claimed a "credit," and this amounted to the simultaneous hiring of a refugee professor. Of course this was absurd. As if the fate of having been made a refugee had been divided up in a way corresponding to the scientific and pedagogic needs of West German universities. In other German states the administration helped itself out to some extent in that they adapted the legal requirement to the total personnel pool. Thus, for every university professor sought and hired, they hired a refugee bathhouse keeper or janitor as satisfaction for the credit requirement. The exacting Swabians thought differently, and so they brought it about that of the eighty teaching positions open in Heidelberg in 1954, twenty-one remained unoccupied because the "credit" requirement was not satisfied. At this precarious moment when everything had come to a grinding halt, I as dean of the Philosophy Faculty made a public appeal. I wrote a newspaper article—naturally without asking my colleagues, who of course would have uttered a thousand reservations. It had the title "The University of Heidelberg in the Chains of the Bureaucracy." In it I split responsibility for the untenable situation carefully between the federal and state authorities. The article was successful. The news magazine *Spiegel* picked up on it, a downcast photo of me illustrated the whole mess, and the Swabian government averted a continuation of this press campaign by filling the twenty-one positions, some of which had lain on Stuttgart desks for years. Presumably this was done only after they had found the necessary number of bathhouse keepers.

In this way the rebuilding of our faculty succeeded, and of course it was a proper *Ordinarius* faculty, consisting of from twenty to thirty full professors. There were no less than thirteen new positions.

This was a body fit for work, and as far as I can make out, the work it did wasn't bad. Admittedly the room for play was much too circumscribed due to all-too-narrow financial politics. And I am also not claiming that this faculty on the whole showed great foresight or breadth, as was the case in other places. For there was no attempt to make timely preparations to meet the demands that coming developments would make on teaching. Only holes were plugged, sometimes in a fortunate manner. One should nonetheless concede to Heidelberg and to the universities as a whole that even when these self-administering bodies showed a breadth of vision, they regularly failed because politicians and administrators themselves did not have enough breadth of vision. Nonetheless, it is still more natural for researchers to fail in taking the correct measure of future developments than for politicians who are put in office for that purpose. On the whole it seems to me that Bertolt Brecht got it right for all concerned when he said that "For this life man is not cunning enough."

It would not be right for me to report here on the successes and failures of my Heidelberg teaching activity. In the course of years children become people. Hardly one of my students simply followed in my footsteps, and it is not my way to judge the new impulses that developed from the old stimuli I gave them. So I shall say only generally that Heidelberg as a place of philosophical education achieved a reputation in the course of the years. It gives me satisfaction to know that after Heidegger stopped teaching, Freiburg lost its reputation. That many foreigners spent their time above all in the Heidelberg seminar and later presented what they had learned there in their home countries—this belongs to the most pleasant of confirmations that come to aging scholars when they go abroad. In many a place there is a true student of whom one was hardly aware. This experience was brought home to me especially in America when, after I had become emeritus, for the first time I dared to use my stuttering English. Similarly with Spanish, Italian, and Greek students and with the countries immediately bordering on us, a lively exchange has existed for a long time. The years of national cultural provincialism are drawing slowly to a close.

In my first years at Heidelberg, I avoided as far as possible all administrative assignments and university politics. I went to no conventions or meetings, and only seldom did I give a paper elsewhere. To give such papers has now become much more usual, and it is certainly defensible that people put their ideas up for discussions outside of their own lecture halls. There the echo effect is so stunningly strong that for the most part one's own words bounce back in a confirming manner. But it must be admitted that each paper one commits oneself to give during an ongoing semester weakens the intensity of one's teaching activity. There should be no illusions about that.

Above all, however, only with the utmost reserve and discipline is it possible to bring one's own scholarly research, as it develops in the context of teaching, to a ripe literary success. *Nonum prematur in annum* — this old principle, that all good things take nine years to ripen, fulfilled itself literally in my own attempt to work out the principles of a philosophical hermeneutics. Repeatedly the new semester would force me to break off work that had gotten into gear during the vacation, although one could perhaps continue working for a few weeks into the semester. When vacations and work time came round again, the problem arose in reverse: Taking up work again was not easy because one was held up reading papers that had accumulated during the semester. How mature publications are supposed to come about with the administrative and pedagogical demands that are made on today's young researchers is a complete mystery to me. Sabbatical semesters such as now exist (but did not in my time) still do not provide for continuity over the years, and that is the important thing.

The integration of my studies of philosophical hermeneutics, which finally took shape in 1959 under the title *Truth and Method*, ended a slow, often broken process of growth. Studies of aesthetics, of the history of hermeneutics, and of the philosophy of history in emulation of Dilthey, Husserl, and Heidegger were united in the end in a philosophical giving of accounts that was not intended to be a narrow construction but, rather, gained its credentials from the broad areas of hermeneutical experience. When the book finally appeared, it was not at all certain to me that it had come at the right time. The "second Romantic age," which had come along with the industrialization, brueaucratization, and rationalization of the world in the first half of our century, manifestly seemed to be coming to its end. A new, third wave of Enlightenment was on the move. Would the word that had been spoken by the great metaphysical tradition of the West and that was still audible throughout the "historical" century, the nineteenth, in the end fall on deaf ears? My hermeneutical attempt, which recalled this tradition, simultaneously sought to go beyond the bourgeoisie's blind faith in education, where this tradition survived, and to bring it back to its original powers. But it might well have seemed alien to a youthful mode of thinking driven by a critical will to emancipate.

That is how it probably was and so it certainly is. Nonetheless, historical movements of the mind are always ambidextrous, and so therefore philosophical hermeneutics could become a force in the present and remain so precisely because people believed themselves to be liberated from every tradition, or at least strive to be.

In any case, my hermeneutic effort began to find increasing interest. At the "baptism" of this book I had banned the word "hermeneutics" to the subtitle on the advice of the publisher, but when the first volume of my *Kleine Schriften* appeared in 1964, the advice of my publisher was now to bring the word into the title. Meanwhile, hermeneutics has become a fashionable term, but this means that it is mostly used as a new hat for old things, especially for a "hermeneutic method" that is not at all new, or even for the nonmethod of divination and enthusiasm, which is as old as the unrequited love for philosophy itself.

But this is not the place to speak about my own philosophical contribution. I mention this only to establish why I appeared more in public in the 1960s and also published a large number of smaller writings, partly intended to supplement the book. After I had concluded this large work and put it behind me, every other task seemed easy. Since then only the return to and completion of my studies of ancient philosophy, which had been piling up for decades, has kept me working and caused me to publish a growing series of small monographs. And in just this way, my studies of poetics wait for a comprehensive working out.

In this context I developed two discussion groups. One was a study circle on the history of concepts, which was supported by a "senate commission" of the German Research Society. It met yearly until finally this became tiresome and younger researchers moved off to form their own work circles. In this area, the *Historische Wörterbuch der*

Philosophie provided the incentive to many studies. Joachim Ritter had brought it to life, and I was also active at its beginning. Hand in hand with the monumental undertaking of the *Wörterbuch* went the *Archiv für Begriffsgeschichte*, edited by Ritter, K. F. Gruender, and myself. The history of concepts seems to me to be a precondition for responsible critical philosophizing in our time, and it is only along the route of the history of words that the history of concepts can move forward. The cooperation of excellent philologists made this circle especially attractive. We took pleasure in the steady support we received from the German Research Society. When it was finally established that we—in contrast to other senate commissions— needed only a small amount of support, the commission was suddenly dissolved and we were thrown back onto the normal procedure. But in the way these things go, the study circle then began to fall apart. Without an obligating project, every academic prefers to follow his own special interests. In my case this meant an increasing concentration on Greek philosophy. For this I could also win the interest of the German Research Society when I needed it.

I had also taken over a multiplicity of other tasks. For a time I was president of the General German Philosophy Society, and in this capacity I organized a 1965 meeting in Heidelberg on the problem of language. The big International Congress for Philosophy in Vienna also took place in this period, and I gave the opening address, "On the Power of Reason." Here for the first time I started to question the worth of such world congresses, occasions when one gets together with others in order to lose oneself in the crowd, to which one is in any event a contributing factor.

Above all, I had now founded a study circle for the furtherance of Hegel studies. I do not want to go into the prehistory of this event, partly distorted by politics. It was not conceived as competition to the already existing Hegel Society of Dr. W. R. Beyer, which sponsored larger, more public congresses. It was conceived, rather, as a forum where researchers could meet and exchange the results of their work in small groups, and as such it did good work, especially in its frequent meetings outside of Germany, in France, Holland, and Italy. The work of the circle was also an advantage to my own Hegel research, which I had been cultivating for years, even if I was able to make only small contributions to the completion of a hitherto altogether too broadly stretched program. These are now to be found in the little book called

Hegel's Dialectic. The growing interest in Hegel, partly stimulated by neo-Marxism, finally led to conferences that had a major public response. Especially significant was the Stuttgart Jubilee Conference of 1970, where I took leave as president of the circle I had founded, and the Stuttgart Conference of 1975, which was organized by my successor in the presidency.

I report on these work circles in only summary form because the results themselves have been published, partly as contributions to the *Archiv für Begriffsgeschichte* and partly as contributions to my Hegel studies. Of course, there are many more or less interesting memories connected with all such gatherings, just as there are with the numerous trips I made in these years within Germany and abroad to give papers. But I shall omit expanding on these things. They are too close to the present and are often too intimate in respect to still living persons for them to be presented as the reflections of a memory grown old. In the final analysis, these remembrances are intent upon holding onto something only because others, younger, are not able to reach back in the same manner.

The Heidelberg Academy of Sciences was another important facility for interdisciplinary exchange in that city. I was elected to it soon after my relocation to Heidelberg. These small academies of West Germany stand in contrast to the large scholarly organizations—the German Research Society, the Max Planck Institutes, and the like—through which hundreds of millions of marks are channeled. They are small support operations that look after a few long-term projects. Thus after the death of Ernst Hoffmann, who with Klibansky had brought to life the Heidelberg Academy edition of the works of Nicholas of Cusa, I was entrusted with looking after this project and did so for decades. I aimed at making good progress, but the edition is still not completed. Other projects of the Heidelberg Academy also run on for decades, but this is not the bad thing an outsider might take it to be. Such projects are simultaneously opportunities for schooling new generations of scholars, and they are not simply to be measured by the mass of printed paper they produce. But it is difficult and time-consuming to make this clear to responsible authorities.

Still more difficult is explaining what happens in the meetings of the academy. In my eyes this is the only kind of meeting worthwhile for an intellectual in contemporary academic life: There is a little bit of administrative work, but only after a scholarly presentation with intensive discussion. This is the correct measure. I later found a similar setup in the Harvard Divinity School. Every faculty meeting there began with an hour-long scholarly part, and I am convinced that such a procedure presents no impairment to reasonable administrative business but on the contrary has a concentrating and intensifying effect. Those who would learn something and who have already confirmed themselves in their intellectual callings through exchanges with others (and therewith simultaneously become aware of the limitations of their competence) will be more inclined to let a collective reason have its say in administrative matters in place of the "private reason" we humans so avidly pursue.

In any case, aside from a few substantial commission meetings and habilitation colloquia, academy meetings provide almost the only occasions in which a learned body can assure itself of its community, and I have a hard time grasping why this side of academic life is not more strongly honored. Certainly not every presentation is worth everyone's time. It can be very boring when highly specialized material excludes one from participation. I remember very well falling asleep during a presentation by Adam Falkenstein, one of the very best orientalists in the world. There were, however, many opposed examples in which the contribution was substantial and the exchanges among persons of different disciplines even provoked really new research discussions. In the Saxony Academy of Science in Leipzig, there was, in contrast, no discussion. What ruled there was a very solemn atmosphere. I well remember my inaugural lecture, before Leipzig had been reduced to ashes. It took place in the rooms of the academy, whose chairs were as comfortable as they were "sat through" in their dignified way. When I began speaking, nearly half of my illustrious and ancient audience began moving toward the podium, each armed with an ear trumpet. It was as in *Macbeth* when Burnham Wood rose up. This was the wood of deaf ears, which the forty-year-old newcomer in the anxiety of his ignorance had to fend off. The grunting recognition of the old gentlemen—Alfred Körte, Alfred Schulze, Heinrich Siber, Erich Brandenburg, and whoever else one met in the coatroom— could not hide the fact that one still had much to learn.

In Heidelberg at first everything also proceeded in an extraordinarily dignified manner, despite the freedom of discussion. This was due especially to the grave traditionalism that radiated from the secretary, Otto Regenbogen. I can still feel my horror when Regenbogen, in answer to a question posed by me, indicated in a threatening tone and with a forcefully rising voice that he was "no mailman." As a newcomer I had committed the terrible offense of addressing him as "the secretary," in the sense of one who did the typing, instead of "Mr. Secretary." Later there were often very profitable discussions. But this was only after we had succeeded in shifting the meetings from Saturday afternoons to mornings and above all after the academy had finally made the transition to representing the entire state of Baden-Württemberg and had ceased being limited to Heidelberg. Then we were able to call upon the leading people from other universities. This was the other possibility for organized solidarity. Either, as in Leipzig, one presumed of every speaker that he was the best in his field, or one was in a small circle of equals and was ready to take instruction from others. We often wielded sharp knives there, and even when one perceived thereby how undeveloped one's own contribution was, this was no shame but rather a genuine gain. The broadening of horizons that resulted from these meetings had a real worth, and at a time when a remedy to the growing separation of the disciplines is sought in interdisciplinary institutions, one should more strongly honor the best institution of this kind that we possess.

I realize that my emphasis on the Heidelberg Academy of Sciences is an echo of my own four-year presidency, taken up after I became emeritus. It was a thankless business. No matter how well one presents one's case, in the age of voter-polling arithmetic, a body like an academy of sciences is a mere decorative prop for the public consciousness — at least in the eyes of vote-counting politicians (Is there any other kind?).

The Heidelberg Academy of Sciences seldom acted in public, except during the annual academic ceremonies, when it served more or less in the role of the humble poor. In this respect, my speeches as president of the academy resembled those of my predecessors and my successors. And yet there are achievements in its existence that in my opinion do honor to the academy but for which it seldom receives credit. Among these is the practice of making the nomination for the bestowal of the Reuchlin prize given by the city of Pforzheim. This has produced a stately row of convincing prizewinners. That I myself would one day be added to this row, through an independent decision of the Pforzheim City Council, was an honor for me and also a confirmation that we had done good work in our recommendations of previous winners. Among these were two winners to whose work and person I stood closer than any other member of our academy. As a consequence I was charged with describing their achievements. These were Richard Benz and Gershom Scholem.

Richard Benz had already lived for a long time in Heidelberg as a private citizen when, at my recommendation, he was elected to membership in the academy. This was an honor that we granted ourselves. In Pforzheim he was introduced with the following *laudatio*:

Richard Benz was in one person a pure researcher and a true lover. In him were united characteristics that would like to go separate ways: a sense of the otherness of a past preserved only in historical memory and the alert sense of a musing consciousness for the living presence of this past in art.

Even as early as his student years and in his dissertation theme, the inner elective affinity that bound him to German Romanticism was clear. His first writings were on the fairy-tale poetry of the Romantics, and as if called forth from the genius local to Heidelberg, he did not simply follow in the footsteps of the Heidelberg Romantics. Rather, filled with their sense and their spirit, he renewed for our century the act of discovery that a century earlier had produced in Heidelberg the collection of fairy tales, folk songs, and folk books. A whole series of German folk books was republished through his work. The Brentano fairy tales were his share of the great Brentano Edition, whose publication began before the First World War. His immersion in the popular literature of the German Middle Ages found its crown in the German translation of the *legenda aurea* of Jacobus de Voragine, which he published with Eugen Diederichs in 1917. All this did not spring from a mere learned interest but was the answer of a finely tuned ear listening to very soft voices. It was an answer that over and over showed itself to be a work of art, in that Benz's spirited prose knew how to restore sound to the things that entranced him.

In the end, however, music proved to be the authentic center of the musing personality of Richard Benz. To it he dedicated his first major work: *The Hour of German Music* (1923). In this book Benz felt called upon to present the classical period in German literature from the point of view of other arts, especially music and baroque architecture.

Especially advantageous to Benz was his fine knowledge of and passionate sensitivity to the voice of music in this brilliant period of German culture. But what distinguished him was above all an unbroken, driving need to pursue the human constellations from which intellectual productivity periodically arose. In this manner, his contributions to eighteenth-century German cultural history present German intellectual history as it could not be presented by any of the individual specialized disciplines. It was not only his musical sensibility that allowed such a panorama of the arts. Also required was his unusual sensitivity to the constellations of human destinies and the conditions of the human creative power, whose interlacing made possible great human achievements.

This work now lies before us in three important volumes: The first to appear, in 1937, was volume three, *Die deutsche Romantik, Geschichte einer geistigen Bewegung.* In 1949 followed *Deutsches Barock, Kultur des 18. Jahrhunderts.* And in 1953 this large undertaking came to its conclusion in *Die Zeit der deutschen Klassik, Kultur des 18. Jahrhunderts 1750–1800.* In these volumes, as if by a new inspiration, the whole sequence of classical German poets rearranges itself into a new order for anyone familiar with the spirit of classical German music that dwells in Bach, Mozart, Beethoven, and Schubert. Names like Wilhelm Heinse and Jean Paul move into the first rank, Wilhelm Wachenroder is seen in a new light as the stimulator of the Romantic movement, while other names retreat. Before Richard Benz, it had never been seen so clearly how the extension of German culture to all of Europe had found its crown in the spirit of German music. As opposed to the heritage of classical antiquity, Benz saw in German culture the authentic completion of the artistic law of the culture of the West: "This truly metaphysical language of music is now the real wonder, the crown of the century."

We owe to the work of Richard Benz a new accent of meaning in cultural history. It is no longer simply a presentation of the general cultural achievements of mankind, showing, alongside the conspicuous dates and happenings of history, the inconspicuous and everyday things that were the discoveries and creations of past ages. Cultural history is in his case a mode of historical self-confrontation of German educational culture with itself. The architecture and painting, poetry and music of our great eighteenth century do not just provide materials that can document the rise of the bourgeoisie of that time to the peak of educational achievement. Rather, all of these things are thankfully and thoughtfully recalled from the perspective of a living and experiencing present age. He was active in an understanding and interpretive way. And as is appropriate to the lively humanity of a spirit that partook of these great artistic traditions, his work builds an atmosphere of human communication that includes the reader along with the described figures of this great epoch of the German spirit. In this sense, we honor Richard Benz as the historian of the aesthetic culture of Germany.

The *laudatio* for Gershom Scholem reads as follows:

The broad field of the historical sciences stems from a long humanistic and neohumanistic tradition. In our day it does not often happen that a lone researcher establishes a whole new discipline, not just a new research direction within a well-known discipline. Gershom Scholem has this rare distinction. With the eyes of the historical researcher, he was the first to look closely at the Jewish mysticism of the Kabbalah and the related phenomenon of Hasidism and the first to give these phenomena significance in the spirit of a critical-interpretive scholarship.

The greatness and strangeness of a Jewish religious movement that fed on hidden traditions became for him and through him an object of immediate intellectual fascination and, simultaneously, one of critical-scholarly enlightenment. A student of the great historical schools of German and Romantic traditions, he was equally a contemporary of the living religious tradition of his people. In defiance of the procedure of leading Jewish researchers of the nineteenth century, his interpretation of Jewish mysticism became a completely new discovery. The liberal error of that generation of researchers was no longer a temptation for the younger Jewish generation of Franz Rosenzweig and Martin Buber, whom the younger Gershom Scholem followed. The liberal researchers had seen in the Kabbalah only incomprehensible errors and the going-to-seed of a past religious belief, and they counted themselves part of a rising and enlightened culture of assimilation. But the waking from the dream of liberal progress brought by the First World War and the astounding confrontation with the evidence of continuing Hasidic piety created new presuppositions for the understanding of misinterpreted mystical appearances in the history of Judaism. The first scholarly fruit of the young Scholem was a 1923 edition of an important work from the early period of the Kabbalah, the book *Bahir*, which he freshly interpreted. This was not merely the achievement of a well-schooled historian and philologist who had learned how to decipher something strange. Despite the critical-skeptical distance with which the enlightened Berliner studied these religious manifestations, nonetheless a startled identification was made, and it would thereafter not leave the imagination and the sharp understanding of the maturing researcher.

That the religious traditions of his people did not dissipate under the bright light of modern scientific methods, but rather unfolded into an array of magnificent dark colors, grounded the young Scholem's belief in his task: This was to help build up the scholarly study of Judaism so that it might spiritually illuminate the roots of the modern political people of Israel. In 1925 he became a teacher at the Hebrew University in Jerusalem; since then he has remained true to his self-appointed task, and not without a good deal of opposition. He has labored not only as a teacher and a researcher but also as an organizer and expert in the area of library science, and with similarly minded people he has worked for the founding of a new scholarly and cultural tradition.

Much of Scholem's work in these long years has been written in the Hebrew language. But a modern researcher cannot dispense with exchanges with other scholars, and thus Scholem was a frequent guest in Paris, London, and America, and also in German up to its self-isolation at the hands of the National Socialists. The format that the researcher Scholem grew into first became known to the German public when in 1957 his major work, *Major Trends in Jewish Mysticism*, appeared in a German edition. This book brought forward the great spokesmen of Jewish mysticism from their ancient beginnings through the blossoming of the Kabbalah in the high Middle Ages up to the Hasidic movement in Germany in the eighteenth century and Poland in the nineteenth century. The book brought together in a single, large historical setting a religious phenomenon of the modern period, one already familiar to German readers through Martin Buber's divinatory and poetic interpretation. The old and the oldest opened themselves up to Scholem's penetrating mind and his brilliant learnedness, and international scholarly recognition was accorded him in rich measure.

My involvement in the Heidelberg Academy of Sciences had an indirect consequence that proved to be significant. Against some opposition, I was successful in the 1950s in getting Martin Heidegger accepted into the academy. This was very nearly as difficult as my successful efforts to present Heidegger with a festschrift on his sixtieth birthday. At that time I received the most astounding refusals and halfhearted acceptances, and in the end I owed it to the decisive independence of Karl Löwith that other friends and students of Heidegger found the courage to participate. Obviously Heidegger's doings in 1933 had made for him many an enemy, especially in Heidelberg.

Heidegger's election to the academy led to a regular series of visits and frequent contacts with my circle of students. Through many years and at least once every semester Heidegger gave a series of seminars, for the most part in my house. These were attempts to reach over generations and bridge the constantly growing distance of the young people from the old master. In my first decade at Heidelberg, the real problem of my teaching was the all too complete devotion of my students to Heidegger's mode of thinking. How could I get it across to them that one cannot begin with Heidegger, but should rather begin with Aristotle if one wants to learn how to think in Heidegger's way? But now communication across generations was becoming more and more difficult. Heidegger took these seminars very seriously, and for my seventieth birthday he gave me the manuscript he had composed as preparation for and consequent to our Heidelberg discussions. He had decked it out with numerous leading questions. It was a true workpaper that documented his power of focused thought, in which he was still superior to any of his contemporaries. The impression here was stronger than that made by Heidegger's personal appearances before my colleagues and students. The distribution of such unfinished working papers through photocopying and of course transcription of the handwriting is perhaps the most important contribution that is yet to be made from Heidegger's papers. This is thinking in action, with questions piling up on questions. Often it was palpably visible how difficult it was for Heidegger in such discussions to bring himself out of himself, how difficult it was for him to understand others, and how he would open up when one of us came onto the way of thinking he had prepared by means of his answers. This certainly did not always succeed, and then he would become very unhappy and occasionally a bit ungracious. But then Heidegger's simplicity, plainness, and warmth won everyone over once we were finished and having an effortless conversation over a glass of wine.

After I became emeritus in 1968, I continued my teaching activity on an unofficial basis insofar as I was not claimed by the activities I now took up in the United States. Meanwhile the climate of university life changed fundamentally. Instead of a prolonged discussion, however, let me here make way for an obituary composed for a colleague of that time who had taken his own life:

Professor Jan van der Meulen, whose death we deplore, was active for more than ten years as a private *Dozent* in the Philosophical Seminar in Heidelberg. As a native-born Dutchman, he received his first and never-extinguished intellectual formation from Dutch Hegelianism, which found itself in ongoing confrontations with the neighboring thinking of English empiricism and its positivistic successors. Shortly before the Second World War, the young Jan van der Meulen came to Freiburg to continue his philosophical studies and simultaneously to get a thorough education in medicine. Certainly it was not as a foreigner that he came to the native land of Idealistic thinking, but rather as a conscious bearer of a Germanic intellectual tradition. In an academic world turned upside-down by the political situation, Freiburg University represented for him a kind of island on which he was met by a transformed spiritual homeland in the powerful form of Heideggerian thinking. He was deeply taken by this, and yet every line he would later write would bear the stamp of Hegel's thinking. There is an inspiration that comes through in Hegel's thinking that has not been exhausted in the work of his academic successors and that still retains something of the essential power and speculative pathos of his language. This happens seldom enough, but one can name some impressive examples, such as Purpus, Cloos, and Brunstädt. Van der Meulen was such a case. He had a lively Hegelian spirit and precisely for this reason was not self-consciously dependent on and enslaved to Hegelian thinking. His was, rather, an unself-conscious, unmodern, and immediate way of negotiating the truth with Hegel. Something of the sovereign power of construction of Hegelian thinking seemed to have been passed on to him.

With the stormy drive that distinguished him as a person and lent him a refreshing immediacy, he developed his thinking in three major books. Aristotle, Hegel, and Heidegger converged in the titles of these books in the catchword of "the middle" that united divisive tensions. Here in fact lay his problem as man and thinker. The eccentric energy that was always storming forth from him provided graphic evidence of how difficult this middle was for him. His spirit recognized clearly its superior truth, and he tested it out in his conversations with the great thinkers of the past and the present. There was something of the vehemence of a Calvinist lay preacher in this man, brought up Catholic but marked by a lofty self-sufficiency. In this respect, all of his work had a genuine radiance to it. His books have the undisputed merit of always going to the whole without allowing subtlety, thoroughness, and faithfulness in detail to be lost. His key theme was "the conclusion"—not the formal conclusiveness of a syllogism but the consolidation of the different, of the general and the particular, of principles and scientific experience—in a word, of the ethical and the sensuous nature of man.

The naive self-certainty of his spiritual temperament might have raised doubts about whether the critical pathos of his thinking remained adequately controlled in respect to sobriety, skepticism, carefulness, and distance, which are the virtues of disciplined scholarly thought. But in the end his remarkable energy, talent, and industry allowed him to establish an independent existence as a neurologist, and the spiritual strength of his philosophical books, the sincerity of his mind, and his pedogogical passion seemed so convincing to the Heidelberg philosophy faculty that they gave him the *venia legendi*, the right to teach.

The faculty thereby made a firm avowal of freedom of research and teaching. For van der Meulen was a loner who did not allow himself to be integrated into an existing work atmosphere or into philosophical directions of thinking that needed to be encouraged. The passionate earnestness with which he practiced his freely chosen calling to teach drove him to take a fearless stand for the inviolable dignity of academic freedom and to take on the pressing political and ideological questions of the present from the point of view of his philosophical principles. Because he was seen as a political opponent, he became the target of coordinated student attacks. This affected him deeply, so deeply that he for his part did not perceive the distress of the unsettled youth of today, who were behaving so intolerantly. But all of us, his students and his colleagues, failed to perceive what the obstruction of his teaching activity meant to this man, a great idealist in the excellent, old-fashioned sense of the word. Without love and without justice he could not live, and so with this despairing admission he went voluntarily to his own death. We have to honor this confession of freedom that he embodied in his person and sealed with his last incomprehensible decision. We have to learn, both we who teach and we who are taught, that freedom of research and teaching is to be defended against all outer pressure, no matter from which side it originates. But also and above all, we ourselves must convincingly represent such freedom, for those who would like to paint us with convenient labels and also for anyone who in distress needs the support of us all.

My retirement from the professorship and above all from administrative responsibilities spared me the demanding experiences of university reforms and the "democratization" of the natural relation between those who teach and those who learn. I was able to leave, to teach and thereby to learn, to learn and thereby to teach, as we say. And I was able to do this on a new continent and in English. It was like a second youth.

Karl Jaspers

Karl Jaspers died in Basel on February 26, 1969, a few days after his eighty-fourth birthday. For two decades he had taught and worked in that city, and through his outpouring of lectures, articles, and books he had earned an international reputation as a writer on philosophy. The positions he took on questions of public and cultural life gave his work an especially far-reaching resonance. Nonetheless, through his whole life and work, Karl Jaspers was indissolubly tied to Heidelberg. He spent the greatest part of his student years here, was a scientific assistant in the Psychiatric Clinic, habilitated in psychology in 1913, and in 1921 became professor of philosophy. After his removal in 1937 he continued to live in Heidelberg. When a new beginning was made in 1945, he was reinstated in his position and taught at Heidelberg in the first years after the war. In 1948 he took up a standing offer from the University of Basel, which he had been unable to accept earlier because of wartime conditions.

To appreciate Jaspers's philosophical achievement, one must be aware above all that he prevailed as an outsider in the philosophical life of Heidelberg. The university was in his time a citadel of neo-Kantianism, especially in the period of substantial development of the national economy and the social sciences at the beginning of our century. Wilhelm Windelband understood that philosophy, too, needed a strong profile. He was the one who extended the transcendental thinking of Kantian philosophy to the broad field of the so-called cultural sciences. As a teacher, he gathered around himself a large number of talented pupils, including Emil Lask, Paul Hensel, Julius

Ebbinghaus, Richard Kroner, Ernst Hoffmann, Fyodor Stepun, Eugen Herrigel, Ernst Bloch, and Georg Lukács. With insight be diagnosed the awakening of a new philosophical interest in Hegel that was taking place in this circle. As brought to completion by his successor, Heinrich Rickert, southwest German value philosophy radiated out into the world as a variety of neo-Kantianism. In the context of this neo-Kantian school, the natural sciences, and especially the science of the human soul, were not granted a privileged position. So Karl Jaspers established himself in Heidelberg outside this school. Starting as a physician and researcher in psychiatry, in the end he became the rare case of a professor of philosophy who had not earned his doctorate in the discipline of philosophy. He was, instead, a doctor of medicine. Only on the occasion of his seventieth birthday did the Heidelberg Philosophy Faculty confer on him the honor of a doctorate.

Jaspers's first major work was still in the field of psychiatry: his *General Psychopathology*, first published in 1913 and reissued in a new edition in 1946. Even this early work showed the specific gifts of his broad, ordering mind. His presentation of the many facets of research in psychopathology revealed him as one to whom all dogmatic narrowness was suspect. This attitude sprang from a deep essential drive, the will to a universal knowledge, something highly distinct from the introversion usually taken as typical of philosophers. In fact, there was in him the sober sense for fact of his Oldenburg homeland. The bright observing eye he directed at his dialogue partner was careful, critical, and above all desirous of taking the measure of the other person, finding his point. This also characterized his relation to the world of books. He was a voracious reader. Even long after his departure from Heidelberg, they still point out the little bench in Koester's Bookstore on Main Street where this man regularly sat and looked through stacks of newly arrived publications, giving them a morning each week of his strictly and carefully divided up time. On each occasion he sought out a huge stack of books, and it was astounding how many things he took note of from his reading. One can easily grasp that for a man of his many interests, the demonic figure of Max Weber, the world's most recent polymath in the cultural sciences, was the great model he admired and tried to emulate. In Weber he came face-to-face with the iron self-discipline of a researcher who productively drove his will to universal knowledge in all directions up to the limits forced upon him by his scientific asceticism and methodical integrity.

The deep irrationalism that lay behind the quixotic magnificence of the champion of sociology as a value-free science presented a true challenge to Jaspers's philosophical need to ground his thinking. This was to be the enduring impulse to thinking that was unfolded in his philosophy. Yet the first major philosophical work that made Jaspers's name known as a philosopher, the 1919 *Psychologie der Weltanschauungen*, remained on the doorstep of the new philosophical deepening to which it drove him. Following Dilthey, but also in the neighborhood of Max Weber's ideal types, Jaspers analyzed in this work the "mental outlooks and world pictures" that, rising out of human life experience, had given philosophy its profile. This was not simply a continuation of the Weber–Dilthey version of a science of philosophy that made philosophy into the object of a scientific theory—known as sociology of knowledge and as anthropological typology. Jaspers's typology implied, rather, a philosophical opposition to the grounding of philosophy in one prin-ciple, for instance in "consciousness itself"—that magic word of neo-Kantian transcendental philosophy. Even if in the manner of a ty-pological attempt at thinking, Jaspers admittedly drew into philosophy themes and inquiries of his *Psychologie der Weltanschauungen* that had no place in the methodological self-understanding of the dominant neo-Kantianism. Ancient human problems—freedom, guilt, death— gained a new distinction as so-called borderline situations in which theoretical reason ensnares itself in contradictions and becomes aware of its limits. Here, too, human existence seeks and finds its support in deeper sources of self-being. In this manner Jaspers's first philo-sophical book above all reflected one of the great philosophical hap-penings of the early twentieth century: the discovery of Søren Kierkegaard, the great critic of German Idealism. This major philo-sophical writer became known due to the Diederichs edition of his work, and he prepared the way for the collapse of Idealism that with the storms of the First World War ended the Age of Liberalism, shaking to its foundation the cultural consciousness of Central Europe. Kierkegaard is everywhere present in Jaspers's book. An essay on Kierkegaard, which formed a chapter of the book, communicated for the first time the new pathos of "existence." And this was roughly simultaneous with the rise of dialectical theology.

In the decade after the First World War, Jaspers had more and more success in neo-Kantian Heidelberg. Alongside the internationally famous Heinrich Rickert and the distinguished historian of philosophy

Ernst Hoffmann, this was no easy task. But even in my student years, Heidelberg was more and more represented by Karl Jaspers among those studying philosophy at other universities. And yet he had published few philosophical writings. Hence the astounding phenomenon that the actual founder and representative of what was then called *Existenzphilosophie* was audible only in the live voice of the lecture hall. When Heidegger's *Being and Time* appeared in 1927, *Existenzphilosophie* was included as a revolutionary critique of the Tradition.[1] Only the initiated knew that Heidegger's work was a new effort in philosophy, one in which Kierkegaard and the philosophical themes of Jaspers's Kierkegaard reception were unmistakable but there primarily to provide points of departure for a fundamentally new inquiry whose reference point lay in very different dimensions. To the larger public this book appeared as *Existenzphilosophie*, but the foundation for this preoccupation had above all been prepared by Karl Jaspers, who in his capacity as an academic teacher in Heidelberg was repeating Kierkegaard's *Existenz* dialectic.

It was not until years later that Jaspers published anything further. In 1931 he offered as the thousandth volume in the Göschen essay series the piece called *Die geistige Situation der Zeit* [translated as *Man in the Modern Age*], a little book with a powerful effect; and its theoretical grounding heralded the author's unique philosophical contribution. Undoubtedly the work was, in its basic lines, a far-reaching cultural-critical argument with the "age of anonymous responsibility," and it glossed in pregnant commentary the dominant streams and tendencies of social life. But its essential kernel lay in what the title's term *Situation* referred to. That a situation cannot be simply an object of scientific knowledge had to come as a penetrating insight. It is all too clear that in this concept is to be found the encircling and the inhibiting, that which prevents the researching subject from gaining distance on the world of objects. The essence of *Situation* demands a knowledge that does not have the objectivity of an anonymous science, one that is

---

1. The term *die Tradition* as used in the Heidegger literature refers to the tradition in Western philosophical thinking, traceable to the Greek classical thinkers, of creating a metaphysical world of objective truths that stands opposed to the real physical world. The restoration of philosophy as an activity that uses ideas as "hypotheses" (Natorp) or "perspectives" (Löwith) or "prejudices" (Gadamer) and thus makes them a part of this-worldly reality is a dominant thread in the life's work of Heidegger, Jaspers, Löwith, Gadamer, and others associated with *Existenz* philosophy in Germany. Thus their effort can be interpreted as one of overcoming the Tradition. [*tr.*]

characterized by a horizon and a perspective, an engagement and an insight into individual existence. The voice of the moralist Karl Jaspers, audible here for the first time, found in this its theoretical legitimation.

All the same it came as a genuine surprise when in 1932 Jaspers published his major work, to which he gave the simple title *Philosophie*. A title is often a program. Even this, the most general and seemingly colorless title that a book of philosophy can possibly have, sounded like a program. Certainly it was not the program of a system, but it was a programmatic explanation of renunciation of the handed-down systematic of philosophy, and it was a centering of a proposed movement of thinking in the existence of the philosophizing person. A meditative thrust runs through the entirety of this work. One must let oneself be pulled into the philosophical argument and must follow it step by step. It is characteristic that there is no general and detailed table of contents in this large three-volume work. Individual chapters carry their contents at their head. Obviously the author wanted to make it difficult to gain an orientation on what he was saying, indeed to discredit any such effort. Or to say the same thing more positively: He wanted to compel the reader to participate in the meditative thrust of the work.

The style corresponds to this position. If you look to Jaspers's philosophical publications for the development and ripening of his style, you will discover some elements in the early publications that later constitute the peculiarities of that highly personal style. For example, the distanced generalization that makes the impersonal "one" the bearer of expression, or the selectively heaped-up paraphrases. But all this is bound into the austerity of a will to style that gives his sentences a crystalline structure. Northern sobriety here pairs itself with a nearly celebratory pathos. Every sentence of Jaspers now sounds inimitably personal and substantial. As glittering fire beams forth from a thousand facets of a pure stone, so the fine-grained brightness of experience, insight, and existential movement shines out from the sentences of Jaspers's philosophy. It is a style of paraphrase. Without rigid formalism, extremes are formulated for the sake of revealing the truth as the middle between the extremes. Developing thinking seeks to break through all dogmatic structures and in the soft washing of the waves of reflection to win the breadth of an open horizon. Jaspers loved to introduce a problem by writing: "It is to be asked . . ." Thus he moved in a medium of notional possibilities, weighing much, not for the sake of persevering at a noncommittal distance, but to make visible in the mirror of reflection what was no longer reflection but rather demanded decision and existential commitment.

Karl Jaspers's philosophical masterpiece repeats the fundamental lines of Kant's philosophical systematic, and not by chance. The first volume of his work, *Weltorientierung* [World orientation], shows under the subtitle *Bewusstsein überhaupt* [Consciousness in general] the limits of theoretical reason, that is, of the scientific expansion of absolute knowledge. To this extent the first volume corresponds to the setting of limits undertaken by the *Critique of Pure Reason*. The second volume, *Existenzerhellung* [Illumination of existence], turns the border experience of theoretical reason into an affirmation. Just as Kant went back to freedom as a fact of reason that cannot be demonstrated theoretically but must be recognized under the claim of the moral imperative, so in the thinking of Jaspers *Existenz* first comes into its own precisely where it is left in the lurch by the anonymity of scientific knowledge. On the basis of such inner existential choice, a new access to the truths of metaphysics finally presents itself. The third volume of the work repeats the great transcendental experience of man in philosophy, art, and religion. To this extent it corresponds to the "moral world view" that Kant and Fichte had established on the basis of reason's certainty of freedom in the so-called postulate doctrines of practical reason. The classical themes of metaphysics, God, freedom, and immortality, which theoretical reason entangled in unsolvable contradiction, attain a new legitimation. As it is with Kant on the way to practical reason, they attain this new legitimation when they are taken as readings of the ciphered script of transcendence seen in the light of a self-enlightening *Existenz*.

This philosophy is no longer the appealing protest gesture with which Kierkegaard had challenged Idealistic thinking. But it also does not simply repeat the irrational split of Max Weber, who may have pushed back the limits of the scientific world orientation on all sides, but who pulled so hard that the decisions that life demands of the individual would have had to have been created out of depths other than that of knowledge. Precisely this—that the science embodied with imperial authority by Max Weber had delivered up what was truly worth knowing to irrational choice because that is what the asceticism of science demanded—had become unbearable to the generation to which Jaspers lent his voice. Jaspers in opposition asked about the knowledge whose brightness leads us when we have to decide and to choose as personally existing beings, with all the conditions and relativity this implies. This is not the infinite progress of knowledge. But it is precisely the finiteness and conditionality of our knowledge that is decisive. Thus behind the notional movement of this philosophy stands the sharp opposition of reason and existence. But there, too, is the insight that the one cannot be without the other.

Jaspers in his analyses follows the deep presentiments of Schelling, the teacher of Kierkegaard, which within Idealistic thinking reflected the separation of the mere possibilities of reason from the basic grounds of reality, on which reason lives. As Heidegger had done in *Being and Time*, Jaspers also made philosophy ring with a new and unfamiliar tone, one that was doubly unfamiliar in the neo-Kantian Heidelberg of those days. He did this especially in the chapter entitled "The Law of Day and the Passion of Night." To this extent it was not a superficial categorization but rather an excellent characterization, if at that time one viewed Heidegger and Jaspers as the representatives of *Existenzphilosophie*. Here the thinking of the great outsiders of the nineteenth century, Kierkegaard and Nietzsche, was brought to the interior of philosophy. Jaspers did nothing less than appeal to the exceptional existences of Kierkegaard and Nietzsche in order to ground the new rules of an existentially bound thinking. In this respect he was so little inclined to an irrational decisionism, as it was taking shape in the politics of the time, that for him *Existenz* and reason meant the reciprocal play of thinking only in their inner relation to each other. He once said of his philosophy that it should systematically execute a transcendence "in philosophical world orientations, for the sake of putting into question all possible attachment to the known things of the world, . . . in shedding light on existence for the sake of remembering and reawakening what human beings actually are, . . . in metaphysics, for the sake of experiencing the last limit and to continue transcendence. . . . There then unfolds a thinking that is not simply a knowledge of something else to which it relates itself as to an alien being. Instead, that same thinking is itself a doing, be it enlightening, awakening, or transforming." The logic of this philosophy, which Jaspers designated "philosophical logic," unfolds the self-confidence of a universal reasonableness and extends itself on the grounds of such an existential movement. The first volume of this work was published in 1946 under the title *Von der Wahrheit* [On the truth]. It was like the broad unfolding of this kind of universal reasonability when Jaspers followed up with a major series of publications that confirmed the classical tradition of philosophical thinking.

The first of these publications was a rare systematization of Nietzsche, and it bound together a masterful control of the sources with a sovereign attitude of reflection. Even the extremely tempting Nietzsche, to whom nothing average was granted or could be sufficient, was related back to the careful middle of this existential reasonableness, in which the experiences of being human are elucidated. Following this was a book on Descartes, a form of accounting for a remarkably different thinker. And then after the war there were, among others, books on Schelling and on Nicholas of Cusa. Above all, however, the first volume of *Die grossen Denker* [The great thinkers] showed what distinguished Jaspers: He extended the borders of philosophical argumentation boldly and broadly. Perhaps only a mind as schooled in observing reason as was that of the psychiatrist Karl Jaspers could succeed in stepping beyond the European tradition of philosophy and the knowledge of it derived from the sources and conjure up the great witnesses of human thinking in the high cultures of Asia. Jesus, Buddha, and Confucius took their places alongside Socrates as the "authoritative figures" of the Western philosophical tradition. One who without knowledge of the original language is in a position to see the philosophical outline of a mode of thinking possesses a rare gift. I would like to call this a "physiognomic thinking," which is able to read the writing rather than the words. Certainly such interpretation cannot grasp what can only be said in the individual elements of articulated speech. Yet it is able to guess and describe the yearning for light that lies at the bottom of all human thought. There is something disproportionate in this execution of universal reasonableness. It goes beyond space and time, and it follows an inner certainty that, with all due respect for the great, nonetheless claims for itself something of a judicial power. *Existenz* answers to *Existenz*. Even in his quarrel with the tradition of philosophy, Jaspers was the great moralist he would later become as a political writer in his Basel period.

It is highly unusual when in Germany the figure of the moralist is recognized in all its authentic legitimacy. The term and the reality originated in the French cultural world, and the great examples of a Montaigne or a La Rochefoucauld are unknown in the Germany of today. Schopenhauer and Nietzsche, who saw in them their great models, remained outsiders to the scholastic tradition of philosophy. What distinguishes Jaspers is that he was at once a great teacher and a great moralist. His all-encompassing spirit had at its disposal his broadly streaming and finely nuanced language, but it also experienced the fate of finiteness, which he never forgot, precisely in the unrealizability of his universal will to knowledge. There was no second volume of the *Philosophischen Logik*. To the first volume of the *Die grossen Denker* only the program for a second volume was attached, and one hopes that we shall at some point be able to read completed sections of this second volume alongside the already named publications. But it is not only in this kind of outer sense that one who values the achievement and essence of Karl Jaspers feels moved: There is no conclusion to Jaspers's impact.

Karl Löwith

Karl Löwith was a man of unmistakable originality. A deep sadness of being poured out of him. Simultaneously he preserved the most worthy composure in the face of the strange and the estranged aspects of being that are imposed on us. An incomprehensible imperturbability seemed to inspire him. In the monotones of his voice, which was hardly ever raised to the soft emphases of the teacher, this imperturbability became something of a physical presence. Even when he was speaking from the podium, it was more like an unending conversation with himself. But everyone who knew him also knew his sudden way of looking up and casting the glance of understanding that unites.

On the foundation of this imperturbability lay a distance that was native to him, a feel for this detachment and a constant consciousness of detachment. He always observed the distance to himself, to friends, to other human beings, to the world. This was his ethos: an illusionless acceptance of things as they are, a recognition of the naturalness of the natural, and also a persevering hold on all that was near him. His way of life corresponded to this. But did he have a home anywhere? He passed his youth in Munich, his term as a prisoner of war high in a castle at Genoa, his student years in Freiburg and Marburg, Florence and Rome, later years teaching in Japan, and his last twenty years in Heidelberg. But even this life history, which laid on him a good deal that was difficult and bitter, could not break through the last barrier of impenetrability peculiar to him. Seeing him standing there, recalling his bearing, his reactions, his silences, one always

sensed something timeless, something Egyptian in him. Neither young
nor old, averse to all extremes and yet hopelessly separated from the
obviousness of conventions—in such ways his unmistakable essence
expressed itself.

He was especially stamped by his youthful communion with the
Latin mind when, just barely escaping death in battle, he recognized
in the Italian soldiers who were guarding him an attitude toward life
that was deeply appropriate to him: a devotion to the moment, a
natural finding of the natural, an acceptance of the inevitable. Thus
Nietzsche and the *amor fati* were the most natural expression of his
feeling for and thinking of the world. He loved the uninhibited and
defended it. Yet the finest discretion was native to his gentle and
introspective essence; this applied to himself as well as to others, and
it did not leave him when his concern was philosophy. Eccentricity
of speculation annoyed him to the point of indignation. Nonetheless
he was repeatedly drawn in for the sake of getting behind or getting
at, so to speak, whatever it was that was behind the speculation. A
thinking interpreter of great creations of thought, he possessed the
astounding gift of being able to ferret out the individual and the
anecdotal from the midst of the most inflexible stuff of abstract conceptual formulation, thereby clearly bringing out the trace of the human. His relationship to Nietzsche, to Heidegger, yes, even his
relationship to Hegel had something tensely ambivalent about it. He
knew how to find the simple, natural, and understandable impulses
of our being human, and this applied as well when someone claimed
to be speaking in the name of the world spirit and kept himself at a
distance. There were two things he found equally understandable and
unreachable: the radical recklessness of thinking encountered in
Nietzsche or Heidegger, and the solidity and skeptical reserve of that
Basel patrician's son, Jacob Burckhardt. His balanced, imperturbable
view took the measure of the most extreme possibilities as the less
likely variants that nature had granted to mankind.

During the last years of his life, Löwith immersed himself in Paul
Valéry, whose Mediterranean skepticism, bright rationality, and natural
paganism moved him in a congenial way. As he put down the last
volume of Valéry's long series of notebooks, those indefatigable self-
reflections and self-interrogations, Löwith's own life also came to an
end, as if at an appointed time.

Let me attempt to present his way of thinking from the perspective of someone who took the same path. That perspectives have value, that perspectives are not only ways to knowledge but are a part of our authentic existence—no one said these things more clearly than Löwith in his first book. This book, *Das Individuum in der Rolle des Mitmenschen* [The individual in the role of fellow man], pursued a highly original concern in the context of the great schooling that we had all received from Martin Heidegger—that of seeing human beings as individuals, as much in respect to the generalities about essence typical of philosophical thinking as to the social roles people play. If one may put into an abbreviated form what Löwith's book sought to bring into philosophical discussion at this time, it was to shed light on what the "thou" in its radical particularity signifies for mankind. In the situation of that time, which in the final analysis was defined in terms of Heidegger's critique of Western metaphysics, especially the metaphysics of the Greeks, Löwith's thinking was a special application of the general opposition that had become apparent in Heidegger's work. The critique of the idea that man was essentially *logos* and that the essence of things was to be found in their *eidos* was here applied to the concept of the person, which had come out of Roman tradition and in recent philosophy had presented one of the most difficult of moral-philosophical and metaphysical problems. When Löwith perceived the "thouness" of man over against the general concept of the person, when he pointed out that in Pirandello the role the individual plays in relation to this one and that one is his most authentic self, he was employing as a partial aspect of the Idealistic tradition the radical criticism that had already found its theological expression through men like Kierkegaard, Buber, Ebner, Barth, Gogarten, and Bultmann. I now believe that one can very nicely characterize the directions of Löwith's whole spiritual development from the first steps he took as a young *Dozent*. His work flows from a point of departure in the critique of Idealism, in that he started by calling up the witnesses for this kind of critique. Characteristically, the first article he did after his habilitation was concerned with Feuerbach's critique of Hegel. Articles on Kierkegaard and Nietzsche, the great opponents of Idealistic speculation, were further signs of this unique way.

A second component showed itself just as early, one that continued the critique of Idealism but took it in a different direction. If I may continue to speak here as someone who took the same path as Löwith, it always seemed to me that his migration into the institutions of the university, however questionable, is not without significance. It explains why Löwith came increasingly to place the social conditioning of the individual alongside the conditioning that occurs through personal and face-to-face relations. In this respect especially, it was the brilliant treatise on Karl Marx and Max Weber that put social inquiry alongside contemplation of the individual. In this work, Löwith demarcated pairs of perspectives. From the point of view of Marx he sought to shed light on Max Weber's intellectual constellation, and vice versa. Then he set Marx and Kierkegaard over against each other, then Burckhardt and Nietzsche, Goethe and Hegel, and in these confrontations there came to pass something like the transformation of the knowledge won in the working out of the first book into a method. Perspectivity— the original insight of that first effort—is at the same time a feature of the true being. It was emphatically not so, as Löwith then still seemed to mean, that the perspectivity of our thought makes it impossible to win insight into an individual's true being in isolation from his particular social relationships. On the contrary, the individual is the sum total of his perspectives. This knowledge of a "Pirandello" ontology enabled Löwith to legitimate his comparative studies on the history of mind.

The method of perspectives is not arbitrarily applied; rather, every perspective raises a strand out of the network of being that is there and is real. If I may continue indicating what I saw emerging and developing, it nonetheless seemed to me that the method that Löwith applied to the history of mind gradually and in continuous exercise resulted in a fixing of definite positions and definite reference points, from which everything else only showed itself in the perspectives, a kind of balancing out of the scales on which truth was weighed. When Kierkegaard and Nietzsche or even Weber and Marx were set alongside each other, then from the relativity of both positions nothing more than relativity could be taken. When, in contrast, Jacob Burckhardt and Nietzsche were put into perspective in a book, it was obvious that Löwith perceived in Burckhardt a higher human truth. And to the same extent one will sense that the position Goethe takes up in reference to Hegel is closer to that of Löwith; that is, it seems truer to him than the opposed position. Finally, this holds for the truth in Nietzsche himself, and this is perhaps the most remarkable development I see in Löwith's thinking: Despite all the qualifications he makes against

Nietzsche, the latter became for him in a certain sense a fixed position, a witness against what he called historicism. For it was evidently Löwith's intention to show that a decisive radicalization of ethical thinking makes visible the limit of historicism.

If we now turn our attention to this balancing of scales between related intellectual appearances, we shall sense the need to ask ourselves: On what basis does Löwith grant certain perspectives an advantage? To answer this question we must first know the position from which this mode of observation is fruitful. What is the common coin, the measuring system with which Löwith measures? I think one can say that above all else skepticism, a traditional motif of philosophical reflection from time immemorial, is the common thread running through all the "state's witnesses" Löwith so loved to quote, and that this skepticism was also his own concern. But like all skepticism, this one gained its definite sense from that against which it was directed and on which it was practiced. In this attempt to follow my own perspective on Löwith, I shall call his skepticism a skepticism against "the school."

Under the term "school" we understand in philosophy the expert form of academic scholarship that has existed since Schopenhauer, in its turn preceded by the traditional form of philosophical education since late antiquity. I recall very clearly meeting Löwith in 1920 in the lobby of Munich University. I had no idea who he was, but my very first indefinite impression was precisely that his personal concern was the critique of academic philosophy, and even the critique of the instructions given to us by Husserl, the master of phenomenological research, and that these concerns brought him near to the then radical revolutionary Heidegger. Critique of the school has for centuries followed the school like its own shadow. The French moralists thrived on it, but this type of criticism may also be found in the nineteenth century—and with special justification—as the philosophy professors won the upper hand and then spent their time repeating and renewing but without ever reaching the consciousness of the times.

In our youth, Löwith's skepticism toward the school gained a first legitimation within academic philosophy in the concept of "the existential," which attained its embodiment especially with Heidegger's emergence. But in the end even Heidegger's philosophy was pursued by Löwith's skepticism. Heidegger's thinking after *Being and Time* took shape in Löwith's eyes as the purest opposite of what seemed to be the existential appeal of the original Heideggerian effort. I cannot go into detail here as to why Heidegger took a direction so different from the one suggested in Löwith's criticism of school philosophy. But it seems to me that it was meaningful for Löwith that his thinking had taken shape in such tensions.

A second aspect of Löwith's skepticism is what seems to me to be a skepticism toward dogmatics as such, above all that of philosophical theology and speculative philosophy of history. All speculative interpretations of history seemed to him unrecognized and illegitimate continuations of the biblical account of salvation. This is the point to which Löwith's skeptical thinking moved, and it brought him close to a central motif of Protestant theology.

Finally and above all there is Löwith's skepticism in reference to history as a whole. This is the motif he drew from Goethe's dissatisfaction with history, from Burckhardt's abhorrence of power, and from Nietzsche's *Thoughts out of Season*. Positively formulated, it is the motif of nature and naturalness brought here into union with the motif of skepticism.

The concept of "nature" seems to me to be especially well suited for the systematic function Löwith gave it. It is not generally known that it is a foreign word which designates for us the most natural of all concepts. "*Natur*" is not a German word, and one has to ask oneself how such legendary power came to be conferred upon this concept, such that it could "waken with a call to arms" in the days of Rousseau and Hölderlin. But I do not want to talk about the history of the word here. I simply want to note that, whether in Greek or in German, the term became relevant and was elevated to the status of a concept only when nature was seen in contrast to the human—for example, in contrast to art or to the supernaturalism of ecclesiastical orthodoxy— that is, only when it meant something more than a mere *natura rerum* or "nature of something." There is a deep, substantial truth in nature that calls out to skeptics. Skepticism is first and last directed at the overblown formulations of the philosophical mind. So in opposition to the speculative dissolution of all that is solid, Löwith seeks to bring nature to bear as the constant of reality, the granite that bears all.

According to content, what comes to words with the theme of nature and naturalness is the oldest motif of Western philosophy—*physis*— admittedly in polemical form and directed against the reflectiveness of philosophy and against the spirit of the technological thinking of the modern period. It actually became Löwith's main concern to win back the problem horizon of the one unified world as a philosophical theme. A series of treatises devoted to the critique of historical existence (1960) and to Christian tradition (1966), as well as some papers he wrote for the Heidelberg Academy of Sciences, served this purpose.

Thus, via skepticism, Löwith became a spokesman for the oldest truths of Western metaphysics. It seems to me that by this arc through which his thinking ran, a true philosophical function of skepticism proved itself through him: to harden what no skepticism can kill because it stands fast as superior truth.

On the Origins of Philosophical Hermeneutics

Many have seen and continue to see in hermeneutic philosophy a repudiation of methodical rationality. Many others misuse the term and that to which it refers by seeing in it a new methodological doctrine that they then use to legitimate methodological unclarity or ideological concealment. This is especially the case now that hermeneutics has become fashionable and every interpretation wants to call itself "hermeneutical." Still others, who belong to the camp of the critique of ideology, do recognize truth in the term, but only a half-truth. It is well and good, they say, to recognize the prejudgmental significance of tradition, but the decisive dimension is missing, namely the critical and emancipatory reflection that serves in practice to liberate us from it.

Perhaps it would help clarify matters if I present the motivation behind my approach as it actually developed. It might thereby become clear that the method fanatics and the radical ideology critics are the ones who do not reflect enough. The former treat the uncontested rationality of trial and error as if it were the *ultima ratio* of human reasonability. The latter recognize the ideological bias of this kind of rationality but then do not give a sufficient accounting for the ideological implications of their own ideology critique.

As I was attempting to develop a philosophical hermeneutic, it followed from the previous history of hermeneutics that the interpretive (*verstehenden*) sciences provided my starting point.[1] But to these was added a hitherto neglected supplement. I am referring to the experience of art. For both art and the historical sciences are modes of experiencing in which our own understanding of existence comes directly into play.[2] Heidegger's unfolding of the existential structure of understanding provided conceptual help in dealing with the problematic of *Verstehen*, now posed in its proper scope. He formerly called this the "hermeneutic of facticity," the self-interpretation of factual human existence, the existence that was there for the finding. My starting point was thus the critique of Idealism and its Romantic traditions. It was clear to me that the forms of consciousness of our inherited and acquired historical education—aesthetic consciousness and historical consciousness—presented alienated forms of our true historical being. The primordial experiences that are transmitted through art and history are not to be grasped from the points of view of these forms of consciousness. The calm distance from which a middle-class educational consciousness takes satisfaction in its educational achievements misunderstands how much we ourselves are immersed in the game [*im Spiele*] and are the stake in this game.[3] So from the perspective of the concept of *play* [*des Spieles*] I tried to overcome the illusions of self-consciousness and the prejudices of Consciousness-Idealism. Play is never a mere object but rather has an existence for the one who plays along, even if only as a spectator. The unsuitability of the concepts of subject and object, which Heidegger had shown in his treatment of the question of being [*Sein*] in *Being and Time*, here let itself be demonstrated concretely. What in Heidegger's thinking had led to "the turn," I for my part attempted to describe as the horizon experience of our self-understanding, as the "effective historical consciousness" that is more being than being conscious. What I thereby formulated was not strictly a task for the methodical *praxis* of art history and historical scholarship, nor did it apply in the first instance to the consciousness of method in these disciplines; rather, it applied

1. I am translating the German term *Verstehen* here as "interpretive," but according to context it may be left in its German form or translated as "understanding." This flexibility corresponds to the normal range within which this word is conventionally translated. [*tr.*]

2. I am here translating *Dasein* as "existence," but according to context it may be translated as "being" instead. The advantage of translating *Dasein* as "existence" is that it preserves a clear distinction when *Sein* is translated as "being." [*tr.*]

3. I am calling attention to the term *Spiel* for two reasons. First it is a key term in Gadamer's philosophizing, and second it is a term whose meaning varies according to context, as is here the case with "game" and "play." [*tr.*]

exclusively or preeminently to the philosophical idea of grounding an argument. To what extent is method a guarantor of truth? Philosophy must demand of science and method that they recognize their own particularity in the context of human *Existenz* and its reasonableness.

In the end the undertaking was obviously itself conditioned by an effective history and rooted in a very definite German philosophical and cultural heritage. Nowhere so strongly as in Germany had the so-called human sciences united in themselves scientific and orienting functions. Or better: Nowhere else had they so consistently concealed the orienting, ideological determination of their interests behind the method-consciousness of their scientific procedure. The indissoluble unity of all human self-knowledge expressed itself more clearly elsewhere: in France in the broad conception of *lettres*, in English-speaking countries in the newly assimilated conception of the humanities. Implied in the recognition of an effective historical consciousness was above all a rectification of the self-conception of the historic human sciences, and this also included art scholarship.

But with this the dimensions of the problem were by no means fully measured. There is something like a hermeneutical problematic in the natural sciences too. Their way is not simply that of the progress of their methods, as Thomas Kuhn has shown in an argument corresponding in its truth to insights that Heidegger had implied in his "The Age of the World Picture" and in his interpretation of Aristotle's *Physics*. The "paradigm" is of decisive importance for both the employment and the interpretation of methodical research and is obviously not itself the simple result of such research. Galileo would have called it a *mente concipio*.

Behind this, however, a much broader dimension opens up, one that is rooted in a fundamental linguisticality or language-relatedness. In all recognition of the world and orientation in the world, the element of understanding is to be worked out, and with this the universality of hermeneutics is to be demonstrated. Of course, the fundamental linguisticality of understanding cannot possibly mean that all experiencing of the world takes place only as language and in language. All too well known are those prelinguistic and metalinguistic dawnings, dumbnesses, and silences in which the immediate meeting with the world expresses itself. And who would deny that there are real conditions to human life? There are such things as hunger and love, work and domination, which themselves are not speech and language but which circumscribe the space within which speaking-with-each-other and listening-to-each-other can take place. There is no dispute that it is precisely such preformations of human opinion and speech that make hermeneutic reflection necessary. In respect to a hermeneutic oriented toward Socratic conversation, it goes without saying that *doxa* is not knowledge and that the seeming agreement in which we live and speak quasi-consciously is no real agreement. But even the exposing of the illusory, as done in Socratic dialogue, completes itself only in the element of linguisticality. Dialogue lets us be certain of possible assent, even in the wreckage of agreement, in misunderstanding, and in the famous admission of ignorance. The communality that we call human rests on the linguistic constitution of our life-world. Every attempt to bring suit against distortions of interhuman understanding on the basis of critical reflection and argumentation confirms this communality.

Thus the hermeneutic aspect itself cannot remain limited to the hermeneutic sciences of art and history, nor to intercourse with "texts," and also not, by extension, to the experience of art itself. The universality of the hermeneutic problem, already recognized by Schleiermacher, has to do with the universe of the reasonable, that is, with anything and everything about which human beings can seek to reach agreement. Where reaching an understanding [*verständigung*] seems to be impossible, because we "speak different languages," hermeneutics is still not at an end.[4] Here the hermeneutic task poses itself in its full seriousness, namely as the task of finding a common language. But the common language is never a fixed given. Between speaking beings it is a language-at-play, one that must first warm itself up so that understanding can begin, especially at the point where different points of view seem irreconcilably opposed. The possibility of reaching an agreement between reasonable beings can never be denied. Even relativism, which seems rooted in the multiplicity of human languages, was already known to Heraclitus. The adult learning a foreign language and the child first learning to speak signify not just an appropriation of the means of producing understanding. Rather, this kind of learning by appropriation depicts a kind of preschematization of possible ex-

---

4. The German terms for "understanding" and "agreement" are closely related and often blend into each other. Similarly in English, we can say that through language or talking we strive to "reach an understanding" or "reach an agreement" and it is hard to establish the difference between the two phrases. [*tr.*]

perience and its first acquisition. Growing into a language is a mode of gaining knowledge of the world. Not just such "learning," however, but all experience realizes itself in ongoing communicative improvement of our knowledge of the world. In a much deeper and more general sense, as August Boeckh intended in his formula for the doings of philologists, experience is always "knowledge of the known." We live in traditions, and these are not a fragment of our world-experience, not a matter of "cultural transmissions" emerging from texts and monuments and communicating a meaning that is linguistically composed and historically documented. Rather, it is the world itself that is communicatively experienced and constantly given over to us as an infinitely open task. It is not the world of a first day but one that is always already handed down to us.[5] In all those places where something is experienced, where unfamiliarity is overcome and what occurs is the shedding of light, the coming of insight, and appropriation, what takes place is the hermeneutic process of translation into the word and into the common consciousness. Even the monological language of modern science wins social reality only by this means. The universality of hermeneutics, contested by Jürgen Habermas with such determination, seems to me to be well grounded precisely here. In my opinion, Habermas has never gotten over an Idealistic understanding of the hermeneutic problem, and he furthermore does an injustice when he narrows me down to "cultural transmission" in the sense of Theodor Litt. (The extended discussion of this question found its documentation in the 1971 volume published by Suhrkamp Verlag entitled *Hermeneutik und Ideologiekritik*.)

In respect to our philosophical tradition, we must come to terms with the same hermeneutical task. Philosophizing does not begin at some zero point but must think and speak with the language we already possess. As in the days of the ancient Sophists, so today, this means leading a language, estranged from its native sense of saying something, back to the common way of saying things and to the communality that supports this way of saying.

Because of the widespread generalization given to modern science by philosophy, we have become more or less blind to this task. In

5. Gadamer used a similar formulation in his first book, written in 1927, where he argued that language and the world are co-original because we are introduced to the world as we are introduced to language. See *Platos dialektische Ethik* (Hamburg: Felix Meiner, 1981), pp. 56–57. [tr.]

Plato's *Phaidon*, Socrates demands that he be able to understand the structure of the world and of natural events as well as he understands why he is sitting there in jail and why he did not take the chance to escape when it was offered him. The reason for not escaping was that he took it to be right to abide by even an unjust judgment. To understand nature as Socrates here understands himself is a demand that Aristotelian physics, in its fashion, satisfied. But this demand is no longer compatible with the science we have known since the seventeenth century, which, as a real science of nature, has made possible a scientifically based domination of nature. Precisely this is the reason why hermeneutics and its methodical consequences have less to learn from the theory of modern science than they do from old traditions that are worth remembering.

One of these is the tradition of rhetoric, which Vico was the last to defend with methodical awareness against modern science, which he called *critica*. Already in my classical studies, I gave a strong preference to rhetoric, the art of speaking as well as its theory. Rhetoric, in a manner that long went unrecognized, has been the bearer of the older tradition of aesthetic concepts, something that is evident as recently as in Baumgarten's definition of aesthetics. Today one must say it with emphasis: The rationality of the rhetorical mode of argumentation, which seeks to bring "feelings" into play but fundamentally validates arguments and works with probability, is and remains a far stronger factor of social determination than the certainties of science. Therefore I oriented myself expressly to rhetoric in *Truth and Method*, and I found confirmation for this from many sides but above all in the work of Chaim Perelman, who looks at rhetoric from the point of view of law.[6] If one insists on making a point of it, this does not mean that I mistook the meaning of modern science and its application in today's technological civilization. On the contrary, modern civilization most certainly entails new problems of transmission. But in principle this has not changed the situation. The hermeneutic task of integrating the monologic of the sciences into the communicative consciousness includes the task of exercising practical, social, and political reasonability. This has become all the more urgent.

---

6. See Chaim Perelman and L. Olbrechts-Tyteca, *The New Rhetoric* (Notre Dame, IN: University of Notre Dame Press, 1969). [tr.]

In truth, this is an old problem that we have been aware of since Plato. Statesmen, poets, and even the real masters of the crafts—all those who claim to have knowledge and appeal to it for support— were convicted by Socrates of having no knowledge of "the good." Then Aristotle defined the structural difference that was uppermost here by means of a separation between *techne* and *phronesis*. This is not a matter that can be talked away. Even when this distinction lets itself be misused and the appeal to "conscience" is veiled in impenetrable ideological obscurities, it is still a misunderstanding of what "reason" and "reasonableness" are, even if one only wants to acknowledge them in the anonymous sciences and as science. For my own hermeneutic theory-building, I therefore became convinced that we had once again to take up this Socratic legacy of a "human wisdom" that is ignorance itself when measured against the divine infallibility of what is known by science. To this end the "practical philosophy" developed by Aristotle can serve as a model. This is the second line of tradition that is to be renewed.

The Aristotelian program of a practical science seems to me to present the only scholarly model according to which the interpretive sciences can be thought out. For in hermeneutical reflection on the conditions of understanding, it turns out that their possibilities articulate themselves in a consciousness that formulates itself in language and does not begin with nothing or end in infinity. Aristotle shows that practical reason and practical insight do not possess the "teachability" of science but rather win their possibility in *praxis* itself, and that means in the inner linkage to ethics. This is worth remembering. The model of practical philosophy must take the place of a *theoria* whose ontological legitimation may be found only in an *intellectus infinitus* that is unknown to an existential experience unsupported by revelation. This model must also be held out as a contrast to all those who bend human reasonableness to the methodical thinking of "anonymous" science. In opposition to the perfecting of the logical self-understanding of science, this seems to me to be the authentic task of philosophy and is so precisely in the face of the practical meaning of science for our life and survival.

But "practical philosophy" is more than a mere methodical model for the hermeneutic sciences. It is also something like its substantive foundation. The special feature of method in practical philosophy is only the result of the "practical reasonability" that Aristotle worked out in its conceptual peculiarity. Its structure is completely ungraspable from the modern concept of science. Even the dialectical fluidity that was won for traditional concepts through Hegel and that served to renew some of the old truths of practical philosophy, threatens a new, impenetrable dogmatism of reflection. The concept of reflection that lies at the heart of ideology critique implies an abstract concept of coercion-free discourse, one that loses sight of the authentic conditions of human *praxis*. I had to reject this as an illegitimate transference of the therapeutic situation of psychoanalysis. In the field of practical reason, there is no analogy to the knowing analyst who can guide the productive, reflective achievement of the analysand. In the question of reflection, it seems to me that Brentano's distinction, traceable to Aristotle, of the reflective awareness of objectivating reflection is superior to the heritage of German Idealism. In my opinion, this holds good even in the face of the demand for transcendental reflection that is directed by Karl-Otto Apel and others at hermeneutics. All of this is well documented in the volume *Hermeneutik und Ideologiekritik*.

Insofar as they are my constant companions, I have been formed more by the Platonic dialogues than by the great thinkers of German Idealism. The dialogues provide unique company. However much we, instructed by Nietzsche and Heidegger, like to take the anticipatoriness [*Vorgreiflichkeit*] of Greek conceptualization from Aristotle to Hegel and up to modern logic to be a border on the other side of which our questions have no answers and our intentions remain unsatisfied, the art of Platonic dialogue also anticipates this seeming superiority, which we take to be our possession from our Judeo-Christian heritage. Certainly it is none other than Plato, with his doctrine of ideas, his dialectic of ideas, his mathematization of physics, and his intellectualization of what we would call ethics, who laid the foundation for the metaphysical conceptualization of our tradition. But simultaneously he limited all his pronouncements by means of mimicry, and just as Socrates with customary irony knew how to reach his ends with his conversation partners, so Plato with his art of dialogue-poetry knew how to strip his reader of his supposed superiority. The task is not to philosophize with Plato but to criticize Plato. Criticizing Plato is perhaps as simple-minded as it is to hold it against Sophocles that he is not Shakespeare. This may seem paradoxical, but only to someone who is blind to the philosophical relevance of Plato's poetic imagination.

Of course one must first learn to read Plato's writings as mimicry. In our century a few things have happened to make this possible, especially through the work of Paul Friedländer, but also through some inspired but not so soundly based books that came out of the circle of the poet Stefan George (Friedemann, Singer, Hildebrandt), as well as through the work of Leo Strauss and his friends and students. But the problem is still far from its solution. That would consist in taking the conceptual pronouncements that are encountered in conversation and relating them with exactness to the dialogical reality out of which they grew. Here is to be found a Doric harmony of deed and speech, *ergon* and *logos*, to which Plato refers with something more than words. It is, rather, the authentic law of life of the Socratic dialogues. In the literal sense they are "loaded" speeches. In them is confided for the first time what Socrates actually intends with an art of refutation that too often works sophistically and drives opponents into the worst of entanglements. Yes, if human wisdom were such that it could pass from one to the other as water can be led from one vessel to another over a strand of wool . . . (*Symposium*, 175d). But this is not the way of human wisdom. A knowledge of our own ignorance is what human wisdom is. The other person with whom Socrates carries on his conversation is convicted of his own ignorance by means of his "knowledge." This means that something dawns upon him about himself and his life of illusions. Or to put it in the bold manner of Plato's *Seventh Letter*: Not only his argument, but also his soul is refuted. This also holds for the boys who believe in their friends but still do not know what friendship is (*Lysis*). It holds for the famous generals, who believe that they embody the virtues of soldiers (*Laches*), or the ambitious statesmen who claim to possess a knowledge superior to all other knowledge (*Charmides*). It holds just as much for all those who follow professional doctrines of knowledge, and in the final analysis it holds for the most ordinary of citizens, who must believe in himself and make others believe that he is a just person in his capacity as salesman, dealer, banker, or craftsman. But obviously it is not a specialized knowledge that is in question here. It is another mode of knowing beyond all the special claims and competences of a knowing superiority, beyond all of the otherwise known *technai* and *epistemai*. This other form of knowing intends a "turn to the ideas" that lie behind all exposures of pretentious knowing.

But even this does not mean that in the end Plato has a doctrine that one can learn, a doctrine of ideas. And if he criticizes this doctrine in his *Parmenides*, this does not mean that he had at that time begun to doubt it. The adoption of "ideas" did not so much signal a doctrine as a direction for questioning, whose implications it was then the task of philosophy, meaning Platonic dialectic, to develop and discuss. Dialectic is the art of carrying on a conversation, and this includes the conversation with oneself and the following out of the agreement reached with oneself. That is the art of thinking. But this is an art of raising questions about what one actually intends with what one thinks and says. With this one sets out on a way. Better, with this one is already on the way. For there is something like a natural human facility for philosophy. Our thinking does not come to a grinding halt because some thinker has framed a system about this or that. Thinking always points beyond itself. Platonic dialogue has an expression for this; it refers to the one, the being, the good that presents itself in the order of the soul, the political constitution, or the nature of the world.

Heidegger interprets the acceptance of the doctrine of ideas as the beginning of that forgetfulness of being that peaks in mere imaginings and objectivations and runs along its course in the technological age as a universal will to power. In consistency with this, he understands even the earliest of Greek thinking about being as preparation for the forgetfulness of being as a happening in metaphysics. But over against this Heideggerian interpretation, the authentic dimension of the Platonic dialectic of ideas has a fundamentally different meaning. The underlying principle of a step beyond everything that exists is a step beyond the simpleminded acceptance of ideas, and in the final analysis a countermovement against the metaphysical interpretation of being as the being of existing beings [*Sein als des Seins des Seienden*].

In fact, the history of metaphysics might also be written as a history of Platonism. Its way stations might be called something like *Plotinus* and *Augustine, Meister Eckhart* and *Nicholas of Cusa,* and then more recently *Leibniz, Kant,* and *Hegel.* But this means all those efforts in the West to question and get behind the substantial being of the idea and the doctrine of "substance" of the metaphysical tradition. By this standard, however, the first Platonist would be none other than Aristotle himself. The goal of my studies in this field would be to make this believable, and indeed to do so against the fact of the Aristotelian critique of the doctrine of ideas and against the essentialist metaphysics [*Substanz-metaphysik*] of the Western tradition. I would not be completely alone, by the way. There was Hegel, too.

This would be no mere historical undertaking. For it would not be informed by the intention of supplementing Heidegger's projected history of the forgetfulness of being with a history of the remembrance of being. This would not be meaningful. It is indeed appropriate to speak of a growing forgetfulness. In my view, Heidegger's great achievement consisted in shaking us out of a nearly complete forgetfulness by teaching us to ask with all seriousness: What is being? I recall how Heidegger ended a discussion in a 1924 seminar on Cajetan's *De nominum analogia* with this very question. We sat there staring and shaking our heads over the absurdity of the question. But since then we have all been reminded of the question of being. Even the defenders of the conventional metaphysical tradition who intend to be critics of Heidegger no longer mistakenly take it for granted that the understanding of being established in the metaphysical tradition shall go unquestioned. They are, rather, given to defending the classical answer as an answer, but this means that they have retrieved the question as a question.

Wherever the attempt is made to philosophize, the remembrance of being happens in this way. But nonetheless it seems to me that there is no history of being. Remembrance has no history. There is a growing forgetfulness, but in the same manner there is no such thing as a growing remembrance. Remembrance is always what comes to one, what overcomes, so that a "re-presencing" [*Wiedervergegen-wärtiges*] offers a brief respite from passing away and forgetting. But remembrance of being is in no way the memory of a prior knowing now "presencing" [*Vergegenwärtigen*]. It is a memory of a prior questioning, a memory of a lost question. But then any question that is posed as a question is no longer a remembrance. As the remembrance of what was once asked, it is the now-asked. This is the manner in which questioning raises the historicity of our thinking and knowing. Philosophy has no history. The first person to write a history of philosophy that really was a history was also the last: Hegel. In him history raised itself to the present of absolute mind.

But is that our present? The present for us cannot be only Hegel, and certainly one should not limit Hegel in any dogmatic fashion. If he spoke of an end to history that would be reached with the freedom of all, he only meant that there was no higher principle than universal freedom. The increasing unfreedom of all that has begun to sketch itself out as perhaps the inevitable fate of world civilization did not constitute an objection to the principle of universal freedom in Hegel's eyes. So much the worse for the facts, he might say. But against Hegel we are also entitled to ask: Is this principle of universal freedom— the first and last in which philosophical thinking about being comes to rest—is this spirit [*Geist*]? The Young Hegelians directed their criticism against just such a notion, but I am convinced that Heidegger was the first to find a positive possibility of good beyond mere dialectical reversal. For this is Heidegger's point: "Truth" is not complete unconcealedness, the ideal fulfillment of which is the self-present [*Selbstgegenwart*] of absolute spirit. He taught us, rather, to think of truth as simultaneously exposure and concealment. The great attempts at thinking in the tradition, in and through which we know and recognize ourselves, stand in this tension. What is spoken out is not everything. The unspoken actualizes and perfects the spoken so that it can touch us. This seems to me to be of a compelling correctness. The concepts in which thinking formulates itself stand up against a wall of darkness. They work one-sidedly in a way that establishes, judgmentally. They call to mind the intellectualism of the Greeks, or the metaphysics of the will of German Idealism, or the methodologism of the neo-Kantians and the neopositivists. They make themselves manifest in their way, but not without making themselves unrecognizable to themselves. They are preoccupied by the anticipated achievements of their concepts.

For this reason, every dialogue with the thinking of a thinker— which we seek to conduct because we strive to understand—is in itself an unending conversation. The conversation is real insofar as we seek to find our own language as the common one. Historical distance and even the placing of one's conversation partner in a historically surveyable course remain subordinate moments of our attempt at reaching understanding. In truth these go to form the self-reassurance with which we close ourselves off from the conversation partner. In conversation, however, we attempt to open ourselves to him, and this means holding fast to our common ground.

If this is so, then certainly things stand badly with a personal position. Does not such dialogical unendingness at its most radical signify a complete relativism? But would this not itself be such a position, and on top of that one that entangles itself in self-contradiction in a known way? In the end, though, it is also this way with the acquisition of life experience: A full set of experiences, meetings, instructions, and disappointments do not conjoin in the end to mean that one knows everything, but rather that one is aware and has learned a degree of modesty. In a central chapter of *Truth and Method* I defend this personal concept of experience against the concealment it has suffered in the institutionalized process of the sciences of experience, and in doing this I sensed myself to be close to Michael Polanyi. Taken from this perspective, hermeneutic philosophy understands itself not as an absolute position but as a way of experience. It insists that there is no higher principle than holding oneself open in a conversation. But this means: Always recognize in advance the possible correctness, even the superiority of the conversation partner's position. Is this too little? Indeed, this seems to me to be the kind of integrity one can demand only of a professor of philosophy. And one should demand as much.

It seems evident to me that the return to the primordial dialogic of the human experience of the world is irreducible. This also applies when a final accounting or definitive argument is demanded, or when the self-realization of spirit is taught. Thus it is of great importance that Hegel's way of thinking be interrogated anew. Heidegger uncovered the Greek background to the tradition of metaphysics and then recognized in Hegel's dialectical dissolution of traditional conceptualization (in his *Science of Logic*) the most radical follow-up to the Greeks. But Heidegger's destruction of metaphysics did not rob Hegel of his achievement: Only then did Hegel's artful, speculative way of stepping over the subjectivity of spirit make itself applicable and offer itself as a unique solution to modern subjectivity. Was the intention here not the same as in Heidegger's turning away from the transcendental self-conception in the thinking of "the turn"? Was it not also Hegel's intention to put behind himself the orientation to self-consciousness and the subject-object split of the philosophy of consciousness? Or are there still other differences? Does not the orientation to the universality of speech, the insistence on the linguisticality of our access to the world, which I share with Heidegger, signify the taking of a step beyond Hegel, a step back behind Hegel?

In order to locate my first attempts at thinking, I could in fact say that I took it upon myself to save the honor of "bad infinity" [*der "schlechten Unendlichkeit"*]. Of course, in my eyes I made a decisive modification here, for the unending dialogue of the soul with itself, which is what thinking is, is not to be characterized as an endlessly continuing determination of an object-world waiting to be recognized. It is this neither in the neo-Kantian sense of an unending task nor in the dialectical sense of the thinking beyond being, over every particular limit. For me, Heidegger had pointed out a new way, in that he had transformed the critique of the metaphysical tradition at a preparatory stage in order to pose the question about being in a new way and had thereby found himself on the way to language. This is the way of a language that is not concerned to pronounce judgment and make a corresponding validity claim to objectivity but always keeps itself concerned with the whole of being. Totality is not an objectivity to be determined. Kant's critique of the antinomies of pure reason seems to me to hold its own in respect to Hegel. Totality is not an object but the world horizon that embraces us.

Heidegger constructed a Hölderlin who was opposed to Hegel and who saw the work of art as a primordial truth happening. I did not have to follow him in order to see the poetic work as a corrective for the ideal of objective determination and for the hubris of concepts. This was certain to me from my own first attempts at thinking. The poetic work constantly provided food for thought for my own hermeneutic orientation, and the hermeneutic attempt to think language up out of dialogue was inevitable for a lifelong pupil of Plato. In the end it meant getting over every fixation through the further development of conversation. Terminological fixations are appropriate to the constructive region of modern science and its task of making knowledge available to everyone, but they become oddly suspect in the region where philosophical thought moves. The great Greek thinkers protected the fluidity of their own language even when they undertook to fix concepts in their thematic analyses. But in opposition to this, there has always been scholasticism—ancient, medieval, modern, contemporary. It follows philosophy like a shadow, and it is almost possible to determine the status of an attempt at thinking in terms of how far it is able to break out of the petrifaction of handed-down philosophical language. Hegel's programmatic attempt, manipulated as a dialectical method, in principle had many precursors. Even a ceremonial thinker like Kant, who took up the Latin of the school, was able to find his own speech. He avoided new constructions, but he gave traditional concepts many new applications. Husserl's place as well is fixed among contemporary and older neo-Kantians precisely because his intellectual power of observation was able to provide terms of art, and the descriptive suppleness of his linguistic vocabulary fused into the unity of a style. Heidegger appealed precisely to the model of Plato and Aristotle to justify the novelty of his language, and he is much more followed in this than might have been expected in light of his first provocations and the amazement it brought on. In contrast to science and the living of life, philosophy finds itself in a peculiar difficulty. The language of philosophizing was not made for philosophizing. Philosophy entangles itself in a constitutive language-need, and this language-need becomes all the more palpable the more the philosophizing person gets out in front of himself in his thinking. In general it is the sign of the dilettante that concepts are arbitrarily constructed and enthusiastically "defined." The philosopher stirs up the observation powers of speech, and every stylistic boldness and act of violence has its place and succeeds in penetrating into the speech of those who would think-with and think-beyond. This means shaking up, extending, and throwing light on the horizon of communication.

The language of philosophy never finds its object but rather constructs it. It is perhaps unavoidable, then, that the language of philosophy does not move and have its life in propositional systems, whose logical formalization and critical testing for conclusiveness and unambiguity could even deepen the insights of philosophy. No revolution will eliminate this or the fact proclaimed by the analysis of ordinary language. Let me give an example: One can win a certain clarity by analyzing the argumentation of a Platonic dialogue with logical means, showing up incoherence, filling in jumps in logic, unmasking false conclusions, and so forth. But is this the way to read Plato, to make his questions one's own? Can one learn from him in this way, or does one simply confirm one's own superiority? What holds for Plato holds *mutatis mutandis* for all philosophy. It seems to me that Plato described this once and for all in his *Seventh Letter*: The means of philosophizing are not the same as philosophizing itself. Simple logical conclusiveness is not everything. This is not to deny the obvious validity of logic. But the thematization of logic limits the horizon of questions to a formal testing and thereby dislocates the emergence of the world that occurs in our linguistically formulated experience of the world. This is a hermeneutic finding that has, I think, a certain convergence with the later writings of Wittgenstein. Here he revised the nominalistic prejudices of the *Tractatus* in favor of conducting all speaking back to the context of life *praxis*. The yield of this reduction remained for him overwhelmingly negative. For him it consisted in the rejection of the undemonstrable questions of metaphysics and not in their reappropriation, no matter how undemonstrable they may be. Such reappropriation could be won only by teasing these questions out of the linguistic constitution of our being-in-the-world. In this respect more can be learned from the word of the poet than from Wittgenstein.

This is exactly the case, and no one argues that it is not: Conceptual explication cannot exhaust the content of a poetic creation. This has been recognized at least since Kant, if not since Baumgarten's discovery of aesthetic truth (*cognito sensitiva*). This is especially interesting from a hermeneutic point of view. In respect to poetry, the mere separation of the aesthetic from the theoretical and its liberation from the press of rules or concepts are not enough. Even poetry remains a form of speech in which concepts come together in relatedness. Hence the hermeneutic task consists in learning how to determine the special place of poetry in the context of the binding force of language, where the conceptual is always in play. How does language become art? This question poses itself here not only because the art of interpretation always involves forms of speech and text and because poetry, too, involves linguistic creations or texts. Poetic creations are creations in a novel sense. They are texts, in an eminent way. Language emerges here in its full autonomy. It stands for itself and raises itself to this standing position, whereas words are normally overtaken by the directed intentions of the speech that leaves them behind.

Here is hidden a particularly difficult hermeneutic problem. It is a special sort of communication that proceeds from poetry. With whom does it take place? With the reader? With which reader? At this point the dialectic of question and answer that lies at the base of the hermeneutic process and springs from the fundamental schema of the dialogical earns for itself a special modification. The reception and interpretation of poetry seems to imply a dialogical relationship of a unique kind.

This emerges especially clearly if one studies the peculiarities of different ways of speaking. It is not only the poetic word that shows a rich scale of differentiation, including epic, dramatic, and lyric. There are other ways of speaking in which the fundamental hermeneutic relation of question and answer goes through peculiar modifications.

I am thinking of the different forms of religious speech, such as pro-claiming, praying, preaching, blessing. I might also name mythical sayings, legal texts, and even the more or less stammering language of philosophy. These provide a hermeneutic problematic of application to which, since the appearance of *Truth and Method*, I have increasingly devoted myself. I believe I have gotten nearer to the thing from two different angles. One is from my studies of Hegel, where I pursue the roles played by the linguistic in its connectedness to the logical. The other is from the point of view of modern hermetic poetry, as the-matized in my commentary on Paul Celan's work. The relationship of philosophy and poetry stands at the center of this undertaking. These reflections have served to remind me, and might remind us all, that Plato was no Platonist and that philosophy is not scholasticism.

Name Index

Index

Index